A Red Boyhood

A Red

GROWING UP

UNIVERSITY OF MISSOURI PRESS
COLUMBIA AND LONDON

Boyhood

UNDER STALIN

Anatole Konstantin

Copyright © 2008 by
The Curators of the University of Missouri
University of Missouri Press, Columbia, Missouri 65201
Printed and bound in the United States of America
All rights reserved
5 4 3 2 1   12 11 10 09 08

Library of Congress Cataloging-in-Publication Data

Konstantin, Anatole, 1928–
    A red boyhood : growing up under Stalin / Anatole Konstantin.
       p.   cm.
    Summary: "A childhood memoir of Stalin's Soviet Union that details
the daily trials of people trapped in this regime. Left fatherless by Stalin's
purges, then forced to flee the Germans and live as an impoverished
refugee in Kazakhstan during World War II, Konstantin eventually
escapes to Western Europe at war's end"—Provided by publisher.
    ISBN 978-0-8262-1787-5 (alk. paper)
    1. Konstantin, Anatole, 1928–   2. Jewish children in the
Holocaust—Soviet Union.   3. Jews—Soviet Union—Biography.
4. Jews—Persecutions—Soviet Union.   I. Title.
    DS134.93.K66A3 2008
    305.892′4047092aB—dc22

                                                    2007050134

⊗™ This paper meets the requirements of the
American National Standard for Permanence of Paper
for Printed Library Materials, Z39.48, 1984.

Designer: Kristie Lee
Typesetter: The Composing Room of Michigan, Inc.
Printer and binder: The Maple-Vail Book Manufacturing Group
Typeface: Adobe Garamond

To the memory of my parents,
Nissen and Raya Konstantinovsky,
and of the countless millions of victims of
international communism.

Contents

ACKNOWLEDGMENTS

Because my childhood was so different from that of my children and grandchildren, I decided to write down my story. I wrote it just as if I were telling it to them in person, without any literary aspirations.

When some of my friends and relatives found out about this project, they asked to read it, and I lent them a copy of the manuscript. Much to my surprise, most of them found it interesting and urged me to have it published. I thank them for all their interest and encouragement.

I particularly thank Carole Millis and Tricia York. Carole (without my knowledge) duplicated the manuscript, circulated it among her friends, and reported their positive comments. Tricia separated it into individual chapters, so that more than one of her friends could read it at a time. When I came for a visit, she organized an informal focus group, whose reaction was very encouraging.

I then showed the manuscript to Jules Koslow, who has published several books on Russia, and to Elizabeth Fuller, author of several books and plays. They both thought that I should endeavor to publish it.

My early editor, Doris Eder, of Eder Editorial Enterprises, not only rearranged the commas and semicolons in the manuscript but also put me in touch with Robert Diforio of D4EO Literary Agency, who has done a magnificent job of representation.

I also thank Evelyn and John Drimmer, for being the first to urge publication; Peggy Breitmayer, Erica Doctorow, Agata Stanford, Mary-Rose Greer, Cindy Puccio, and Jonathan York, for their enthusiastic support; Maxima Trambert and Rhoda Soloway, for their helpful suggestions; and, last-but-not-least, my wife, Rosaria, and children, Rachel, Neal, and David, for their understanding, support, and patience.

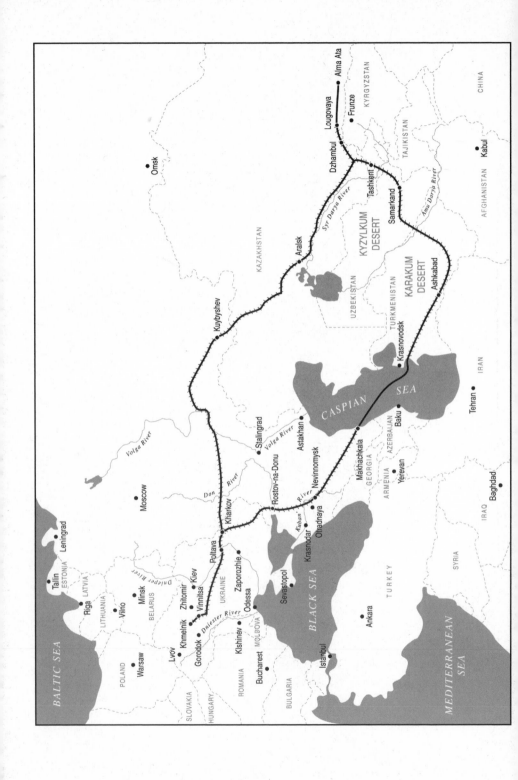

A Red Boyhood

PROLOGUE

I was startled by thunderous banging on the door. Father jumped out of bed, hurriedly turned on the light, and rushed into the hallway. Mother also got out of bed.

"It's three o'clock, who could that be?" she said haltingly, and there was fear in her voice.

There were heavy footsteps in the hallway. Father came into the room, ashen and shaking. Three NKVD men followed him, pistols in hand.

"They came to arrest me . . ." Father's voice was quivering and scratchy. "There must be some mistake . . ."

Seeing that only Mother, I, and the baby were in the room with Father, the men put the guns into their holsters.

Mother, wearing only her nightgown, sat down, or rather fell on the bed, staring at them with wide-open eyes and biting her knuckles, as if trying to suppress a scream.

I sat on my bed with my nightshirt pulled over my knees and looked from one man to another. The one in charge was big, swarthy, with heavy cheeks and bushy eyebrows. I knew his name was Dziuba, because his son was in my school. I did not know the names of the other two.

"You search the kitchen," Dziuba, who came in behind Father, ordered the second man, who appeared to be older. "And you search the other room," he told the third one, who was young, thin, and blond and, unlike the other two, did not appear to be angry.

"If you would tell me what you are looking for," said Father, his voice trembling, "I may be able to help you . . . " He seemed to be at a loss as to what to do.

"Get dressed!" barked Comrade Dziuba as he searched in the wardrobe, pushing aside Mother's dresses and going through drawers. When he came to my erector set on the table he stopped and regarded it with suspicion. I watched him closely. Then he frowned and pointed a chubby finger at the spring motor.

"What is this?" he asked in a strident voice.

"It is an erector set," I said. "It is a toy." I remember actually smiling at his ignorance.

He noticed my smile and for a moment stared at me with suspicion, as if expecting the erector-set motor to blow up in his hand.

Mother began moving around slowly, as if in a dream, gathering some of Father's clothing into a small suitcase. Then, all of a sudden, she collapsed to the floor.

I froze with fear. Father was in the other room getting dressed. Comrade Dziuba looked startled and only the young NKVD man rushed into the kitchen and brought Mother a glass of water. She came to, and the young man and Father helped her to get up and guided her to a chair.

Father closed the suitcase and sat next to Mother, holding her hand and repeating that it was all a mistake and he would be back as soon as things were sorted out.

After what seemed like an hour of searching and not finding anything suspicious, Comrade Dziuba shouted: "Let's go!"

Father shook his head as if waking up to what was happening. "Please, let me collect my immigration papers, I completely forgot about them . . ."

"Never mind!" angrily barked Comrade Dziuba. "Where you are going you will not need any papers!"

Afterwards we often thought about the meaning of his words.

CHAPTER I

1928-1938

I was born on April 24, 1928, in a small Ukrainian town called Volochisk. The town is split in two by the River Zbruch, which between 1918 and September 1939 formed the border between Poland and the Ukrainian Soviet Socialist Republic. From 1815 after the defeat of Napoleon until 1918, this was part of the Russian Empire. In 1991, when the Soviet Union fell apart, Ukraine became an independent country.

My father, Nissen Konstantinovsky, who was then twenty-five years old, came from Kishinev, which is now Chisinau, the capital of Moldova. From 1918 to 1940 Moldova belonged to Romania, but before that, when Father was born in 1902, it was part of the Russian Empire and was called Bessarabia. In 1940 the Soviet Union took it away from Romania and, until the beginning of the war in 1941, Kishinev was the capital of the Moldavian Soviet Socialist Republic. During World War II Romania, which was allied with Germany, took Moldova back until 1944, then the Soviet Union reoccupied it until 1991, when it became an independent country.

Father was a photographer and was working in a studio in Volochisk when he met Mother, Rachel "Raya" Breitgand, who had been born there. They were married in 1927, only two months after having met. According to Mother, she was sixteen years old, but according to her brother she must have been at least eighteen. She looked very young: she was slim, a little over five feet tall, and took care of her appearance. Many times I heard her telling the story of how once at the movies Father was asked whether he needed one adult and one child ticket.

Two months after I was born my parents moved to a little town called Gorodok in Russian and Horodok in Ukrainian, which actually means "little town"; here Father opened his own studio.[1] There was already a photographer in town when Father moved in, and there was no love lost between them. Father always referred to him as the *partach,* which is Russian for someone who does shoddy work, and for a time I thought that this was his name. The town was a county (*rayon*) seat and had three or four thousand people, of whom about half were Jews, about a third were Poles, and the rest Ukrainians. All the peasants in the area were Ukrainian and worked in collective farms called *kolkhozes.*

Father's father was Emanuel or Rachmil Konstantinovsky, which means "the man from Konstantinov." There is a town in the Ukraine called Staro-Konstantinov (Old Konstantinov), as well as one called Novo-Konstantinov (New Konstantinov), where his family could have been from. Emanuel served in the Russian army during the Russo-Japanese War of 1905. The Russian army was defeated and he returned home a total pacifist. He bought several cows and became a milkman.

Father's mother was Assya "Hadassa" Konstantinovskaya, the ending "aya" in Russian being reserved for females.[2] I do not know much about Grandmother, other than that she was an energetic, take-charge woman, while Grandfather was a mild man, greatly affected by his war experience. I know nothing about my great-grandparents on either side.

Father had two sisters: Aida, who went to Uruguay in 1920, from where she illegally crossed into Argentina, and Ester, who, together with my grand-

---

1. The Russian language does not have the "h" sound and uses hard "g" instead. The Ukrainian language, on the other hand, does not have "g" and uses only "h." That's why the name of our town in Russian is Gorodok and in Ukrainian is Horodok; in Polish it is Grudek.

2. The Russian, Ukrainian, and Polish languages all have word endings that specify a person's sex. In Ukrainian and Polish, the female ending would be "a." In addition, in Polish there is a different ending for a "daughter of," which is "ouwna," so that a daughter of someone named Kowalski would be Kowalskouwna. This creates a problem with names ending with "g," such as Goldberg, for which the daughter becomes Goldbergouwna: the word *gouwno* means "excrement." The problem is resolved by calling her Goldbergzhanka. The poet Heinrich Heine delved into this labyrinth in his story "Memoirs of von Schnabelewopski," but he probably was not aware of the *ouwna* dilemma.

parents, died of typhoid fever in Uzbekistan during the war. Ester's husband and two children were killed during the bombardment of Kishinev by the German Luftwaffe in 1941.

At the age of twelve Father became an apprentice to a photographer. To learn the trade in those days one also had to learn to mix the developer and the fixer, and also to retouch negatives by filling in light areas and scratching out blemishes. Later on he found a job in the Romanian city of Yassy. When, in the early 1920s, he was about to be drafted into the Romanian army, he decided to join his sister Aida in Argentina. The Romanians looked down on the Moldovans; Romanian soldiers mercilessly beat the Moldovan minority soldiers, particularly if they were Jewish. Father knew men who had returned home from the army with most of their teeth knocked out.

Father packed his two cameras and found a freighter sailing to Naples. He wrote to Aida from there, asking her for advice on how to get to Argentina. Because the mail in Romania was censored, he was afraid to write to her from home, for fear that the authorities would find out that he was planning to emigrate instead of going into the army. Aida wrote back, telling him not to come because things were very bad in Argentina. She regretted this for the rest of her life and blamed herself for what would eventually happen to Father.

Not being able to return home, Father faced a dilemma. He spoke only Russian, Romanian, Moldovan (which is a dialect of Romanian), and some Yiddish. He was afraid to go to a country whose language he did not know and where he did not know anyone. Then he found a Russian freighter going to Odessa and, in exchange for photographing the captain and the crew, was taken on board. After stopping in Genoa and Istanbul, he arrived in Odessa, where he had some distant relatives, and eventually found the job in Volochisk.

Mother's father was David Breitgand. Breitgand is a Russification of *breite hand,* which in Yiddish or German means "broad hand." I have never encountered another Breitgand. The family legend has it that grandfather David's father, Solomon, was one of several sons and was subject to be drafted into the Russian army, which, before 1874, meant he would serve for a term of twenty-five years. Since only sons were not drafted, my great-great grandfather bought new identities for the rest of his sons, and they settled in different places under invented names, each claiming to be the only son of his father.

Grandfather David was born in 1874 and died in 1961 of gangrene that developed after he broke his leg and refused to go to a hospital—he had never been in one in his whole life. My grandmother's name was Eta. She died of smallpox during the epidemic after World War I, and Mother had to quit school to take care of her three younger brothers. Grandfather David was in the egg business. He bought eggs from farmers, candled them, and then resold them. To candle eggs is to look at them in front of a light, to see if the embryo has begun developing, in which case they are sold for hatching rather than for food. Since there were no chicken farms where the hens were separated from the roosters, all eggs were fertilized, and if they were to be eaten, it had to be before red blood vessels began forming in the yoke.

Before I was born, Mother decided that if her baby was a girl, she would be named Eta, after her mother, but my parents did not have a name for a boy. Mother resolved this by naming me Etan, with the accent on the "a," which she claimed to have invented, even thought there is a biblical name Eytan, meaning "strong." In my case it turned out to be mostly headstrong.

Since in the Ukraine the name Etan did not exist, it evoked a great deal of teasing—I feel sorry for any child condemned to carry an unusual name. To make matters worse, where I came from, a child is called by a diminutive of his name, which in my case became Etanchik. This did not sound right and was abbreviated to Tanchik, which in Ukrainian means "little dance." I was driven to tears when, upon seeing me, kids would point an index finger to the sky and spin round and round, or would ask me to perform my little dance. Only teachers called me Etan and it remained so until the war, when I could claim that my birth certificate was lost and that my name was Anatoly.

Father did not quite know how to cope with the name Etan. Many years later, when my aunt Aida died in Argentina, her daughter sent me a baby picture, on the back of which Father had written that this was his son Izzy.

My first memory is that of a low-slung old building with crooked walls in the center of town, at the intersection of the only two cobblestone-paved roads. You entered a long, unlit hallway, at the end of which, behind a plywood partition, was kept a wooden barrel filled with drinking water and periodically replenished by a water carrier, who brought water from a distant well in two buckets suspended on a yoke. A huge glass bottle in a wicker basket, containing kerosene for lamps and for the primus burner used for cooking, was also kept there, and a wooden ladder led from there to the attic. In the attic in a wooden cage, several chickens were being fattened with corn before being taken to the slaughterhouse, where a bearded man in a bloodstained apron slit their throats and hung them by their feet on a hook over a smelly metal trough to bleed. He plucked them while they were still warm and threw the feathers into a barrel, the stench of which was detectable at a great distance. Watching Mother dissect chickens, I had learned early a great deal about anatomy. I was particularly interested in the tiny eggs, which I insisted Mother cook for me right away.

From the hallway one entered Father's office, part of which had been turned into a darkroom. A door from the office led into the room where the three of us lived, and a permanently locked door led from our room to the rooms belonging to our landlord. The studio, or what Father called the gallery, was a separate wooden structure, its front wall and ceiling consisting of 18 x 24 centimeter glass panes made from photographic glass negatives stripped of their photosensitive emulsion. The wall and ceiling had sectional curtains, the metal rings of which made a scratching sound when Father manipulated them with a long stick to get proper light on the subject. There was no electricity, which meant Father could not take pictures on very cloudy days. At the back of the studio was a table with a mirror and a kerosene lamp, on which country girls heated the tips of long, metal tongs, one side of which was concave and the other convex, with which they curled their hair before being photographed.

The floor of the studio was covered with sand, which I once stuffed into my mouth until it made me sick. On the end wall hung a gray linoleum backdrop with pictures of fancy furniture in the bottom corners, so that photographs might create the impression of having been taken in an opulent living room. There were several bentwood chairs and a tall, round stand on which standing persons could rest one elbow and lightly support their head, perhaps placing an extended index finger on the cheek—a fashionable pose that implied wisdom.

The front of the house was long enough for Father to paint in two-foot-high letters *Fotografia Konstantinovskogo,* the ending "ogo" meaning "be-

Anatole Konstantin with Father, 1936.

Father, 1935.

Father, Anatole, and
Mother, 1935.

Mother, 1936.

longing to a male." He spent a couple of weeks on the ladder, first dividing the space with a ruler and a flat carpenter's pencil into five-centimeter squares, then drawing the letters and filling them with black paint and, finally, drawing in perspective the third dimension and painting it red. The result was the biggest sign in town. There was also a display case, called a *vitrina,* full of photographs of happy grooms, radiant brides, pudgy babies, and glowering officials, who must have assumed that a fierce look made them appear more important. Father was a very good draftsman, which his competitor, the *partach,* was not, and he had a monopoly on "vignettes," groups of individual photographs of organization members, which he arranged on a large sheet of cardboard and decorated with ornate scrolls. The size of the photograph and the number of scrolls around it corresponded to the rank of the person photographed. Father copied the scrolls from pre-Revolutionary money bills, but Communist officials did not seem to mind looking like czars. Father also drew a pretty heading with farm animals for *kolkhoz* vignettes or stars with hammers and sickles for party conferences. He then photographed the whole thing and made multiple copies. It was a lucrative business.

Another source of income was provided by the Ukrainian custom of families being photographed behind open caskets of their deceased loved ones. Even during the starvation of 1933, when squads of Communist goons confiscated all grain from the peasants to force them to "voluntarily" join collective farms, we had enough to eat. Father took the sad photographs of open caskets in exchange for a few eggs or some buckwheat grain.

Our building was actually part of an inn. The living quarters were attached to a large barn that could accommodate several wagons and horses. Peasants from distant villages who had brought their products to the market used to stay overnight at the inn, where they and their horses were fed and had a place to sleep. In my time, keeping a private inn was illegal and only occasionally were old customers allowed to sneak in after dark.

Our landlords were an elderly couple named Berkovich. He was tall and thin, with stooping shoulders and red-rimmed, watering eyes. He had "sat for gold," which means that he had sat in prison until ransomed. Since he had been a businessman, the authorities assumed that he had money hidden away, presumably in the form of pre-Revolutionary ten-ruble gold coins, about the size of a penny, which for some unknown reason were nicknamed "piglets." All former storekeepers and craftsmen—in Gorodok mostly old Jews—were ordered to turn in their gold. Those who claimed that they did not have any were imprisoned and kept on bread and water until their relatives sold their belongings and procured some gold coins, which was very difficult and dangerous to do. There were rumors that the recalcitrant ones were given only herring to eat and no water; many did not survive. Another rumor had it that at an opening night of the opera in Odessa, when the people were leaving, the NKVD men stood at the door and robbed everyone of their jewelry, including wedding rings and earrings, then thanked them for their contribution to building communism.

As I grew older, I refused to stay in our room and became a nuisance to Father, particularly when Mother was not home. Occasionally Father would slap me on the behind and sometimes, after having been slapped, I would stand at the door and complain to any passing militiaman: "Uncle militiaman, please arrest my father, he spanks me!" Little did I realize that someday this would actually happen. Most of the time they pretended not to hear me, but those who knew Father would come in and have a good laugh with him.

Eventually, Father got to know most of the people in town and I remember once, at the end of the day, the chief of the NKVD (People's Commissariat for Internal Affairs, which later changed its name to Committee for National Security, or KGB) dropped by. He was a huge man, with a huge face that fit his last name—Mordovets. (*Morda* is a Ukrainian word for animal face.) He was in a jolly mood and told Father a joke that well illustrated NKVD humor. It was about a manager of a ball-bearing factory who was being accused of producing undersized bearing balls. The manager was summoned to a party meeting, to which his accuser, the head of the factory party cell whose job was to second-guess management, brought a measuring gauge. After making a long speech accusing the manager of sabotage, the accuser triumphantly inserted a ball, which all this time he held in his hand, into the gauge. It fit perfectly, because during his long speech it had expanded from the heat of his hand.

The chief laughed uproariously and Father obviously tried to force a laugh. I did not understand the humor until much later, when I could visualize the petrified factory manager accused of sabotage, which meant long imprisonment or worse, sighing a huge sigh of relief.

Because we were located right in the center of town, our street had a stone-block sidewalk; most other streets turned into ankle-deep lanes of mud after a rain. Facing the street, to the right of us, in a single-story red-brick building, was the County Party Committee, from which one could hear the constant clicking of typewriters. Next, in a beautiful gray stone house, which like all the other buildings in the center of town had belonged to merchant families before the Revolution, was an office of the government bank that dealt with financing of collective farms and of other county offices. Individuals did not do any banking and there were no checking or savings accounts. Then, in a long warehouselike building, there was the movie house that showed silent movies accompanied by a pianist, who banged away on an old upright piano. The talkies did not arrive until about 1935. I remember the first time I was allowed to go to the movies by myself. The movie was H. G. Wells's *The Invisible Man*. When the man began unwinding the bandage from his head and there was nothing there, I became frightened and tried to leave, but the doors were locked. Finally, someone heard me crying and let me out.

Next came a beautiful Greek Orthodox church, white with green, onion-shaped domes. Its priests had been arrested, and it was used for storing grain. All over the churchyard were scattered hundreds of glass prisms of many shapes from the huge church chandeliers. The chandeliers had been thrown out, together with icons, priests' robes, and other ecclesiastic paraphernalia that the militiamen did not want to take home for fear of being suspected of secret belief in God. Children collected these prisms and caught sunbeams, which scattered into all the colors of the rainbow.

Next to the church was a pleasant white-brick house, where lived the movie manager. He had the unusual name of Mitbreit, which in Yiddish means "with bread"; his seventeen-year-old daughter, Lisa, a spindly, curly-haired girl, was Mother's best friend. Before the Revolution, Comrade Mitbreit owned the movie house; now he was just an employee. To me their house was the epitome of luxury. They had a piano and soft, velvet-upholstered furniture in the living room, plus a separate dining room with a shiny table and credenza on which stood a bowl of artificial fruit. Above the credenza hung a large painting in an ornate, gilded frame that very realistically depicted dead pheasants, ducks, and rabbits hanging by their feet, which I found utterly disgusting.

Across the road from the movies was a park with a large, white, two-story building. The building had very thick walls, small windows, and vaulted hallways running between two rows of rooms on each floor. This had been a Polish monastery and was being used as the County Executive Office. Theoretically it was the county government, but it was constantly scrutinized and second-guessed by the County Party Committee from across the street, even though all the executives were also members of the Communist Party. The park was very old, with huge trees and a magic circle of large lindens, each about three feet in diameter. I loved to read while sitting on the grass in this circle of giants, in whose hollows resided gray bats and in whose branches nested bright bluebirds. In the summer, when the lindens bloomed, their fragrance was overpowering. We collected their blossoms, dried them in the sun, and brewed fragrant linden tea that was supposed to be good for our health. The bats' nest hollows had an opening at each end. When we spotted such hollows, one of us would poke a stick into one opening, while another boy held his hat over the other and captured the screeching bats as they tried to escape. If they were still alive after we played with them, we let them go.

We were very cruel to bumblebees, tearing them apart and sucking the drop of honey from their tiny honey sacs. Also, we pushed thorns through a folded strip of paper and into the leg of a May bug (which we called June bug) so that it would fly in circles when we slipped a finger through the loop of the paper.

Next to the park was a cobblestone-paved square with a wooden speaker's platform in one corner. Here, on the first of May and the seventh of November, the two official Communist holidays, were held the "spontaneous" demonstrations with flags, portraits of leaders, and banners. Here the party big-shots bored each other and their captive audiences with practically identical speeches praising the Communist Party and Comrade Stalin and exhorting the workers, peasants, and "laboring intelligentsia," which encompassed all white-collar workers, to overfulfill their work quotas in building socialism and to be vigilant against class enemies. There was also a brass band that played the Soviet anthem—the "International"—at the beginning and at the end, as well as other revolutionary tunes between the speeches. It was the only brass band in town and I had seen it many times at the head of funeral processions, all of which seemed to pass in front of our house, mournfully playing the funeral march by Chopin.

Once, when the deceased must have been a party functionary, the funeral procession was led by two sad-faced young women carrying a portrait of Stalin framed by black ribbons. I assume this was supposed to symbolize the functionary's devotion to the great leader, but it appeared as if it were Stalin's funeral. As they were passing in front of the party committee, someone ran out and wrestled the portrait out of the women's hands, leaving them standing with their mouths wide open and terror in their eyes.

Adjacent to the square, directly across the street from us, was the Jewish school, where the primary language was Yiddish and which, according to my mother, produced "linguistic cripples." While Mother did not have much of a formal education, she was an avid reader and spoke beautiful Russian and Ukrainian, good Polish, and some Yiddish, which she and Father used only when they did not want me to understand what they were saying.

The graduates of such schools usually wound up with heavy Yiddish accents, which they were unable to shed and which not only impeded their careers but, during the German occupation, may have doomed them. Many years later I had a friend, Michael Klaus from Odessa, who had such an accent. He had been a prisoner of war in Germany and managed to survive the Holocaust only by pretending to be a Chechen, an ethnic group from the northern Caucasus that also spoke Russian with an accent and, being Muslim, were circumcised like the Jews. He was a physician in the prisoner-of-war camp, and many of the prisoners were from the Caucasus. One day, an important Chechen chieftain visited the camp to recruit volunteers to fight against the Soviets, and at night, around a bonfire, they danced the native dance called the *Lesghinka*. Naturally, Michael had never danced it, but when he was pushed into the circle he had to dance for his life and did it so well that the chieftain praised him for preserving native customs.

Across the side street from the school, where once stood a magnificent red-brick Catholic cathedral, remained only ruins and mountains of debris. The ancient, three-foot-thick walls were being taken apart brick by brick. Once, Mother had taken me to this church to hear a visiting organist, and I remember being very impressed by the highest ceiling that I had ever seen, by huge chandeliers blazing with candles, and by the glittering, gilded frames of giant paintings. I did not appreciate the music and thankfully, since there was standing room only, we did not stay long. This was Mother's idea of exposing me to culture in all its forms.

Mother could not understand boredom, and when I occasionally complained of being bored, she asked me whether I would like her to hire an orchestra to entertain me or, more frequently, suggested that I bang my head against the wall, which would give me something to do. If I complained about food or such, she inquired whether I thought I was the Prince of Wales and was entitled to something better.

Farther along the road there were private houses, each with its own garden of fruit trees, vegetables, and flowers, and then there was the pond, formed by a wooden dam across the small river called Smotrich. The water from the pond turned a waterwheel, which during the day powered a flour mill and in the evenings, after dark, turned the electric generator that supplied electricity to the few houses of big-shots and to several streetlights. At the point where water entered the pipe leading to the waterwheel, there was a whirlpool that left a hole in the water as big as a man's hat. When Father pointed it out to me and warned me that one could be sucked into it if one swam too close, there was a bloated purple drowned pig going round and round in circles, with its tail upwards. No one bothered to remove it and it remained there until the stench became unbearable. Father also told me that if this whirlpool were in the Southern Hemisphere, it would be swirling clockwise rather than counter-clockwise, even though he was not sure why.

I loved the warm summer evenings when Father and I went bathing in the river, upstream from the dam at a small, pebbly beach in a clearing between reeds. Father swam out to the other shore and brought me furry cattails while I splashed around near the shore. He showed me how to pull out the reed plants by the roots without cutting one's fingers on their sharp blades, and how to braid them into whips. The leaf blades were pink at the point where they were joined together and when pulled apart exuded a wonderful pungent fragrance.

There were only three cars in the whole town: one belonged to the County Party Committee, one to the County Executive Committee, and one to the NKVD. These cars were copies of model "A" Fords, built in the Soviet Union under license. The NKVD also had the only truck in town. All other transportation was by horse carriages and wagons in summer and by horse-pulled sleighs in winter, when the snow covered the ground from late November to late March.

The River Smotrich was narrow and shallow except for deeper holes here and there. The water looked clean and some people used it for cooking, in spite of the fact that people and horses swam in the deeper places and laundry was washed upstream near the bridge. I liked going to the river with the neighborhood boys, wading in the shade of weeping willows and eventually learning to swim. There were many river mussels mixed in with pebbles in the shallows. They were considered inedible, even though during the famine some people survived thanks only to them.

Once someone discovered in the pond a battlewagon called a *tachanka* that during World War I must have fallen through the ice over one of the deep holes. It was a regular horse carriage with iron armor plates and a Maxim machine gun in the back. This find gave rise to a rumor that during the war the Polish army must have retreated over the frozen pond in the winter, and that there might be all kinds of treasures on the bottom. The next thing we knew, a bypass canal for draining the pond was being dug by the neighboring *kolkhoz*. It took several months to dig the canal with hand shovels and, when it was finished, the whole town assembled to watch as the last bit was dynamited and water rushed into the breach. After three days of draining, to our great disappointment, the only thing that appeared was another rusted-out *tachanka* and some animal bones near the waterwheel inlet. In the meantime, the town was without electricity for more than a month.

On the other side of our building was a fire station with two horse-drawn pumps and water barrels. It had a red observation tower about four stories high, from which one had a view over the whole town. Once I overheard a whispered joke that, even though the NKVD building was only two stories high, one could see from it farther away than from the tower—all the way to Siberia. Next to the firehouse was a store, called Univermag, or "Universal Magazine," where, when they were available, one bought products distributed by the government such as sugar, salt, cigarettes, matches, and vodka. They also sold food items that were made of grain delivered to the authorities by the *kolkhozes,* such as flour, farina, spaghetti, or buckwheat and millet cereals.

On summer days a seltzer pushcart appeared in front of the Univermag, manned by a friendly woman who, for one kopeck, sold you a glass of plain seltzer or, for three kopecks, squirted in some delicious syrup of your choice from one of several tall glass tubes filled with colored liquids. One had to drink this on the spot and return the glass, which the woman placed upside down on a round platform with a handle. When she turned the handle, water squirted into the glass and around the rim from the outside. The water came from a container suspended from a post above the pushcart and it drained into a bucket below the platform. I had to enjoy this ambrosia in secret, because Mother thought that the rinsing water was recirculated from the bucket back into the overhead container, which I suspect was true.

Fruits and vegetables were available only in season at the weekly market. They were sold directly to the public by the *kolkhozes* or by individual farmers from their home plots and gardens. The marketplace was right behind the firehouse. It was an open, cobblestone square, half of which was used for the farmer's horse wagons, while women sold their goods on the other half. They sat in rows on small stools or straw-filled sacks, displaying their wares on empty sacks spread before them on the ground. This gave rise to the saying that one cannot be simultaneously at two markets with one behind.

The market women sold bunches of vegetables, pound loaves of butter or cottage cheese wrapped in cabbage leaves, little mounds of fruit or berries, and live chickens with their feet and wings tied. Before buying a chicken, a woman would feel its belly to see whether it was meaty and blew at the short feathers under the tail to check the color of its skin. Yellow skin signified that the bird was fat, which was desirable. The fat was rendered with bits of skin and fried onions and used instead of butter on bread, or for frying and cooking. This was long before people knew about cholesterol; fat was considered to be healthy. Thick slices of salted pork fat were served on bread, the crust of which had been rubbed with a clove of garlic dipped in salt— it was delicious.

Market day in Gorodok was Thursday. Early in the morning one heard the steel-rimmed wagon wheels rattling on cobblestones. By nine o'clock wagons filled the square, bringing goods to the market or the sick to the polyclinic, which was two streets away. The sick were mostly elderly and they lay in the wagons on straw, covered with sheepskin coats even in the summer. They looked at the passersby with their pale watery eyes, which I thought were full of silent reproach, as if they saw some kind of injustice in us being young and healthy while they were sick and dying. I tried to avoid looking at them.

This section of the square was pretty much covered with horse manure, and I did not go there unless I needed a new fishing line. Then I had to find a horse with a long white tail and, when the farmer was not looking, snatch out a couple of hairs which, tied end to end, formed a fishing line invisible in the water. There was danger of being hit by the farmer's whip, but if one wanted to fish, there was little choice, since fish did not bite if they could see line made of string.

Next to the polyclinic was a pharmacy, to which patients had to bring their own bottles for liquid medicine and where powders were dispensed in folded white paper wrappers, the ends of which were tucked into one another. But before resorting to doctors and medication, the old-fashioned remedies, such as leeches and cups, were employed to suck out bad blood and pull out bad humors. Leeches were available in every pond. The cups were small, tulip-shaped glass jars, from which air was expelled by a flame before they were slapped onto the back of the patient. They sucked in the flesh about an inch deep, slowly turning it black and blue. Usually half a dozen cups were applied at each treatment, and some people claimed to feel better when they were removed. Father thought that they felt better in the same way they would if someone stopped beating them.

Right behind Father's studio began the Jewish section, which extended down to the river and enveloped the marketplace on two sides. The narrow, crooked streets there were unpaved, and after a rain they were covered with deep, sticky mud that pulled the galoshes right off one's shoes. It was better not to venture there without rubber boots. The clay-wall houses were old and crooked, leaning in all directions, with sagging, rusty tin roofs. There were no yards, no trees, no flowers, and no vegetable gardens. The only vegetation was a few weeds, which here and there broke through the bare ground.

The doors of these houses opened directly onto the street and their garbage heaps were only as far from the doors as women could throw the refuse on a rainy day without getting wet. On hot summer days a heavy stench hung like a cloud over the whole area, spilling into the neighborhood along with a multitude of flies. There were no wells in the area and water had to be either carried from a well almost a mile away or purchased by the bucket from the waterman, who peddled it from a barrel. The barrel was mounted on a two-wheeled wagon, pulled by a sad-looking old horse with protruding ribs and black, hairless patches on its sides where the rope harness rubbed against its skin. We did not buy from the waterman because he was suspected of filling his barrel from the river, rather than pulling it bucket by bucket from the deep well at the edge of town. A new well was dug in the center of town but its water turned out not to be good.

With the exception of the two cobblestone roads, the streets in town were unpaved, and one of my earliest memories is being carried by Mother in the street while reading store signs. Some signs were real tongue twisters, such as *parikmakherskaya,* which meant "barbershop" (for some historic reason the Russian language adopted for "barber" a German expression for a "wig maker.") My reading made Mother proud and she urged me to demonstrate my abilities whenever we encountered someone she knew. However, I am not sure whether she carried me because I was so young or because the streets were so muddy.

At the age of about four, I went to a sort of preschool, run in the home of a sweet, elderly widow named Elizaveta Fedorovna Morozova. Her husband had been a surgeon, and she lived with her teenage granddaughter in a two-story house that had several rooms filled with overstuffed furniture downstairs and several bedrooms upstairs. In comparison with our quarters, this house was very luxurious. There were two other children in the group, a boy whose nose was perpetually running and who was not interested in anything, and a cute little girl who was smart and scheming.

Elizaveta Fedorovna was a small, thin, gray-haired woman with large, bulging dark eyes and a rudimentary mustache, which made her look like a giant mouse. She had many toys. I remember square boards with rows of holes in which we arranged colored marbles in various patterns and color schemes, as well as flat squares, rhomboids, triangles, and rectangles, which we were encouraged to arrange into various shapes. There were also many books and bound volumes of a pre-Revolutionary magazine called *Niva* that we were allowed to look at. I remember asking Elisaveta Fedorovna about a frightening picture showing a man being burned at the stake, and her answering that his name was Giordano Bruno and that his last words were: "Nevertheless, the earth rotates!" I don't think I understood the difference between the church dogma that the sun orbits the earth and Bruno's insistence that it was the other way around, but I did not think that it justified burning anyone alive, and I have hated inquisitions of all kinds ever since.

One day Elizaveta Fedorovna was very upset. I overheard her telling Mother that she had been told by the authorities that private schools were not allowed any more; she would have to close it and she did not know how she would be able to make ends meet. She cried and Mother tried to console her, but that was the end. I wrote a few words and drew a card for her and insisted on delivering it in my tin mail truck, even though the streets were full of mud.

The next fall I went to the government preschool, where there were many children, very few toys, and the teacher did not have time to spend with each of us. When I returned from school after a few weeks, Mother discovered a louse on me and withdrew me from this school.

For my sixth birthday my parents gave me an erector set and from that moment on I wanted to be an engineer. First I built everything in the book, then I began constructing things of my own invention. When father brought me a clock motor, it created more possibilities, and I spent endless hours devising all kinds of machines. I also took apart our alarm clock and, naturally, was unable to put it back together.

At about that time we moved out of the cramped room into two rooms with a kitchen in a house on the other side of the park. It was owned by a Ukrainian woman who lived there with a son named Pet'ka who was a little bit older than me. It was a different world from the one we had inhabited before, and I loved being surrounded by gardens where the miracles of nature could be observed. On the right side of the house was a flower garden; on the left was a vegetable garden; in the back were cherry and plum trees. The house had a thatched roof, clay floors, and whitewashed walls, but no electricity. The garbage pit was behind the vegetable garden, far enough away so as not to offend, and the outhouse was behind the flower garden. Its walls were made of dry cornstalks and it had no roof; it consisted of a hole in the ground, over which lay two boards. While using the outhouse in warm weather one could learn a great deal about insects, larvae, cocoons, maggots, and worms. In the winter we used a chamber pot.

There was a wood-burning oven built into the wall between the rooms, with a metal chamber where one could keep pots of food warm. On cold winter mornings Father got up first and stoked the oven, while I shivered under my blanket, waiting for the room to warm up, as my imagination interpreted the fine cracks on the ceiling into faces, animals, or mountains. In the kitchen there was a wood-burning cooking stove with concentric metal rings, some of which were removed to fit the pear-shaped cast-iron cooking pots, and an oven for baking bread, which Mother did once a month with the help of a peasant woman named Handzia. Handzia was egg-shaped like one of those wooden dolls called *matrioshkas* that fit into one another. She had a pug nose with black nostrils, no neck, and was almost as wide as she was tall. Her arms were as thick as her thighs, so that she had no trouble carrying two buckets of water on a yoke from the distant well.

Handzia also assisted Mother with the monthly wash, for which they used rainwater that had been collected in barrels, supplementing it with water from the river, which was somewhat closer than the good well. Large pots of water were heated on the stove and poured into a galvanized trough. Then Handzia lathered the laundry with brown soap and rubbed it on a washboard before depositing it in another trough for rinsing, and after that wrung the water out with her powerful hands while Mother hung the laundry to dry on the clothesline.

In summer, Mother and Handzia made a charcoal fire under a huge copper basin in an outdoor pit and cooked cherry preserves. I volunteered to crouch over the kettle and skim the white foam from the simmering cherries, disposing of most of it in my mouth. Some cherries were placed in large glass bottles with layers of sugar and were kept in the sun on a windowsill; as their juice fermented, it turned into sweet cherry liquor. I was not allowed to drink the liquor but I could eat some of the cherries.

When Mother and Handzia baked bread, it was a big production. A sack of rye flour was mixed with water and some salt in a wooden trough, then the dough was kneaded and set aside to rise. In the meantime wood was burned in the bread oven until there was enough glowing charcoal to keep it hot for a long time. By then the dough had risen and large round loaves were formed on a flour-covered board. The loaves were shoved into the oven on a wooden shovel, and after a couple of hours fragrant dark loaves were extracted and set out to cool. The bread was dark and dense, and it kept for a month.

Behind the house was a cool cellar, which was just a deep cave in the ground, its entrance covered by a thatched roof. A dozen steps led to the interior where the landlady kept potatoes and fruit and we could keep butter, meat, and milk in the summer.

A path led from the house to a dirt road and down an incline to the intersection with the cobblestone roads where Father's studio was located. After heavy rains, the mud on the road was up to the axles of the horse wagons that carried sugar beets to the sugar mill outside of town, and the drivers had to jump into the mud to help the horses, while whipping them mercilessly. Other boys and I made sticks with nails on one end and, while the drivers were preoccupied, snatched sugar beets with them from an ambush behind roadside bushes. This took place in the fall after potatoes had been dug up and there were mounds of potato stalks to be burned. We grubbed like pigs in the loamy black soil until we found some potatoes that had been missed by the farmers and baked them together with beets in the red-hot ashes. Nothing ever tasted as good.

After the rain, streams of water rushed through the drainage ditch on the side of the road and we raced paper boats and built dams and canals. We also made mud logs about an inch in diameter and built log cabins and elaborate log castles and fortresses, in the process becoming covered with mud from head to toes to the great disapproval of our parents.

Between our house and the road was a two-story stucco house that belonged to a formerly well-to-do middle-aged Polish couple named Maletski. They lived in the back rooms with an old man who had a long drooping mustache and always wore a cap with a shiny black visor. The house had a gray Spanish tile roof, a flower garden in front, and a large, fenced-in fruit garden with several varieties of plums, cherries, pears, and apples, as well as several beehives, in the back. When the fruit began to ripen, the old Maletski moved into a shack among the trees and spent days and nights there, foiling our attempts to snatch some of the fruit. However, when the fruit was well ripened, he himself let us in, pointed out the trees with the ripest fruit, and allowed us to pick all we could stuff into our pockets and shirts. We devoured most of it and usually wound up with severe bellyaches.

The front part of this house was split into two apartments, in one of which lived the director of the Yiddish school, Citizen Studnitz, with his wife and a son, Boris, who was a few years younger than I. In the other part lived Comrade Hnidenko with a beautiful, blonde, blue-eyed wife and a baby. He held a big job in the County Party Committee, but he and his family were very friendly and I had visited them with Mother, who exchanged books with the wife. To me the house appeared most luxurious. It had electric lights in the evening, a solid wooden outhouse behind the barn, and a doorbell that I liked to turn. One day, Mother told me that the Hnidenkos were leaving and that we would be moving into their apartment. From overhearing my parents, I found out that Comrade Hnidenko had been "purged" from the party and that they were being exiled to Siberia.

I had difficulty visualizing how someone could be "purged," but eventually understood the process. There was only one political party in the whole country and that was the Communist Party of the Bolsheviks. At some party congress before the Revolution, the Communist Party had split into Bolsheviks, meaning the majority, and Mensheviks, the minority.

There had also been other parties that took part in the democratic revolution against the czar in February 1917, but they were all outlawed when the Bolsheviks seized all power in October 1917. Now the Bolsheviks wanted to make sure that no enemy, who might have belonged to another party in the past, would sneak into their ranks, and they decided to investigate all party members. One by one people were called in to a meeting where they had to prove their loyalty, to justify their decisions on the job, and to be second-guessed if those decisions did not work out. Their family background was thoroughly investigated to make sure that they were honest-to-goodness proletarians. This was a great opportunity for personal vendettas and settling of scores, and every now and then one heard of the victims having strokes or heart attacks during the process. Since Comrade Hnidenko was not local, inquiries were made into his background; it turned out that his real name was not Hnidenko, but Hniden, and that he was a son of a *kulak* or well-to-do farmer who employed (or, as it was called, "exploited") farm helpers. Since as a son of a *kulak* he could not advance under the Bolshevik system, he added the "ko" to his name in his documents and moved to a distant city, where he joined the party and eventually was assigned to Gorodok.

While we felt sorry for them, we still enjoyed moving into a large, airy room with wooden floors, high ceiling, and tall windows. Because it was only part of a larger apartment (the other part being occupied by the landlords) there was no kitchen, and Mother had to cook on the "primus" in a small hallway. But now we had an electric bulb suspended from the ceiling in a glass lampshade.

Only one lightbulb was allowed per room and it could not be more than 25 watts. Every now and then, inspectors unexpectedly knocked on doors in the evening demanding to examine the bulb. The penalty for having a larger bulb was an immediate discontinuation of service. Once they caught us with a 45-watt bulb, and Father made up a story that I broke the 25-watt one with a billiard cue.

Father had designed a billiard table and a cabinetmaker made it for us using strips of tire rubber on the sides and flannel for covering. For balls, we used ball bearings, which Father got from the tractor repair station that served the *kolkhozes* in the area. Whenever Father showed someone the pool table, he retold Mordovets's joke about the ball bearing.

Father had also made a projector with which he could create portraits by projecting photographs onto large sheets of photographic paper pinned to a wall. For this he needed a 200-watt lightbulb. When he was making portraits, we hung blankets over the windows and either I or Mother acted as lookouts in the street, watching for the inspectors.

Father worked at home late into the night, developing the glass negatives, retouching them, and printing photographs. He had a fairly good voice and usually sang quietly as he worked, mostly arias from operettas and operas. One of his favorites was Mario Cavaradossi's aria from *Tosca,* which has a line that, in Russian translation, is: "I've never thirsted for life as much as I do now." It was as if Father had a premonition of what was going to happen to him; I still hear his voice every time I hear this aria.

In the meantime, a lot was happening to others. Father subscribed to the Russian newspaper *Izvestia* (the News), published by the executive branch of the government in Moscow. The other big paper was *Pravda* (the Truth), published by the Central Committee of the Communist Party. There was a joke, which I did not hear until many years later, that in the "News" there was no truth, and in the "Truth" there was no news.

In addition to the usual glowing reports of overfulfilled grain delivery quotas and progress on building the canal between the Baltic and White Seas, which no one ever read, the newspapers provided multi-page reports on the show trials in Moscow. Former associates of Lenin, who had led the putsch in October 1917 against the democratic Temporary Government of Alexander Kerensky that had overthrown the czar in February 1917, were accused of being spies and saboteurs. After Lenin died in 1924, the leader of the Bolsheviks became Stalin, who was from Georgia, and whose real name was Dzhugashvili. Georgia is located between the Black Sea and the Caspian Sea in the Caucasus Mountains that separate Europe from Asia. Even though the Georgians are Christians—as a matter of fact, Stalin had been a seminarian—geographically, as well as by the degree of violence prevalent there, Georgia belongs to the Middle East.

Stalin's main competitor for power was Leon Trotsky, the man who had organized the Red Army that had won the civil war. To get rid of him, Stalin accused him of being a left deviationist from the party line and had him first exiled and then murdered in Mexico. Of course the party line was whatever Stalin said at that moment. The power of Communist propaganda was so great that when the news of Trotsky's death was announced, we kids danced for joy, chanting that the traitor was finally dead. Next to be killed were the top Red Army generals: Yakir, Gamarnik, and Tukhachevsky, who were also revolutionary heroes. One day I told Mother that a boy had told me that these generals were accused of being traitors. She turned pale and warned me never to repeat this to anyone. But it turned out to be true, and they were soon shot.

Then the same fate befell those who were accused of not being politically correct by deviating from the party line either to the left or to the right. Like Ivan the Terrible in the sixteenth century, Stalin killed everyone who disagreed with him, no matter how slightly, or who could become a rival for power. Eventually he killed all of Lenin's associates. It was difficult to understand why tough revolutionists would stand up in court and confess to all kinds of espionage, sabotage, and assassination plans in which they were presumably involved.

Only many years later did I read of some of the ways that this was brought about. About a year before the trials began, a law was promulgated according to which children over the age of twelve could be tried as adults. This law was used by the chief of the NKVD, Nikolai Ivanovich Yezhov, who threatened the accused that, unless they signed a confession and followed a prepared script at the trial, he would arrest their wives and daughters and have the man he employed as his torturer, an apelike, pox-marked gorilla, rape them in front of their eyes. Since the accused knew that they would be shot anyway, they did everything requested of them to spare their families. Incidentally, the chief prosecutor at these trials was Andrey Vyshinsky, the same man who later became the Soviet representative to the United Nations, with its commitment to human rights.

During this time, from 1936 to 1938, the U.S. ambassador to the Soviet Union was Joseph E. Davis, who bought the Soviet propaganda line and wrote in his book *Mission to Moscow* that he could tell just by looking at the defendants that they were guilty. He also wrote that the ultimate purpose of the Soviet state is to promote the brotherhood of men, and found excuses for every Soviet crime.

At all meetings it was mandatory for speakers to glorify the party and

Comrade Stalin, whose name always evoked a standing ovation. There was something almost religious in this glorification: only God is praised this way in the Bible. A problem arose when no one, including the speaker, wanted to be the first to stop applauding, because the NKVD kept an eye on all meetings. So they stood and applauded to save their lives, until their devotion to Stalin became so obvious that the speaker dared to raise his hand. In the newspapers this comedy was described as "stormy, extended applause, growing into an ovation."

In addition to praising Stalin, speakers often glorified some of the other leaders, particularly those in their area of endeavor. Expressing devotion to them might lead to a promotion. However, when these leaders were arrested as enemy agents, those who had praised them were accused of being their accomplices and were also arrested. This chain reaction created a potentially unlimited number of enemies, and no regional chief of the NKVD dared to report that he had run out of people to arrest or had caught fewer enemies than the chief of the neighboring region. A report like that could signal inadequate vigilance on his part, or perhaps even a cover-up of enemy activities, which could lead to his own arrest.

Such competition created a wildfire of terror and an unlimited supply of slave labor for various projects. The first big project of the Gulag (Central Administration of Concentration Camps) was to build a canal between the Baltic and the White Sea, a project that was billed as vital for the country and an example of what a Communist system could accomplish. It was built with picks and shovels at the cost of many thousands of human lives, but turned out to be a total waste, since it was used very little.

Another great accomplishment was a giant eight-engine airplane named *Maxim Gorky*, which after only a few flights collided with a small plane and crashed. A large delegation of Communists from all over the country, to whom this plane was being demonstrated, died in the crash; a second plane was never built. The biggest showplace of communism was going to be the Palace of the Soviets, which was to be taller than the Empire State Building. It was to be crowned by an enormous statue of Lenin and was to have moving sidewalks and air conditioning that would perfume the air with fragrances, so that the members of the Soviet could enjoy the smell of roses or violets while they were pondering the problems of the world. The Palace looked great on paper, but when they began excavating the foundation, they discovered more underground water than they were able to pump out, and the project was abandoned.

The NKVD chiefs were frequently shifted from one place to another, probably to prevent them from forming friendships and attachments. Soon Comrade Mordovets was gone and his place was taken by Comrade Belikov, whose cute blonde daughter was in my third-grade class. I remember her because, while no private person was allowed to have firearms, she once brought a .22 caliber rifle for our class play. Her father used it to shoot sparrows, which he fried and ate. One day she did not come to school and we later found out that both of her parents had been arrested; she and her baby brother were sent to an orphanage.

My parents did not comment on such events in my presence, but I saw that they were disturbed. This did not affect my own life very much. I started the first grade when I was six, a year earlier than I was supposed to, because two of my pals were going and, after the first-grade teacher met me, she agreed with Mother that I would not have any difficulties. I could read and write, which was more than most other kids my age could do. At that time the school had ten grades and was taught in Ukrainian. There was also a Polish and a Yiddish school in town.

In the second grade I hated calligraphy, in which we had to repeat individual strokes hundreds of times along the lines of slanted graph paper. I did not do a good job of it, which still shows in my horrible handwriting. Being bored, I whispered to my neighbors. When the teacher, a young village woman named Polyna Ivanovna, caught me at this, she pinched and pulled my ears so hard that they remained red and hurt for hours. After a while, I refused to go to school, pretending that I had headaches, and my parents had to drag me there by force. This lasted until I went into the third grade, with a new teacher and more challenging work. There I enjoyed all subjects except for the singing hour, which was just another name for brainwashing. I still remember one of the songs:

My dear little rifle, kill! Kill!
My dear little rifle, kill! Kill!

My dear little Red rifle,
Have no mercy on capitalists!

The word "Red" did not mean the color—it meant Communist, as in Red Army. "Capitalist" meant anyone who had any kind of business or provided employment.

The only health problems that I had were intestinal worms, which were common to all children and domestic animals, since we played a great deal in the mud. Most worms looked just like rain worms except that they were pale, but I also had another kind called "hair-heads," which had a nasty habit of crawling up my throat and choking me. Once in the middle of the night Father had to fetch a doctor, who made me swallow a spoonful of diluted turpentine, which chased them back down.

The other problem was with my eyes, which were red and tearing. The doctor said this was because I read too much. I had to limit my reading, particularly at night by the light of a kerosene lamp.

I managed to escape the scarlet fever, which was frequently fatal to children. In school we had to memorize a poem about a little girl who got sick with scarlet fever. Her "superstitious" mother gave her a medal of a saint to hold, but being a "militant atheist," she threw it away and died as a good Red Pioneer.

Every summer Father traveled to Odessa to buy his supplies, and twice Mother and I went with him. I still remember having my first cream soda at the Odessa railroad station and being convinced that this was the most delicious drink in the world. We had rented a whitewashed "chicken coop" practically at the edge of a cliff that dropped to the Black Sea, and stayed there for a month. I loved walking on the sandy beach, turning over stones, catching tiny shrimp and crabs that hid there, and gathering shells and smooth, colorful pebbles. The breeze smelled of seaweed and the air was full of spray that left a salty taste in one's mouth and dried to white powder on the skin. The village was a German colony called Lustdorf, which in German means "Village of Joy." In the evenings when it cooled off, we frequently took the streetcar to the nearby town called Arcadia, which had magnificent formal flower gardens and an ice-cream vendor. To this day, whenever I smell fragrant petunias, I am transported back to that garden by the time machine that resides in our olfactory sense. There was also another very fragrant plant, *mattiola,* which had tiny purple flowers with an incredibly strong fragrance that emanated from them at sunset. I have been insisting all these years that flowers in Eastern Europe were much more fragrant than flowers here, and everyone smiles benignly upon hearing this. However, years later I saw on television the painter Marc Chagall who, on his visit to Russia, was handed a bouquet. He immediately passed it to his wife, saying: "I've been telling you all these years that flowers in Russia are more fragrant than in the West, and here is the proof!"

When I was nine, my brother, Vilya, was born. I remember only that after Mother broke water she had to walk about a mile to the hospital, since there was no way of getting a carriage in the middle of the night. There was no ambulance in town and there were no private telephones. Individuals were not even allowed to own a horse. One could own only one cow and, when a calf was born, it had to be kept until it was weaned and then turned over to the government for a small payment. One could also own a pig, but when it was slaughtered, the skin had to be given to the government and there was a large penalty if this was not done.

Not far from our house, beyond the orchard and potato plots, behind a row of stately, perfectly shaped poplars, was the Polish cemetery, where we played hide-and-seek among the graves. Every one of the larger graves that had a burial vault had been broken into by robbers. I remember peeking into one vault and seeing an open coffin suspended from the ceiling on four chains; in it was a skeleton that still had some reddish hair on its skull.

We also liked to play war with realistic-looking machine guns, made by older boys. They had a wooden gear turned by a crank and a strip of bamboo from old coat hangers, which made a loud noise as it jumped from one tooth to the next. Our favorite game was something similar to baseball, but without a ball. We made an oval hole in the ground about two inches deep and five inches long, into which we placed a stick that was about six inches long, so that it protruded from the hole at an angle. The idea was to hit the end of this stick with another one, like a bat, so that it popped up in the air and could be hit horizontally, like a baseball. There were two teams, and the one that hit the stick farthest over several turns won. We also played a lot of soccer in which I, not being very aggressive, was always the goalkeeper.

Before the cemetery, in an overgrown apple orchard, stood the Palace of Red Pioneers. In the fall, when apples began to ripen, the orchard was guarded day and night by a man armed with a shotgun. According to rumors, the shotgun was loaded with rock salt that would make a painful but nonlethal wound. Whether or not this was true, it discouraged most of us from attempting to sample the apples on the way from school, and those who dared and succeeded were considered heroes. The large white building with columns had been the home of a wealthy merchant. It had high ceilings and large windows, and now housed a library of propaganda pamphlets, a theater for propaganda plays, and meeting rooms for activities associated with acquiring points for various pins, such as first aid, chemical defense, and "militant atheism." In front of the building was a soccer field, and at the side of the building was a meadow full of wildflowers and dandelions. No one seems to like dandelions, but I like their fragrance because I associate it with this meadow and think that, if sunshine could be smelled, it would smell of dandelions.

We all knew the names of all the flowers, grasses, and trees, which we could identify by their leaves, their bark, or even by the shape of their branches. We also knew which tree flowers were edible, such as those of white acacia—they tasted like early pea pods. Another delicacy was the sweet sap of cherry or plum trees, which dried as it seeped from cracks in the bark; it had the consistency of licorice candy and stuck to one's teeth.

My favorite pastime was reading. When I had a good book, I would rather stay home and read even when friends called me to play. I did not always like what they considered to be entertaining, such as building a barricade of stones and branches on the path leading to a blind woman's house and watching her stumble and curse.

Since my eyes were tearing and a doctor had told my parents not to allow me to read so much, we had many arguments on this subject. Love of books was instilled in me by Mother, who herself was an avid reader. She gave me children's stories by writers such as Turgenev and Tolstoy, magic tales by Pushkin, stories by the Brothers Grimm, and fables by Krylov, which were mostly translations of fables by Lafontaine, who in turn had translated them from Aesop. She emphasized that these were classics of literature, known to all literate people. Some stories were very sad and I remember shedding tears as I read Turgenev's "Mou-Mou," in which a homeless dumb man finds a dog and teaches him tricks so that they could appear in a circus show and escape their misery. When they finally succeed, a small boy in the audience recognizes his lost dog and calls him. The dog runs to the boy, leaving the man with tears running down his cheeks. Tears ran down mine too.

I also subscribed to a magazine called *Pioneer*, which, in addition to the mandatory articles about the glories of communism, contained some good features on science and culture. I remember reading a story about Rembrandt that described his technique of using light and shadow, illustrated by the portrait of an old man with a turban entitled *Portrait of an Old Jew*, and a story about Murillo and his paintings of street urchins. I also waited impatiently for the next monthly installment of an interesting Georgian epic poem, *Knight in a Tiger Skin*, about a beautiful princess named Tina-Tina by, I believe, medieval Georgian poet Shota Rustavelli.

One of the poems in the magazine explained to me what had happened to the Hnidenkos. It was by the Communist poet Vladimir Mayakovsky and was about the death of the great Russian poet Pushkin, who was killed in a duel with a French officer named Dantes. It went something like this: "Son of a bitch Dantes, who killed Pushkin. If you had asked him who were his parents and what were they doing before the revolution, it would have been the last you'd heard of him!"

What he was saying is that anyone whose parents were well off was an enemy and should be banished or liquidated just for belonging to the "capitalist" class, just as a few years later the Nazis were liquidating people for belonging to an ethnic group. While Mayakovsky was a fine and innovative poet, he was also a revolutionary propagandist. When he later realized what kind of a monstrous system he had helped to create, he blew out his brains.

The magazine also contained a very interesting section on technology; after I read each issue, half a dozen neighboring boys gathered in the evenings to hear me talk about machines, airplanes, and weapons. I was quite flattered by the fact that they were older than I, some by two or three years and one even by four. We spoke Ukrainian, which greatly displeased the mother of two of the boys, Lionek and Mun'ko, who were Polish, and on whose fence we usually sat during these sessions. Whenever their mother heard us, she would shout to them: "Lionek, Mun'ko, don't speak the peasant language!" The other kids—Vovka, Zhorka, Pavka, and Pet'ka[3]— were Ukrainian, and those were very awkward moments.

After having read Jules Verne's book *From Earth to the Moon,* I decided to write some science fiction stories myself and, together with two friends, formed a writers club. First of all we needed a place to work and made a table from a sheet of plywood and sawhorses in our woodshed. Mother invited us to write in the house, but we needed privacy. However, the club did not last very long. My story was about a cosmonaut's visit to all the planets of the solar system and the kinds of dangerous creatures he encountered there. Unfortunately, each visit occupied only a page or two before the subject was exhausted. The literary efforts of my friends were no better and, after a few sessions, the club was disbanded. Besides, it was getting rather cold in the shed and we could not write with mittens on.

I also began collecting stamps, which was not a simple matter, because one could not buy foreign stamps in our town, but had to acquire them by trading. Since we were getting letters from Father's parents in Romania, I had plenty of spares to trade. By looking up the relevant countries on a map I learned quite a bit about geography and began collecting maps of various countries. Some years after the war, I noticed that Tannu Tuva, a small country between the Soviet Union and Mongolia which issued beautiful stamps with pictures of animals, had disappeared from the map. It turned out that during the war, while the world's attention was focused elsewhere, the Soviet Union had gobbled Tannu Tuva up. Later on, I read in the biography of the Nobel Prize physicist Richard Feynman that he had noticed the same thing and for the same reason.

3. We called each other by the very familiar rough form, used mostly by children. Their proper names were Vladymyr, Zhorzh, Pavel, and Petro. I did not see the problems with using any language, but the Poles considered themselves to be above Ukrainians. I loved all languages. At home we spoke Russian and I found it fascinating to compare Russian, Ukrainian, and Polish for similarities and differences. When I was in the third grade, someone gave me an old German textbook; I tried to gather from it whatever I could without knowing the pronunciation, and looked forward to learning German in the fifth grade.

One day, an airplane landed in a field on the outskirts of town. None of us had ever seen a plane close up, so the whole town ran to look at it. It was a biplane, with one canvas wing above the other and an open cockpit. The pilot wore goggles and a leather hat with chinstraps. He landed because he did not know where he was. After someone found the place on his map, he started down the field, bouncing in the rills left by the plow, and we all cheered when he finally took off.

I watched, all entranced, as the plane became smaller and smaller, and thought how wonderful it must be to fly as free as a bird and not be tied down to one place. But how could something so heavy fly? I decided there and then that I had to find out.

Occasionally, I overheard serious discussions between Mother and Father that I did not understand until later. They concerned the fact that all private businesses were being pressured to join a cooperative called an *artel*. The only private businesses still remaining were one-man operations, since employing help would have been considered "exploitation" and was not permitted. The government continually increased their taxes and, at the same time, they were told that joining the *artel* was voluntary and that if they did not like being in it, they could leave again at any time. Mother advised Father to join, but he resisted and was one of the last holdouts. Eventually Mother prevailed and Father joined, which meant that he turned in all of his income in return for a salary. This salary was based on the divided income of the whole *artel*, which included cobblers, tailors, the water seller, the watchmaker, the barber, and also the competitor *partach*, which galled father probably more than anything else.

Before Father joined the *artel*, his earnings had been very good, because at that particular time everyone had to obtain an internal passport with a photograph. Before, only city-dwellers had to have these, but not peasants, which was a way of holding the peasants in the *kolkhozes*, because they could not move anywhere without a passport. The official explanation was that with all the suspected enemies, saboteurs, and spies around, the government needed everyone over age sixteen to have a photo identification. Father was

busy every day—photographing during the day and developing and printing at night and on Sundays. On Saturdays people stood in line outside the
door for hours, waiting to be photographed.

The salary Father received from the *artel* turned out to be only a fraction
of what he had been earning on his own, so he took the authorities at their
word and, in spite of Mother's objections and pleading, quit. Not only did
he quit the artel but also, despite Mother's even more violent objections, he
bought from the Berkoviches a plot adjacent to his studio and began building a new brick studio, leaving room for future living quarters for us. Mother was afraid that by doing this he was demonstrating that it was better not
to be in the *artel*. Given the political climate and the fact that Father was
born abroad, she thought that building a new studio could be dangerous.
Father's reply was that he was told by the authorities that membership in
the *artel* was voluntary, and he did not believe that they did not mean what
they said.

The construction took the entire summer of 1937 because, when it was
half-finished, Father discovered that a large part of the front wall was out of
plumb and it had to be torn down brick by brick and rebuilt. After that he
made sure every day that the walls were truly vertical by checking them with
a plumb line.

For a while, the arrests and trials took place far from home, in Moscow
and Leningrad, and affected only members of the Communist Party. The
party's infighting had been going on ever since Lenin died in 1924 and Stalin came to power in spite of Lenin's will, in which he had warned against
giving power to Stalin. But the will disappeared and Stalin, who had been
in charge of party personnel and had appointed many of his followers to
high positions, was elected by the Central Committee to Lenin's job as the
first secretary of the party, which was the equivalent of being president. According to rumors, a dynamic secretary of the party in Leningrad, Sergey
Kirov, was going to compete with Stalin for the position of first secretary at
the next session of the Central Committee in 1934, but Kirov was assassi-
nated in his office when for some unknown reason his NKVD guards left

their posts. Stalin immediately accused his potential rivals of plotting to assassinate party leaders and ordered the arrests of his opponents and a purge of the party.

In the Ukraine, a man named Golubenko was shot for presumably plotting to assassinate the Ukrainian party secretary, Pavlo Petrovich Postyshiv, who, several months later, was himself arrested and shot. I had heard that Postyshiv used to dress in peasant clothes and visit various offices to see how a peasant would be treated. This could have made him popular, which Stalin would have found threatening.

In 1936, when Genrich Iagoda, the chief of the NKVD who had supervised the show trials, was arrested and shot, terror spread throughout the whole country. A whole new group of old Bolsheviks who had helped Lenin grab power in 1917 were accused of plotting against Stalin, sabotaging industry, and spying for the capitalists. Since they had been in charge of various departments that controlled everything in the country, all of their supporters and underlings in the provinces also became suspect.

In industry, if a machine broke down in a factory, particularly if it had been imported and spare parts were not readily available, the managers and engineers were accused of sabotage and frequently were executed. Production was coming to a halt because so many people had been arrested; those who remained did not dare to make decisions.

The terror did not bypass the NKVD, either. The new chief, Yezhov, began exterminating Iagoda's men, who knew too much; now the old torturers were tortured by new torturers and the old executioners were executed by new executioners. They were so terrorized that, as I read later, sometimes, upon hearing a knock on their office door, they jumped out of the window or put a bullet through their heads. Occasionally they may have done this when the knock was at the office next door. I could not help gloating when I read these stories.

"Yezh" in Russian means a hedgehog, and posters appeared all over the country showing Yezhov in a pointed cavalry hat, wearing spiny hedgehog gloves, and choking a squirming capitalist with bulging eyes and a long, dangling tongue. The inscription said: "Choke the enemy with hedgehog gloves!"

When the concentration camps of the Gulag had been filled, the NKVD began executing prisoners in ditches in the forests by shooting them one by one behind the ear. The name "concentration camp" was coined by Lenin in 1918. According to Aleksandr Solzhenitsyn's *Gulag Archipelago,* approximately five million people were killed in this way. Then, in 1940, Stalin told Yezhov that he had broken too many dishes and had him arrested and tortured until he admitted being a spy and saboteur. Then he was taken to a slaughterhouse that he had built and was shot. As they say in Russian: "A dog deserves a dog's kind of death." The new head of the NKVD was Lavrenti Beria, another Middle Eastern despot who was one of Stalin's old pals and who had been the NKVD chief in Georgia.

Amidst all this slaughter Stalin had issued a new constitution, which he appropriately named after himself. It was proclaimed to be the most democratic constitution in the world, guaranteeing freedom of person, freedom of speech, and freedom of assembly. Except for stating that all land and all means of production belonged to the state, it might have been acceptable anywhere in the world. It even guaranteed individual republics the right to secede, and this at a time when tens of thousands of people were being shot on accusations of nationalism and of wanting to secede.

Then events came close to home. After the local NKVD chief, Belikov, disappeared, the father of one of my classmates was arrested, presumably for being a Polish spy. His parents lived in Poland, and he had corresponded with them. In Soviet parlance, this meant that he had contact with a foreign country. All this information was rumored, since the local newspaper, which, like all newspapers in the country, was published by the government, did not say a thing.

Mother became very worried because Father was corresponding with his parents in Romania, and again urged him to rejoin the *artel.* However, Father remained calm, saying that he did not believe that someone who did not commit any crime had any reason to be afraid. Then our apartment neighbor—Comrade Studnitz, the director of the Yiddish school—and several of his schoolteachers were arrested on the same night because they presumably had been Zionists. According to rumor, the NKVD found a list of people who as children had attended a Zionist summer camp in the early 1920s.

I happened to be near Father's studio very early in the morning when I saw Studnitz and five of his teachers on the back of the NKVD truck, guard-

ed by two NKVD men with rifles. He sat there holding his chin and looking at the floor. His face was the color of ash.

Every morning a truckload of prisoners who had been rounded up during the night departed from the NKVD courtyard. Rumor had it that it was
the local watchmaker, by the name of Gluzman, who signed the denuncia-
tions. Being an obnoxious person, he had many enemies and presumably at
first settled personal scores, but then he began signing whole lists prepared
by the NKVD.

In spite of the fact that the NKVD was outside the law, they were very
punctilious with regard to procedure. In order to arrest someone, they had
to have a signed denunciation. Even the dreaded *troikas,* teams of three
anonymous NKVD judges who sentenced millions of people to death without even seeing them, had to procure signed confessions. How the confessions were obtained did not matter; whole armies of sadistic torturers were
employed in obtaining them. The new NKVD chief, Beria, was quoted as
having said that within three days he could make any man confess to being
the Prince of Wales. If the prisoner died under torture this was not a problem, since such deaths were attributed to natural causes and the corpses were
never released to relatives for burial.

Many years later, a friend of mine, Walter, told me that his mother had
been arrested and sent to a Siberian concentration camp without having
signed a confession. It appears that the interrogator did not want to torture
a woman and falsified her signature. Somehow Walter's father managed to
prove this to a new head of the NKVD in their city; she was released and
the interrogator was imprisoned.

At three o'clock in the morning of April 17, 1938, Mother's worst fears
became reality—Father was being led away into the night.

Trembling, he hugged and kissed Mother, me, and Vilya, who woke up
crying. The NKVD men pulled out their guns, and Father was gone.

After the door closed behind them, Mother and I sat together holding
one another and sobbing. When it grew light, Mother said, "Go ask Lisa
Mitbreit to come over. Tell her I am having some problems with my milk,

and I need her help with the baby." Mother had just begun weaning Vilya, who was nine months old.

I ran to the Mitbreits, who were just sitting down for breakfast, and managed to transmit Mother's request without breaking down. Lisa promised to be right over. When she did not come after some time, Mother asked me to go there again. This time I broke into tears as soon as I entered the house and barely managed to make clear what had happened. They looked at one another and Lisa went with me quickly. At that time I did not realize that being seen at our house might have endangered Lisa's father, but very soon people began crossing the street so that they would not have to greet Mother, and Lisa began coming only after dark.

One day, after looking around to make sure that no one would see him, the young NKVD man who had arrested Father came up to Mother in the street and told her that he was very sorry, that it was not his doing; it was just his job. Mother was moved to tears.

After several days without any news from Father, Mother went to the NKVD headquarters to find out where Father was and what he was being accused of, but was told to inquire in the nearest city, Proskurov. She arranged for Handzia to stay with us and took a train there, hoping also to bring Father a parcel with food and clean clothing and his immigration papers. She returned on the third day completely exhausted and disheartened. Parcels were accepted only in the mornings, and there were hundreds of women standing in line. In order not to lose their place they slept in the roadside ditch for two nights. When she finally reached the window, she was told that father was not there: he had been transferred to Vinnitsa, the regional capital.

The following week she went to Vinnitsa, but after a similar experience in the line she was told that Father had been transferred back to Proskurov. This went on for about a dozen trips, back and forth, with the same results.

The great Russian poet Anna Akhmatova, whose husband, poet Nikolai Gumilev, was executed in the 1920s and whose son, Lev, was imprisoned in 1935, had also stood in lines at prisons and described this experience in her poem *Requiem, 1935-1940*. In 1996 the poem was selected as one of the "Books of the Century" by the New York Public Library. I will cite only the dedication in my own translation which, like most translations of poetry, conveys what the poem is about, but does not fully recreate the images and feelings. She wrote:

Instead of a Foreword

During the frightful years of the Yezhov terror I spent seventeen months waiting in lines outside prisons in Leningrad. Once, someone has recognized me. Then a woman with purple-from-the-cold lips, who stood behind me in line and who had never heard my name, was roused from the common torpor and whispered in my ear (over there we all spoke in whispers):

"Can you describe this?" And I said: "I can." Then, something resembling a smile slipped over what had once been her face.

Dedication

Before this sorrow, mountains bow
And mighty river halts its flow,
But strong are prison's locks
In front of penal burrows
And deathly longing—
For someone fresh breeze blows,
For someone sunset lingers—
We do not know, we're all alike,
We only hear the awful screech of keys
And soldiers' heavy steps.
We rose as if for early prayer,
Dragged our feet through jungle of the town,
There we have met, as breathless as the dead,
The sun still low and the Neva outspread,
And hope sings always far ahead.
The sentence . . . And the tears break through,
Severed from all,
As if the life torn out from heart,
As if knocked down flat,
But still is walking . . . Wobbling . . . All alone . .
Where are my friends against their will
For two disastrous years?
What do they see in the Siberian storms,
What do they fancy in the circle of the moon
To them I say—farewell

March 1940

Most of the time, while Mother shuttled between prisons, I was left in full charge of Vilya. Handzia or Lisa stayed with us overnight, but it was I who had to feed him, to clean and comfort him. We were never sure when Mother would be back. It all depended on the length of the lines at the prisons. Usually, she returned within three days, but we never knew. She developed huge black rings under her eyes and a wistful, distant look, lost a lot of weight, and never smiled. Her three brothers came, one at a time, but they could not stay for more than a week.

One evening, Grisha-the-Elder (there was also a Grisha-the-Younger) asked Mother why she had left the window open in the pantry. She responded that she had not, and it turned out that the window had been removed by a burglar. This added another worry, namely that a burglar, knowing that there was no man in the house, might strike again, perhaps when Mother was not home.

About a week after Father was arrested, groups of peasants whom Father had photographed for their passports began appearing at the house, demanding either their photos or their money back. There was no way that Mother could know who had actually been photographed and who had not, because, being overwhelmed by the demand for passport photos, Father stopped giving receipts and depended on the photo itself to identify the customers. Fortunately, Mother had occasionally helped Father and, working straight through many nights, somehow managed to develop the negatives and print the photos. The work had to be done at home at night because she did not want to be alone in the darkroom at the studio and there was no way that all daylight could be excluded in the room at home.

Then the Finance Department descended upon us demanding payment of income tax. The name of the chief of the *Finotdel* was Povolotsky, and Mother's expression always changed to furious whenever his name was mentioned. He was tall and thin, with a pockmarked face, bald head, and an upturned mustache. He had an obnoxious, fat son named Kiva, who never missed an opportunity to bully me.

When the hopelessness of her prison trips became apparent, Mother decided to go to the headquarters of the NKVD in Kiev, the capital of Ukraine. There, instead of standing in a line, she had to register and to come back every day until called, which could have taken weeks. The only alternative was to give a substantial bribe, which she did, but upon reaching a high official she was told that they had no information about Father and instructed to inquire in Proskurov, where she had started. In desperation, she decided to go to the very top—to Moscow—and see Vyshinsky, the chief procurator, an equivalent of attorney general, who had been the chief prosecutor at the show trials. It took all the money we had left to pay the enormous bribes required at each step, but when Mother finally made it to the anteroom of his office and the secretary announced her, she heard him yell: "Who the hell let her in? Throw her out immediately!" Of course she did not get back any of the bribe money.

Mother returned home completely distraught. "There is nothing I can do any more," she said. "I've spent all the money trying to find out Father's fate, but I've been beating my head against a wall. There must be a trial or something; he cannot just vanish as though swallowed by the ocean!"

Some days later, Mother said: "You know, son, there may be something that you can do." Whenever she called me "son," I knew it was serious. "People say that Comrade Stalin probably does not know about these arrests. The posters say that he is a friend of children; *you* must write to him." Indeed, there were posters everywhere showing Stalin holding in his arms a young girl in a sailor suit and proclaiming: "Stalin—Friend of Children!"

I felt blood rushing to my head. "I can't, Mama! I can't beg him as if he were a czar!"

"You must!" she screamed in tears. "I have done all I could! It is your turn to do something! Don't tell me you are too proud to beg for your Father! I am not!"

She pushed a notebook in front of me and brought a pen and an inkwell. "Write!" she ordered. With a shaking hand I dipped the pen into the inkwell and began:

"Dear Comrade Stalin!

"I am ten years old," dictated Mother. At this point my tears began to run and drip onto the paper. I can still taste their bitterness. "I will start from scratch," I said. "No," said Mother, "let him see your tears, perhaps they will soften his heart."

I wrote down all the data about Father's arrest, begging Stalin to look into his case and let us know where he was and why he was arrested. Then I addressed the envelope: "Moscow, Kremlin, To Comrade Stalin." In the Soviet Union the name of the city is written first and the name of the recipient last. I took the letter to the post office and asked the clerk to send it by registered mail. He read the address, regarded me with pity in his eyes and shook his head without saying a word. I am sure that this was not the first such letter that he had seen.

Now that we were broke and could not pay the rent, Mother decided to move into the studio office. It was now our turn to sell the plush furniture that we had bought two years ago from a German couple by the name of Melkhert, when they were being exiled to Siberia. For several generations they had owned a cast iron foundry, which was confiscated after the Revolution, though Mr. Melkhert was retained as manager. One summer evening I visited them with Father and we bought several chairs, a table, and a couch upholstered in green velvet. They were an elderly, gentle, sad-looking couple and they offered us tea and cookies. Now *we* became the Melkherts and I understood how they must have felt when strangers invaded their house, picking, pocking, and bargaining.

Mother also hoped that by moving into the studio, it might not be confiscated as threatened by the cursed Povolotsky, whom she challenged to prove that Father's sentence specified confiscation of property. Seeing the charges against Father could reveal what he was being accused of and perhaps what had happened to him. Povolotsky told her to inquire again at NKVD headquarters, where she was told that Father had been sentenced to ten years for anti-Communist activities, under Chapter 58, Paragraph 10 of the Criminal Code, without the right to correspond and with confiscation of property. When she asked where he was and for a document stating the sentence, she was told to get out and never show her face again, or she also would be arrested.

Forty years later I read in Solzhenitsyn's *Gulag Archipelago* that sentence without the right to correspond did not exist, and that it meant that he had either died during interrogation under torture or had been executed.

On January 16, 1989, there was a Ukase of the Presidium of the Supreme Soviet of the USSR entitled: "On Additional Actions to Restore Justice Regarding the Victims of Repressions Taking Place in the Period of 1930-1940 and the Beginning of the 1950s."

Soon afterwards, when Mikhail Gorbachev came to power and instituted glasnost, which means "openness," my uncle Samuel gathered enough courage to send a letter to the NKVD, now renamed the KGB, inquiring about Father's fate. About six months later, he received a reply from the "Military Procurator of the Red-Banner Sub-Carpatian Military Region," dated December 5, 1989:

Certificate

This is to confirm that citizen Konstantinovsky, Nisson Rachmilevich, born March 1, 1902, was repressed on September 26, 1938 by the decision of a NKVD troika, having been accused of espionage. In accordance with the Ukase of the Presidium of the Supreme Soviet of USSR of January 16, 1989, he is being rehabilitated (posthumously).

Documents of this case do not contain information on the place of burial.

Colonel of Jurisprudence F. K. Shepetov.

The "troika" were three NKVD "judges," who sentenced whole lists of victims according to what they were accused of, but without having seen

them. Actually, there was no need to confront them because, under torture, they had already signed their confessions. The word "repressed" was the NKVD's euphemism for "executed." In his book *1984*, George Orwell describes a totalitarian society where words mean whatever the party says they mean and the thought police execute prisoners by shooting them in the back of their head, unexpectedly, as they walk down a hallway. This method was not cruel enough for the NKVD. As one executioner told in a televised interview after the disintegration of the Soviet Union, the prisoners were lined up on the edge of a ditch and he went from one to the next putting a bullet behind each one's ear. He said he did it for endless hours and complained that his trigger finger hurt very much.

As to not knowing the place of burial, I was told later that the NKVD had kept meticulous records of everything. However, they could not tell us because that would have disclosed the location of the killing fields.

At the time, of course, we did not know any of this, and every day we eagerly awaited the mail, hoping that this would be the day we heard from Father. In the meantime we lived by selling things. The only objects that Mother swore not to sell were Father's two cameras. The cameras had to be there for Father whenever he might return.

When my hair grew so long that I began looking like a girl, Mother, over my violent objections, decided to cut it herself to save money. She sat me down in a chair, wrapped a bedsheet over my shoulders, and began to clip away with Father's paper scissors, which pulled my hair instead of cutting it. I screamed and carried on but she clipped away, every now and then stopping to look at her handiwork. Then, all of a sudden, she put down the scissors and said, "I am sorry, I made a mess of your hair. Go to the barber and have him fix it."

When I looked in the mirror, I could not believe my eyes. Bunches of hair protruded at odd angles and I looked like a mangy dog. I screamed, "I want you to come with me and explain to the barber what you have done." But Mother would not hear of it and I did not have much of a choice. The barber had a good laugh and, since it was beyond repair, cut off all my hair with manual clippers.

Chapter 2

1938–1941

In August we received the order to move out of the border zone. It did not leave any room for interpretation: we were given two weeks to disappear. If we did not, we would be forcibly resettled in an unspecified distant region, which to us meant Siberia. Our building was being confiscated and would become state property. I remember overhearing Mother telling someone later that she had received a proposition from a powerful Communist official, who said that if she would meet him in the lovers' lane (which in Gorodok was the cemetery) the order might be rescinded.

The only relative to whom we could turn for help was my mother's father, David, who with his three sons lived far away in Zaporozhie. However, Zaporozhie was a big industrial city and it was impossible for a family of an "enemy" to obtain a police permit, called a *pripiska,* to live there. What were we to do?

Since we did not want to move far away in case Father should return and look for us, Mother began making day trips to towns just outside the fifty-kilometer border zone, hoping to get a permit to move there. I learned to cook farina porridge for Vilya, who had just been weaned, and to change his diapers. He was a cuddly little fellow and not very demanding. Finally, as the day of exile approached, Mother found a small town called Derazhnya, about forty miles (sixty kilometers) east of Gorodok, where the chief of militia took pity on her and granted the *pripiska.*

Mother sold whatever she could; some things were left with friends, and our most valuable possessions—Father's two cameras and the shiny, nickel-plated samovar—were dispatched to Grandfather. We bundled up whatever the two of us could carry and headed for the railroad station in a hired horse wagon that belonged to some government office, whose driver was trying to make money on the side.

On her previous trip, Mother had rented a room in the house of a farmer, not far from the railroad station. The house had a thatched roof and clay floors. It consisted of only one room, which was ours, and a kitchen, where the farmer with his wife and their small son lived and slept on a wide bench behind a rough wooden table. There was no electricity, and the drinking water was kept in a bucket in a small entryway. We had a bed with a straw-filled mattress and the use of a plywood wardrobe. The walls were white-washed, and if one accidentally leaned against them, the whitewash rubbed off onto the clothing.

But it was summer, and there were cherry trees outside the window and flowers along the wooden fence. There was a swinging gate and next to it a cut-out in the fence about two feet wide and a foot and a half from the ground, with a horizontal plank, so that one could step over the low part of the fence without having to open the gate. The purpose of this contraption was to keep in the cow and piglets, but to keep out strays, which roamed around feeding on whatever was available.

The farmer and his wife were about Mother's age, around thirty. As a welcoming gift, they presented us with a pitcher of cool milk and half a loaf of delicious crusty, dark, home-baked bread. They both worked in a *kolkhoz,* which also provided day care for their boy. I rather liked the place and in a few days made friends with a neighborhood boy named Mitia, who was my age, and with a girl named Lena, who was a few years older. They both ran around barefoot, as did our landlords and most of the farmers. Shoes were worn only when they were needed, just as one wore gloves only when they were necessary. Not to be different, I also walked barefoot, and after a couple of weeks of discomfort, the soles of my feet became tough and I did not miss the shoes, or rather the leather slippers or sandals that I usually wore in the summer. The dirt roads were covered with fine dust, which felt pleasantly silky between the toes, as did walking on the grass.

The kids showed me around the yard of the *kolkhoz.* The cow barns and horse stables were made of adobe with thatched roofs, and were surrounded by mountains of manure, which was used as fertilizer. The blacksmith's forge had large bellows, operated by a pull chain. At its nozzle, in the burning coal, a piece of iron glowed brighter with every squeeze of the bellows. The stocky blacksmith in a dirty leather apron gripped the glowing iron with long tongs and brought it to the anvil where after several strikes of his hammer, it was transformed into a horseshoe. Then it went back into the fire and again came out red hot and the blacksmith pierced it in several places, making nail holes, and then quenched it in a bucket of water, where it hissed and raised a cloud of steam.

On the threshing floor, two men pounded sheaves of winter rye with flails, which consisted of two sticks connected end to end by a leather strap. The men swung the flails rhythmically one after the other, until the kernels fell out of the spikes. Then the straw was removed and the grain, with its husks and bits of straw, was gathered by women and poured into the hopper of the hand-cranked winnowing machine. As it fell from the bottom of the hopper, wind created by a fan blew away the husks and other debris and clean rye kernels flowed into sacks. Another machine was used to chop up the straw into short pieces used for animal food in the winter as well as for making adobe bricks. It had a large cast-iron wheel with a crank that turned a set of blades. The straw was pushed into the blades in small bunches by hand; I was told that many a careless finger had been chopped up with the straw.

I also got to ride a horse for the first time, but without a saddle, I did not feel very safe on the undulating back of the beast, even though the horse was old and did not move very fast.

Somehow Mother managed to enroll Vilya in a day care for children of railroad workers near the railroad station. While for Vilya and me things were reasonably satisfactory, for Mother the situation was very different. The only job she was able to find was digging peat moss in the turf bogs. She had to cut out rectangles about a foot wide, a foot and a half long, and four inches thick, and stack them like bricks to dry, so that they could be used as fuel in the winter. The first problem was that the clothes she brought with us were the best she had, since she was hoping to find a job as a waitress or in a store. There was nothing she could buy in Derazhnya, so there she was, about five feet tall, slim, in her navy-blue suit and light shoes, trying to dig peat in a soggy bog beside husky peasant types in rags and heavy boots. Pay was based on the output and after one week, with huge blisters on her hands, ruined shoes, and only pennies to show for it, she gave up. In the stillness of the night I heard her sobbing and bit my lips so as not to start sobbing myself.

Her next job was stacking bricks in a brick factory. Coming home, she was barely able to step over the fence. She staggered into the room, fell on the bed, and did not even bother to wipe the tears. I was at a total loss. On the one hand, I wanted to hug her and cry with her, but on the other, I felt a duty to be strong. I was the "man" of the family and could not afford to show weakness.

One day the landlady, who was very kind to us, asked me what happened to my father, and I told her. When she gave me a strange look and said that she thought he had died, I realized that Mother had been afraid to tell her the truth, and that I had spilled the beans. I became terrified.

When I told Mother what had happened, she hugged me tight and, through tears, whispered in my ear: "It is all my fault, I should have told you. You are not a child any more," and we cried together, intermixing our tears.

The next morning the landlady asked Mother to sit down at the table. "You know, I had a terrible nightmare last night," she said. "I dreamt that you had disappeared and had taken our greatest possession, the *kilim* that we keep in the drawer of the wardrobe in your room." Mother did not say anything. After a moment of silence, the landlady asked: "Why did you not tell us the truth?"

"I was afraid you would not take us in," whispered Mother. "I am very sorry."

"But there are hundreds of families like yours here," said the landlady. "Half of the workers at the railroad station have been arrested. There is no one to do the work."

That night the landlord had a long talk with Mother and assured her that we had nothing to fear. I liked him a lot. He was a big, friendly man with blue eyes, curly blond hair, and huge hands. He had introduced me to Mitia and Lena and, like I, he could not roll his "r's".

In the meantime, Mother's older brother, Grisha-the-Elder, who lived with Grandfather in Zaporozhie, became engaged to a secretary at the militia headquarters, where they issued *pripiskas*. While she could not arrange a *pripiska* in the city for an "enemy family," she managed to get one in a nearby village called Khortitsa. This was wonderful news because Mother was just about to collapse, so, after thanking our kind landlords, we were on our way to Zaporozhie, where I would arrive in time for the beginning of the school year, going into the fourth grade.

Mother's father and three brothers, Grisha-the-Elder, Samuel, and Grisha-the-Younger, lived in a suburban settlement for factory workers. It was called the "First of May Settlement" and was located just outside of Zaporozhie, about two miles from the end of a streetcar line. The reason there were two Grishas was that the real name of the younger one was Hershel, but he preferred to be called Grisha. His Ukrainian wife, Lyuba, called him Hryts'ko.

My three uncles met us at the station and carried Vilya and the luggage to the house in the settlement. Mother and Vilya stayed with Hryts'ko and Lyuba, who was pregnant, and I went with Grisha and Samuel, who were single and lived with Grandfather.

They were renting a room in a small bungalow, number 42 Krasin Street, that had a large backyard with a vegetable garden and peach, plum, and cherry trees. The room itself was only big enough to accommodate two rough wooden bunks along the walls and a small table in between, under a window. Grandfather and Grisha slept in one bunk, and Uncle Samuel and I in the other. The bunks were not meant for two people. The mattresses were burlap sacks stuffed with straw and were as lumpy as a camel's back. A bare lightbulb hung from the ceiling in the middle of the room.

From outside, one entered a small hallway furnished with the usual water barrel. Water had to be brought in buckets from a hand pump at the end of the block. From the hallway one entered the kitchen, which had a wood-burning stove with two nests of cast-iron rings. The cast-iron pots used for cooking were pear-shaped, with the small end downward. By removing some rings from the stove opening, one could regulate how far the pots protruded into the fire. About two feet away from the stove was a bench, then a rough table and, at the wall, another bench, a wider one, that served as a bed for another tenant, a young man named Izzy. He had been recently discharged from the army; not having any other clothes, he still wore his uniform.

The door straight ahead led to our room; the door to the left, to the sitting room, where there was a couch on which slept a young woman tenant. Behind the sitting room was a small bedroom where the landlord slept with his wife, their son Zhora (a year older than me), and their daughter Lyuba (a year younger than me).

The landlord was Comrade Ivan Grigorievich Protsenko, who was a candidate for membership in the Communist Party. This meant that twice a week after work he had to attend lectures on the history of communism and on the current party line that were supposed to prepare him for full membership. In the evenings, he liked to sit on the kitchen bench with his elbow on the table and his index finger alongside his nose. He repeated whatever he could remember of those lectures about the latest party ukases and current international developments. During these discourses my uncles exchanged glances and suppressed smiles, because this comrade was way out of his depth; it appeared he parroted polysyllabic words without understanding them. He was a laborer at the "Communar" harvester factory, where Uncle Grisha-the-Elder worked as a welder and Uncle Samuel as a foundry-man.

After a few days, Mother and Vilya left for Khortitsa, where Mother found a job in a nursery school. This meant that Vilya could be with her and they could also eat there, but Mother's earnings were barely sufficient to pay the rent for their tiny, furnished room.

The school in our settlement was taught in Russian rather than Ukrainian, which made no difference to me. Since my uncles were at work every day and Grandfather's Russian was not very good, I went to the school alone with my third-grade certificate and, much to the amazement and amusement of the director and teachers, registered for the fourth grade. Remembering the problem I caused in Derazhnya, I told them that my father was dead and that I had come to live with my grandfather. Everyone was very sympathetic and my teacher, a tall, red-headed woman with an encouraging smile, gave me a list of textbooks and introduced me to the class as Etan. This unheard-of name raised a few eyebrows and evoked some teasing, but it ended a few weeks later when on the way home from school I gave one of the bullies a bloody nose.

Uncle Samuel, roommate Izzy, Grandfather David, and Grisha-the-Elder, 1937.

Grandfather David in
Russia during World War II.

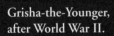
Grisha-the-Younger,
after World War II.

At that time the government had abolished days of the week. Schools and factories functioned for five days and were closed on the sixth, so that instead of having two days off we had only one. This created so much confusion that in less than a year everything reverted back to a Monday-through-Saturday-noon workweek, which was also the school week.

Both of my uncles were in their twenties and, in order to get ahead, they had to join the Communist Youth Union known as Komsomol. They duly reported that their sister was married to an "enemy of the people," but since by now most families had "enemy" relatives, they were not kicked out. In addition to attending meetings and spending one Saturday a month working without pay on the so-called *Subotnik* (in Russian, Saturday is called *Subota*), they also had to "agitate," that is, to propagandize among the benighted about the splendors of communism. For this they were given a guidebook and a special report notebook, which they had to submit every month. Once, when they were agitating our next-door neighbor, I had a chance to listen in. This neighbor was at least twice their age, held a white-collar job, and did not socialize with his blue-collar neighbors. His house was larger and nicer than the one we lived in and was enclosed by a tall fence.

My uncles waited for him to come out of the house after dinner. One was watching the front door while the other kept an eye at the rear. When he appeared, they asked very politely if they could come over to talk about the new constitution; with the NKVD on the rampage, he did not really have much choice. They sat on a bench behind the house, and while my uncles took turns explaining all the wonderful freedoms guaranteed by the new constitution, the neighbor silently but gravely nodded his head. They were somewhat disappointed that he did not ask any questions, because their "Agitator's Companion" had all the answers, but they had done their job and, with my help with their spelling, wrote a nice report.

One day my uncles did not come home from work at the expected time. Grandfather was very worried since they had not told him that they would be late. He prepared dinner at the usual time, around seven. When they did not show up by nine, we all began to worry. They finally appeared around ten, beaming from ear to ear, proudly displaying a book, which they had stood in line for more than three hours to obtain. The book was the *Abbreviated History of the All-Union Communist Party of the Bolsheviks*. They were convinced that studying this book would help them advance in the ranks of the Komsomol, which would in turn help them to get better jobs.

Leafing through this "magic" book, I noticed that it followed chapter-by-chapter the *History of the Soviet Union* textbook that we studied in school, except that the chapters were longer and contained much more detail. This gave me an idea. For the next history class I read the assigned chapter from our book, then the corresponding chapter from my uncles' book. I memorized as many details as I could about a certain party congress, where it took place, who said what, and all the rest of the boring material. When the teacher asked us a question, I raised my hand and responded in much more detail than was given in our textbook. As I spoke, her eyes opened wider and wider and then her jaw dropped as she stared at me in disbelief. I told her about the other book but she remained impressed by my interest and effort. From that day on I became her favorite pupil and she even left me in charge whenever she had to leave the room. I continued doing this through the rest of the year and graduated from the fourth grade first in my class with a letter of commendation, which was the highest honor. The school director himself commended me on my interest in communism, telling me that he was very glad to have in his school a dedicated student who made such efforts to learn about the history of the party, which was the more impressive since I was so young. If he had only known the truth!

In 1939 a new political plague struck the country just as arrests had somewhat subsided. It was decreed that employees who came to work more than five minutes late were to forfeit their pay for three months, while those who skipped a day without permission were to be sentenced to six months at forced labor. Comrade Protsenko, our landlord, explained to us the need for work discipline. He said the whole country would go to hell if people were allowed to goof off, but by the way he was hesitating, I did not think he really believed what he said. Even his wife, Olga Petrovna, who worked as a cleaning woman at the factory office and always looked at him with adoration and respect when he pontificated, this time questioned the justice of all this. "What if the sickness lasts only one day and when the person sees the company doctor on the next, he is already well?" she asked. "Should he be imprisoned for that? And what if the streetcars are so packed that a person has to walk and comes in a little late, how is he going to feed his family for three months without pay?" No one had an answer for her. My uncles pretended not to have heard her.

One evening, Olga Petrovna's sister came to the house in tears. She told us that her husband had not felt well that morning and stayed home, intending to go to the doctor the next day and obtain sick leave permission, but they had a leak in the roof and he decided to fix it. When the company functionary arrived to check why he had not shown up for work, he found her husband on the roof. He was arrested that afternoon, and she had come to see whether her party candidate brother-in-law could do anything to save him from imprisonment. However, Comrade Protsenko could not promise her anything and just mumbled something about discipline.

He also believed in maintaining discipline in his family, and every time Zhora transgressed, the following little drama was performed:

Comrade Protsenko: "Zhorka (a rough form of Zhora), bring me the strap!"

Zhora (whimpering): "Daddy, I will never do it again, I will never do it again . . ." repeated continuously as he heads toward the bedroom dragging his feet and shuffles back with his father's belt in his hand.

Comrade Protsenko: "Drop your pants and lie down on the couch!"

Zhora (crying much louder): "Daddy I will never do it again, never do it again, never, never, never . . ." as he drops his pants and lies down, with his bottom up.

Comrade Protsenko would strike Zhora's bottom with the strap, counting aloud the blows, the number of which was proportional to the transgression, while Zhora screamed his mantra louder and louder with each blow. This spectacle was repeated at least once a month. The girl, Lyuba, usually got away with just a slap on the behind.

On a sunny October Sunday we went to visit Mother and Vilya. First we had to walk about two miles to the streetcar, which took us across town to New Zaporozhie, a city being built near the hydroelectric power plant at the huge concrete dam across the River Dnieper that had been built by Americans. I had read a great deal about it and the miracles made possible by the electricity produced by the dam. One of them was a glass greenhouse where vegetables grew year round and where the writer reported having tea prepared without having to make a fire—you just plugged the tea kettle into an outlet in the wall.

I marveled at the tall buildings, some five stories high, and at the asphalt pavement, which, unlike cobblestones, was smooth as glass. Another street-car took us across the dam, which was even more impressive in reality than I had imagined from pictures. Water cascaded from it onto huge rocks, which centuries ago had forced the Vikings, on their way to the Black Sea, to carry their boats around the rapids and be subjected to ambushes by native tribes. This, in turn, forced the Vikings to build fortifications along the river. The city of Kiev was founded in this way. Zaporozhie was another such settlement, the tribes around which became known as the Zaporozhian Cossacks. They later fought the Tatars in the south and the Poles in the west, both of whom at various times attempted to control the area.

After crossing the dam, we had to walk another couple of miles through empty fields before we reached the house where Mother was renting a room. It was a small house, like the one we lived in, and the settlement was similar to ours, except much neater. The population was mostly German, invited to settle there in the eighteenth century by Catherine the Great. After the war, I heard that some of the residents were helping the Nazi bombers to navigate at night by placing lamps in chimneys. Presumably, one night a Soviet pilot noticed these lights, and the settlement was bombed to smithereens.

Mother and Vilya were doing well in the nursery school, but she was not earning enough to bring me over, so she had to find another way of reuniting us.

There was no moonlight that night and we walked back through the fields in complete darkness, singing and hollering, not quite sure that we were on the right track; we barely caught the last streetcar home.

I got along very well with the landlord's children. I helped Lyuba with her homework and Zhora, who was a year older and quite a bit stronger than I, protected me from older kids. I also liked the other tenant, Izzy, who worked in an aircraft engine factory and took drafting courses. He showed me how to divide a line into two equal parts using only a compass—which I still remember how to do. Occasionally he came home slightly drunk and told off-color stories, which we kids thoroughly enjoyed. The woman tenant was not very communicative. She was huge and given to fits of crying. She had a suitor, a tractor driver from a nearby *kolkhoz*, who brought her flowers. On cold winter evenings, when everyone congregated in the warm kitchen to drink tea, she and her friend sat right behind the door in the sitting room, without turning on the light. The door had a glass pane, and we marveled at how they could sit motionless for hours, mouth to mouth. Later on I was told that after they got married, it turned out that he was a drunkard who beat her.

Grandfather's cooking consisted mostly of potatoes, which we ate with herring or with tiny pickled fish called *camsa,* which we ate heads, tails, and all. On weekends we also had a piece of meat or chicken soup, some awful salty goat cheese called *brynza,* and pickled tomatoes and cucumbers, or sauerkraut. My breakfast consisted of a glass of milk with a piece of dark bread. For lunch I took a bread-and-butter sandwich, called for some reason *Butterbrot,* which is "butter and bread" in German. The dark bread was brought home by my uncles from the factory, but to obtain other food Grandfather had to stand in long lines, which occupied most of his day. People in these lines got to know one another and had worked out a system for keeping each other's place so that they could be in several lines at the same time.

Every Saturday I went with Grandfather to the communal bathhouse, where he loved to flog himself with oak switches in the steam room until his whole body became pink, then to douse himself with cold water. He said it was good for him, but I did not think it was good for me. He was sixty-five and his health was fine except for a hernia, for which he wore a contraption called a truss that consisted of a flat steel spring that wrapped itself around his waist and pressed on the ruptured area in his groin. He had been keeping house for his sons ever since they moved to Zaporozhie from the country.

In the 1920s, parcels of land that had been confiscated from large landowners were being given by the government to those who would cultivate them. Grandfather and the three boys, then in their teens or early twenties, left Volochisk, where there was no future for young men, moved to a small village near the River Dnieper, and became farmers. They knew very little about farming, and the first two years were disastrous, but with four strong men working hard, the third year brought a good crop. Part of the crop they had to turn over to the government, another part had to be kept for seeds. They were free to sell whatever was left. Unfortunately, the third year happened to be the exact time at which Stalin decided to take back all the land from the farmers and form *kolkhozes*. The idea of *kolkhozes* was supported by those who had nothing to lose, but opposed by those who had worked hard and were successful. These successful people the Communists called *kulaks*, which literally means "fists." The term implied that they had acquired their property by taking it away from the poor. Since in every village some peasants were better off than others, every village had its *kulaks*. Some were shot or hanged, just to set an example, but most were exiled to Siberia and Kazakhstan.

One day, Uncle Samuel went to deliver their grain quota to a distant government granary. He was away for two weeks, and since after the harvest both Grishas took jobs building the Zaporozhie dam, Grandfather was left alone on the farm. Just at that time a request from the NKVD came to the village committee to name the area's *kulaks*. This was not a pleasant task, since the villagers all knew each other, knew how hard they all struggled, and knew that the accused would be impoverished and exiled. Uncle Samuel was a member of the committee, but he was away. In his absence the committee decided that, since Grandfather and the boys did not have wives or children, they had a better chance of surviving punishment and therefore they should be the *kulaks*. However, because Grandfather and my uncles did not have any hired help, which was the definition of a *kulak*, the committee could only report them as being sub-*kulaks*. But the NKVD was not interested in nuances, so Grandfather was immediately arrested and taken to prison. Because the NKVD men spoke Russian, he did not understand what he was being accused of and was frightened out of his wits.

When Uncle Samuel returned, he found an empty house and starving chickens. He rushed to Zaporozhie and together with the two Grishas managed to convince the NKVD that they were not *kulaks*, nor even sub-*kulaks;* instead they were building the dam for the glory of communism. They also produced documents proving that they had just delivered grain to help feed the proletariat in the cities. Eventually, Grandfather was let go, but he remained deathly afraid of all authorities and for a long time did not leave the house and never went to work. The family immediately sold the horses, ate the remaining chickens, and moved to Zaporozhie, where Grisha-the-Elder and Senya got jobs at the Communar harvester factory. Grisha-the-Younger became a lathe operator at the aircraft engine factory number 29. It was so secret that, unlike all other factories that had been named after Communist leaders or other propaganda heroes, such as *Sacco and Vanzetti,* it had no name.

While Grandfather had very little education, he knew a great deal. He could multiply two-digit numbers on his fingers much faster than I could do it on paper. I tried to learn his trick, hoping to dazzle my teacher once more, but I never mastered it. Another one of his tricks that I remember was to determine which months have thirty-one days by looking at one's knuckles (excluding the thumbs). The knuckles represent months that have thirty-one days, while the spaces between the knuckles represent those that do not.

On Friday nights in good weather, Grandfather hid his frayed prayer book and an equally frayed prayer shawl under his shirt and disappeared without telling anyone where he was going. This was dangerous, because if the NKVD had found out where the prayer meetings were held, it would have meant disaster for all, but particularly for the owner of the apartment, since unauthorized meetings were strictly forbidden in spite of "guarantees" by Stalin's constitution.

In the late fall, Grisha the Elder got married. His wife, Manya, had several sisters, one of whom, Lisa, was my age. Every Sunday, Uncle Samuel gave me an allowance of one ruble. If the weather was good, I put on my only suit, the *capitanka*—a navy-blue captain's suit with shiny anchors on its brass buttons—and set off for the city. On the way I stopped at Grisha-the-Younger's house and collected another ruble. Sometimes he and his pregnant wife were still asleep when I knocked on the door and there were some very awkward moments.

With two rubles in my pocket, I took the streetcar to the center of Zaporozhie, had an ice cream, and either went to the movies or to a matinee at the theater on the main street—Sobornaya (Cathedral) Street. On the front wall of the movie house there was usually a gigantic painting of one of the movie scenes in full color, but the movies themselves were in black and white. While we waited in the foyer for the earlier performance to end, there was entertainment by a band and a lively singer performing the latest patriotic songs. Most films, such as *Battleship Potemkin,* glorified the Revolution. Some were historical, such as *Alexander Nevsky;* other were based on adventure books by authors like Jules Verne, or they were imported, like Charlie Chaplin's movies. Most were just Communist propaganda, in which the hero paid more attention to his tractor or his factory machine than to his girlfriend; they were reconciled only after she became as enthusiastic about building socialism as he.

The theater was built before the Revolution and had red velvet upholstery and a row of loges. It was usually only a quarter full and, while I bought the cheapest ticket, I could sit wherever I pleased. I did not like sitting so close to the stage that I could see the actors' makeup, and usually sat in the fifth or sixth row. The plays were mostly about heroic workers building socialism or about the NKVD uncovering spies, saboteurs, and other "enemies of the people." Every now and then they would perform Ukrainian operettas, which I loved—I knew most of the songs by heart. The operettas were about Cossacks and love and featured pretty ladies in pretty costumes and beautiful music. It is interesting that while there were many Ukrainian operettas, there were no Ukrainian operas, and while there were many Russian operas, there were no Russian operettas, which must have something to do with the national character of the two peoples.

Every now and then I went to the house of Grisha-the-Elder and collected another ruble. He and his wife lived in a part of a compound of small, old houses situated around a courtyard that had previously been an inn, at 85 Michailovich Street. His in-laws also lived there and sometimes I stayed to play with Lisa and a neighbor boy named Vilya, who was a good chess player. He was the only child of middle-aged parents who had given up hope of having children before he arrived, and he was very spoiled but very bright.

One day, Mother came to visit us. She looked very upset and her face was ashen. She sat down without saying a word and finally whispered through tears that Vilya had been run over by a truck. I began to cry, and only then did she reveal that it was not our Vilya but the other Vilya, who had run out into the street after a ball. It was normally a very quiet street with very little traffic and this was a sad illustration of being in the wrong place at the wrong instant.

We all went to the funeral. At the head of the sad procession marched the town idiot swinging a cane and pretending to be playing a flute every time the brass band struck up the funeral march. (This man's mother had died when he was a child and ever since then, if not chased away, he tried to lead all funeral processions.) Vilya's father must have been an important man because there were several hundred people following the truck with the casket. Before lowering the casket into the ground, it was opened and a man flashed a pair of scissors over his head for all to see, before making several cuts in poor Vilya's suit to discourage grave robbers.

One spring day, I heard a loud roar growing in intensity and ran outside to see what was going on. A fleet of four-engine heavy bombers was approaching us from the north at a fairly low altitude. Before long they covered the whole sky and hid the sun. They moved rather slowly and appeared clumsy but there were hundreds of them, and I thought that, just as the patriotic songs we sang in school proclaimed, the power of the Soviet Union was invincible and eternal.

That summer Mother began traveling in search of a place where we could be together and where she could find a better job. She left Vilya with us, and several times was away for a week at a time. One day she returned with the news that she had found a job as a waitress in a town called Khmelnik. It was close to Gorodok and, if Father were to return, it would not be difficult for him to find us there. We moved in August so that I could start fifth grade in September.

Khmelnik had about twenty thousand people, including the surrounding villages, and was situated on an island in the Southern Boug River, which split into two channels at one end of town and merged again at the other end. The river was only knee-deep over most of its course, with only an occasional swimming hole. There, the water was over our heads and on hot summer days we could dive and drink the clear, cool liquid, which tasted of water plants. In most places the river was less than fifty feet wide. It flowed from the north to the south and its western shore was steep because, so I was told, the rotation of the earth from east to west forced the water against it and undercut its edge. I loved wading along this shore, feeling with my hand under the water line for cavities, and satisfying my hunter instinct when occasionally a crayfish pinched the tip of my finger and I grasped it with a sudden thrust. Having caught a few, I hurried home and boiled some water into which I dropped them and watched them turn bright red. The thought of sharing my catch with anyone never entered my mind. In the winter, when the river froze, we skated all around the island. It was a distance of several miles and, by the time I returned home, my shins and ankles were so sore that I had to stop several times, completely exhausted, and could barely take the last few steps to the door.

It was a quiet and peaceful river, except for around the end of March, when the ice broke. Then it overflowed its confinement, and thundering ice floes crashed against the steel rails of the ice breakers that protected the bridge supports, climbing one upon the other in a seeming attempt to cross over the bridge and continue their way south to the open sea. People gathered along the shores and marveled at the great upheaval of the ice, which only the day before had been glistening placidly in the sun.

Another favorite place of mine was the forest. It was several miles away from town, beyond fields of wheat and rye that were sprinkled with flaming red wild poppies, like with drops of fresh blood, and with cornflowers of intense, almost iridescent blue looking like tiny bits of sky dropped down to counteract the violent impression created by the poppies. Whenever the weather was good on a Sunday, I went there with my friend Dima and his kid brother Vitya to gather mushrooms. Each part of the forest had its own kind of mushrooms: one kind hid in the thick carpet of pine needles, another in the grass of the meadows at the feet of white birches, whose bark peeled like paper, and still another in the Black Forest, where the trees were deciduous and tall, and the sun did not penetrate the dense canopy. We were armed with thick sticks engraved with spiraling snakes to protect ourselves from their kind, but we never saw one. Only occasionally something would rustle in the undergrowth and we would thrash at it furiously, though it was probably only a mouse. We were dwarfed by the huge trees, some of which must have been five feet across, but we feared neither beast nor man, because there were no wild animals in this forest and in those days we had never heard of child molestation.

The town had spread across the river and consisted mostly of single-story houses with gray tile or red tin roofs. Their walls were constructed of sticks that were slid between grooved posts and covered with clay mixed with finely chopped straw and horse manure, which I was told added strength to the mixture. Only here and there one saw a brick house, which before the Revolution had belonged to a well-off family but had since been converted into a government office.

We were renting a room in a house at the edge of town from an elderly couple whose last name was Bida, which I found very funny, because in Ukrainian it means "disaster." They were Jewish and secretly tried to maintain their religious customs, which was good for me, because on Friday nights and Saturdays they were not supposed to turn on lights or light a fire, and I earned pocket money by performing these tasks for them. Our room was about ten feet wide and perhaps twenty feet long, with one window at the end. There was a small table under the window, with my bed on the right side of the table and Mother's bed on the left. On the wall over Mother's bed was our prized possession—a Moldavian *kilim* carpet which was sort of pink with sharp, geometric designs that reminded me of wolves and llamas, even though I knew very well that there were no llamas in Moldavia.[1] At the end of Mother's bed was the ubiquitous wardrobe, since built-in closets were unknown, and then Vilya's bed. At the end of my bed was another one, in which slept a peasant girl of about eighteen named Varka who took care of Vilya while mother was at work. Varka worked for room and board and a small amount of money that she was saving for her wedding. She was pimply and not at all pretty and she tried to boss me around, which I strongly resisted. But she had a pretty girlfriend who was playful and did not mind wrestling with me, which made Varka's offensiveness tolerable. Cooking was done on a primus—a kerosene stove, on which one could cook only one thing at a time. I became quite proficient at starting up the primus. First I poured some kerosene into a little tray around the flame head and ignited it. When it burned out, the tubes of the head became hot so that when I pumped air into the tank, it forced kerosene through the hot tubes, where it evaporated and squirted out of the nozzle as burning gas. The nozzle had to be frequently cleaned by a thin wire, crimped at a right angle to a tin handle.

Mother worked as a waitress in a restaurant where I went once a week at

1. Upon gaining independence in 1991, Moldavia became Moldova.

the end of dinner time and the friendly cook and Mother's friend, Aunt Gorokhovskaya, prepared my favorite pork chops, which she tenderized by pounding them with a wooden mallet. Since this was the only restaurant in town, all the big-shots ate and drank there. Vodka was served by weight, the smallest portion being a half-full water glass that contained one hundred grams, but quite often the measure was a full water glass, or two hundred grams. After a few of these, which were usually drunk bottoms-up, because sipping was not considered to be macho, the guests became quite mellow and left generous tips, which helped us considerably. The only problem was the assistant manager, Comrade Rokhberg, a dour, redheaded man who never smiled and was the head of the restaurant's Communist Party cell. He begrudged the waitresses their tips and even the leftovers they took home. He was universally hated by the staff and I could not have my dinner when he was around.

At the highest point in town, overlooking the river, loomed a grim, gray stone castle. It looked medieval but was actually built in the early part of the eighteenth century by a Polish count who had owned the surrounding villages before serfdom was abolished in 1861. The castle had a tall tower and was surrounded by a high gray stone wall, with smaller towers on each corner which, as rumor had it, were connected to the castle by tunnels. For some years it had served as the headquarters of Gulag #211, a regional concentration camp, whose prisoners were building a railroad in the area. Every now and then the iron gates opened with a penetrating screech, and trucks full of sullen men with sunken eyes, dressed in gray quilted jackets, sped down the road, followed by another truck filled with armed guards and dogs. According to rumors, these prisoners were kept in the tunnels. They were the "enemies of the people."

There were many "enemy" families in town. By most conservative estimates, the number of people arrested in the 1930s was around 10 million. Since the average family had two children and at least two grandparents, this means that about 60 million people out of the Soviet Union's population of around 180 million were classified either "enemies" or families of "enemies." This does not include brothers and sisters, who were also affected in one way or another.

Nevertheless, in spite of the numbers, it was not easy to be a son of an "enemy." Mass arrests began in 1937 when I was in the second grade. The son of the first man to be arrested in our town was in my class. He was mercilessly hounded by the rest of the kids, who peered at him through crossed fingers and chanted "That's where your father is!" until tears rolled down his cheeks as he kept repeating: "A son is not responsible for his father! A son is not responsible for his father! . . ." Soon after, his mother was granted a divorce and they both assumed her maiden name.

By 1939 there were so many of us in this situation that the teasing had subsided, because no one knew whether that very night the secret police might not come for their father. There were not many divorces any more, either.

"How would you like to visit Gorodok?" Mother asked me one morning about a month after we had settled in Khmelnik.

"Sure! Can we get a permit to travel there?" I asked with excitement.

"Not we, just you. I found out that children under twelve can enter the border zone without a permit," she replied, "and you are still eleven. It is only about one hundred kilometers from here, but you will have to change trains in Yarmolintsy. Perhaps you will be able to find out something about Father. Perhaps there is a letter waiting at the post office."

On the very next day I put on my *kapitanka,* and with many admonitions not to forget to change trains, was put on board of the passenger train to Proskurov. It was the first time that I was traveling alone and I felt very grown up. I was somewhat worried that I might miss the station where I had to change trains, but I did not miss it. After having changed trains, I was confronted by a burly conductor in a blue uniform. I thought my heart would pop out of my chest. He took my ticket. "Your border zone permit," he said extending his hand.

"I am only eleven," I said, "I don't need a permit until I am twelve." I handed him my birth certificate, trying to sound calm.

He looked at the certificate, then at me, then at the certificate again, then at me again, as if deciding what to do. Then he punched the ticket and handed it back to me, together with the certificate. I took it and turned away so as not to betray my excitement and fear.

The railroad station in Gorodok was several kilometers from town and even had a different name: Victoria. I always liked this name: it sounded foreign and mysterious, like the lake in Africa. But there was nothing mysterious about the wooden shack surrounded by sugar-beet fields of the nearby sugar mill. I started walking toward town but someone who had hired a horse wagon asked me to climb aboard and was kind enough not to take money when I offered to share expenses.

As soon as we got into town I ran to the post office and, my heart beating fast, asked if there was a letter for us *post-restante,* a phrase used to describe a letter sent to the post office and held there until the addressee asked for it. There was no letter.

Then I walked through the streets where I knew every stone, but I had no feeling of being back at home. At every corner I half expected to run into Father, even though deep down I knew that this would not happen. His studio was being used for an office. The outdoor showcase, which he called the *vitrina,* was gone, but the huge sign on the wall was still there.

I stayed overnight with the family of Mother's friend Lisa. They were very surprised to see me, since Mother had not written to them because receiving mail from "enemies" was not safe and the NKVD knew who was receiving what from whom. As I approached their house, I saw them sitting on the porch, sneaked up to it, and popped up, saying "Good afternoon!" They had not heard anything about Father, but some "enemy" families had been informed that their men had been sentenced to anywhere from ten to twenty-five years for "counterrevolutionary activities," according to Statute 58, Paragraph 10 of the criminal code. This paragraph specified the "crimes" for which one could be given these sentences, such as spreading rumors or maligning the government, such as by telling anti-Communist jokes. Other high political crimes included belonging to a non-Communist party before the Revolution, having been a businessman, a policeman, or an army officer, or, in general, being a "socially dangerous element."

The next day I briefly visited some of my friends and then left for home, carrying a gift bundle of clothes for my mother.

I started the fifth grade, which in our European-type school included algebra, physics, geography, botany, history, the German language, and

Ukrainian and Russian grammar and literature. We had classes six or seven hours a day and five hours on Saturdays.

Since no one in Khmelnik knew us, and considering the consequences of having told the truth to the landlady in Derazhnya, I decided not to tell anyone about Father being an "enemy of the people." But, if asked, what should I say? Well, if I was going to lie, I was going to lie big! What was the best thing to which one could aspire? To me, at that time, it was being a pilot. However, for some reason I do not remember, I decided to say that Father was at the Moscow Flight Academy training to be a pilot. How could anyone prove that he was not?

This went over quite well for a while, until I became friendly with my classmate Lyonia. When he asked about my father, I told him the tall story.

"What a coincidence!" he exclaimed. "My older brother is also at the Moscow Flight Academy!" This was the last thing I had expected to hear in a Ukrainian hick town. After all, there were many thousands of towns, and probably only a few hundred students at the Moscow Flight Academy. The chance of such a coincidence was infinitesimal! But, as the Russian saying goes: "A word is not a bird, once it escapes it cannot be recaptured."

One day, Lyonia and a boy named Kadik were talking with me during class recess, when Lyonia asked what we had heard from my father at the Flight Academy. "Flight Academy?" queried Kadik. "What Flight Academy?" "In Moscow," I mumbled, with a premonition that something was not right.

"Then how come I overheard your mother talking with my mother about not knowing where our fathers had vanished after having been arrested?"

"Really," said Lyonia. "My parents wondered whether your father would not be too old for the Flight Academy. They wanted to meet you." All I could do was turn purple.

I did not have to hide anything from my best friend, Ben. He was about my height, with a freckled face and red hair. He lived with his parents and five brothers and sisters, ranging in age from a baby to about fifteen, in one room and a kitchen that were attached to a shed where his father, a cooper, was making barrels. Having been forced to join a cooperative *artel*, he had to hand over all of his income, in return for which he received a measly salary, insufficient to support the family. To help make ends meet, his mother baked bread in a large oven in the kitchen and sold it illegally to people she knew. When Ben first told me about this, he appeared to be embarrassed that his mother was doing something illegal, but when I told him about my father, his uneasiness disappeared. After all, what was a minor violation of the law in comparison with being an "enemy"?

Occasionally, when people came to buy bread, they looked at me with suspicion, but Ben's mother acted as if I was one of the family, and I felt good about their confidence that I would not betray them. Their house always smelled of freshly baked bread, and their shed of fresh oak shavings. In spite of being poor and having to wear patched hand-me-downs, it was a happy family. Both parents were full of smiles and if I was there around mealtime, they insisted that I share their food no matter how much I refused. I suspected that upon seeing the way I devoured the freshly baked dark, crusty bread, they knew that I was just being polite.

Like me, Ben also liked books, and together we read *The Sea Wolf, The Adventures of Tom Sawyer, The Adventures of Huckleberry Finn,* and other books about distant and marvelous places that we did not even dream of being able to visit. No one could go abroad without being sent there by the government, and those who had gone were frequently imprisoned upon their return. They were suspected of having been influenced by what they had seen, and possibly of having been recruited by foreign intelligence agencies.

Also, we both were interested in airplanes and talked about the possibility of going together to a technical school for aviation mechanics, which we could do after the seventh grade.

Dima was another friend from whom I did not have to hide anything, since he also was the son of an "enemy." I visited him frequently and on the way to his house passed the nice brick house of Dr. Mazuruk, an elderly pediatrician. Once, through a crack in the window curtains, I saw the doctor on his knees, praying before a candle-lit icon. This was a dangerous thing to do; it could have cost him his job at the clinic. It was very careless of him not to have checked the curtains.

Dima had another interesting neighbor, a man who on a certain day every summer began drinking moonshine and continued until he started hallucinating—seeing white mice crawling all over him. Usually it took several weeks for him to reach this point. He got drunk every morning and slept it off in the shade on the grass outside of his house, where he also spent the nights, because his wife would not let him in. We threw pebbles at him to see if he would stir, but even if he did, he was in no condition to chase us. When the hallucinations began, he would stop drinking and move back into the house until the next summer.

Being the son of an "enemy," I was not accepted into the Red Pioneers, which was the Communist version of the Boy Scouts. This was fine with me, because I would rather have read a book than stayed after school for their silly meetings in which, according to my friends, they were lectured by their leader, a pimply girl from the ninth grade. She was a member of the Komsomol, and her father was a big-shot in the secret police. Most lectures were on how horrible life was in capitalist countries and how wonderful it was in the Soviet Union. The Red Pioneers were also expected to report any suspicious or anti-Communist activities to the authorities. They were urged to follow the example of Pavel Morozov, as described in the book *The Red Pioneer Pavel Morozov,* which was mandatory reading. We were told that it was a true story and were assigned to read and discuss it. According to this book, Pavel's father was stealing grain from the collective farm where he worked. Pavel and his little brother discovered this and reported their father to the authorities. When the father found this out, he killed both of them and hid the bloodstained knife behind the icon of a saint, which stood on a shelf in the corner of the room. The story did not sit well with me because I could not imagine why a killer would hide a knife in such a prominent place where, of course, the militia found it right away. But many songs were composed about Pavel Morozov, many schools were named after him, and he was constantly cited as an example of a true Soviet patriot, whom all children should emulate. There was not a child in the country who did not know his name.

I did participate in some after-school activities, where we learned about military defense and for which we received medal-like badges. Some of the badges were large and pendulous, suspended by two thin metal chains from screw clamps that left holes in your clothing. It was a matter of pride to wear these badges every day, so that some upperclassmen jingled as they walked, with one or two rows of badges and pins covering the whole left side of their jackets. To earn them one had to pass the appropriate tests. The badges that I remember were for "Preparedness for Chemical Defense," where we learned all about gas masks, how to recognize various poisonous gases, and what to do in the case of a gas attack. Another one was for "First Aid in Defense," where we learned how to take care of wounds and fractures. There were also badges for "Air Defense," which taught us to identify enemy planes by their silhouettes, and for something called "Be Prepared for Labor and Defense," for which we had to march, run, jump, and learn to take apart and reassemble rifles. I was good only at hundred-meter dashes. The older students also trained with .22 caliber rifles and could earn "Voroshilov's Sharpshooter" badges, named after the commissar of defense, Clementy Voroshilov—but I was too young for that.

The most absurd badge was given to members of the Union of Militant Atheists. To add injury to insult, to be a member one had to pay monthly dues of something like ten copeks. I would not have bothered with it, but Mother insisted that I join it because, as the "son of an enemy," my refusal could be interpreted as an anti-Soviet act. Lenin's slogan, "Those who are not with us, are against us!" was taken very seriously, and I knew very well what it meant. To earn the badge one had to attend meetings after classes on Saturday afternoons. We were told that God does not exist, and that Lenin called religion the "opiate of the masses," devised by capitalists to keep the people docile by promising them rewards in the next world. We were also ordered to "agitate" against religion with believers. When I asked my grandfather why he was going to clandestine prayer meetings since there was no one to pray to, he answered: "I want to be on the safe side, just in case there is."

I was greatly worried by the fact that colleges did not accept children of "enemies." I had read a book entitled *Our Wings,* translated from the English, which described in great detail how airplanes were constructed, and I decided that I wanted to be an aircraft designer rather than just a mechanic, as I had discussed with my friend Ben.

In the Soviet Union airplanes were known by the names of their designers rather than by their manufacturers; I dreamed about planes with my initials, just like those known as ANT, standing for Anatoly Nikolaevich Tupolev, who became my hero. I even wrote a poem about the silvery birds with my initials on their wings which, like night meteors, sped into storms, battles, and into outer space. Not being able to go to college would put an

end to these dreams. I did not find out until much later that Tupolev had
also been an "enemy of the people" and languished in a concentration camp
until he was needed during the war.

Our school was a gray, two-story brick building situated on the main
cobblestone road between the Ukrainian cemetery, with its mostly wooden
crosses, and the Polish cemetery, with its marble monuments and chapels.
Even in death it was easy to tell who had ruled whom. On warm summer
days I liked to go there to read, lying in the grass in the shade in peace and
quiet near a square, tapered, black marble column, my favorite of the monuments. I did not feel at all uneasy there and had no morbid thoughts.

The school housed grades five through ten, in all about three hundred
children. There was no running water or central heating. In winter, tem-
peratures of twenty below Centigrade, or five below Fahrenheit, were quite
common and made going to the unheated outhouse a formidable task. One
could not go without a coat; one had to bring a piece of newspaper to use
as toilet paper, and there was no place to wash your hands. The classrooms
were heated by coal-burning stoves that were built into the walls between
rooms, so that two classrooms were heated by one stove. Drinking water
was kept in a wooden barrel with a spigot that stood in the hallway. A tin
cup was attached to the barrel by a chain, and we all drank from it so that
when one child had a cold, the whole school had a cold.

We lived on the opposite end of town, about a mile and a half away, and,
since there were no snowplows, we had to wade through deep snow until
paths were established along the road. Most kids wore knee-high boots
made of hard felt, with galoshes, and fur hats with earflaps. Snow usually
fell in November and remained on the ground until late March.

I liked studying. My curiosity was limitless and, for me, the purpose of
education was to be able to understand everything around me: nature, culture, science, technology, and everything else there is in the world. To me,
the universe was full of knowledge, and it was my task to acquire at least
some of it on every possible subject. I read every book I could obtain on any
topic. Many of them were way over my head, but I still tried to absorb them,
because they were part of the universe that I had to explore. My favorite

subjects were science fiction, travel, and adventures. In addition to domestic authors who wrote on these subjects, I also read books by Jules Verne,
H. G. Wells, James Fenimore Cooper (who reads much more easily in Russian translation than in English), Jack London, Mark Twain, and Mayne
Reid, who wrote cowboy stories, but who seems to be unknown in the United States. I had also read *Uncle Tom's Cabin,* which was mandatory reading,
but we were not told that it described events of almost a hundred years ago.

Books were very hard to get because many of those published twenty
years ago, that is, before the Communist Revolution, had been destroyed as
being politically incorrect. This made them, in Communist lingo, "socially
dangerous." Just owning one of them could be dangerous, and lending one
to someone might be considered spreading "counterrevolutionary propaganda," for which one could be sentenced to ten years of hard labor. The library shelves were periodically combed for books that might depict life before the Revolution in a favorable light. To be on the safe side, anything even
remotely suspicious was removed. However, unlike in Germany, where books
were burned, in the Soviet Union many were used for wrapping things. One
never knew what one might read on wrapping paper. If the paper was not
glossy, it was used for rolling cigarettes. There was a joke about one man
asking another: "Do you like the newspaper *Izvestia?*" "Yes," said the other,
"It is a very good paper." "And how about *Pravda?*" "I don't know that one,"
said the other. "I've never smoked it."

To keep on the right side of the law was not easy. No sooner was the *Great
Soviet Encyclopedia* published than several leaders mentioned in it as great
revolutionary heroes were declared enemies of the people and executed.
Right away, all encyclopedia owners (the encyclopedias were sold only by
subscription, one volume at a time) were ordered to remove the subversive
pages. They had to substitute revised pages sent to them later. Other books
mentioning these people had to be destroyed: they became "nonpersons,"
just as in Orwell's book *1984.*

In addition to dangerous books there were also dangerous words such as
"officer," "general," or "policeman." These words were symbols of the old
system and could not be mentioned in a positive way. The policemen were
now called "People's Militiamen." Instead of shoulder straps signifying rank,
army uniforms now had red collar tips, to which were attached red rhomboids, rectangles, squares, or triangles as signs of rank. The ranks themselves

were division commander, platoon commander, etc. Therefore I was greatly surprised when one day, as my mother was reading a newspaper, she said,
"Look at this, the army is reintroducing the old titles, like general, colonel,
lieutenant, sergeant and so on."

"That's funny," I said. "Before you know it, they will bring back shoulder straps." I had just been reading a book about a red partisan hero named
Chapayev, who fought against the czarist White Army. It described a scene
where a drunken man put on his pre-Revolutionary uniform with shoulder
straps; for this crime the red partisans put him against a wall and shot him
on the spot.

Mother did not find this funny at all. "Do you know what you are saying?" she screamed. "Do you want to follow your father? Don't you ever dare
say things like that anywhere!"

I liked most subjects in school, except grammar, in which we had to
memorize endless rules and, what was worse, all the exceptions. What I did
not mind memorizing was poetry. Russian literature was taught by a corpulent middle-aged woman with a large square face and curly brown hair.
We addressed her by her first name and patronymic, Nadezhda Stepanov-
na. She was the wife of an "enemy," exiled to Khmelnik from a large city,
and spoke Russian with a beautiful city accent that normally would not have
been heard in a provincial Ukrainian school. She had no discipline problems since her bulk intimidated even the large, half-witted bullies, who had
been held back so many times by the time they reached the fifth grade that
it looked like they already needed a shave. They could not wait to become
sixteen so that they would not have to go to school. Other teachers did not
fare so well. One of them, Betya Davidovna, a small, birdlike woman who
taught botany and zoology, was occasionally provoked to the point of crying and pulling her hair, which greatly amused the bullies but made me feel
very uncomfortable.

Nadezhda, as we called her behind her back, encouraged us to write poetry, and I was her star pupil. Therefore, when the Soviet Union signed a
nonaggression pact with the Nazis in 1939 it became my assignment to find
a suitable replacement for the derogatory references to Germany in the patriotic song we were obliged to sing at assemblies. In place of a stanza describing how we had beaten the Germans after the Revolution and express-

ing regret that we had not finished them off, I wrote one about the punishment we had inflicted upon the Finns. Also, from then on the word "Fascist" was forbidden and the Germans had to be referred to as "National Socialists." Since we lived in the Union of Soviet Socialist Republics, to us one Socialist was as good as another. While earlier, during the Spanish Civil War, we were urged to hate Hitler and Mussolini as evil Fascists and warmongers, now Hitler became a good comrade Socialist, and the British, French, and Americans became evil warmongers.

I looked forward to Nadezhda's classes and did not mind memorizing pages and pages of poems by Pushkin, Lermontov, Nekrasov, and other, lesser-known poets. In the West it is considered pretentious for someone to start spouting poetry at the sight of something beautiful or inspiring, but to me it is one of life's pleasures, and I still frequently recite to myself poems that express what I am experiencing, in much more beautiful language than I could find for it myself. Perhaps the fact that my enthusiasm was shared by a pretty girl named Lusia, with long blonde tresses and sparkling blue eyes, made it even more exciting.

I was also an editor of our class "Wall Paper," which was a bulletin board with handwritten articles about class events, criticism of poor students, poems by students, and announcements of upcoming events such as class plays. In spite of my being editor, the school director complained to Mother that I did not participate in preparations for the Communist holidays, such as the day of the October Revolution, which was actually held in November because, after the Revolution, the calendar had been advanced by twelve days. This happened when the Julian calendar (introduced by Julius Caesar in 46 B.C.), which was still being used in Russia, was replaced by the Gregorian calendar used by most countries.

The other big holiday was on the first of May, the day of "solidarity of the world proletariat." Preparations consisted of making huge placards with portraits of Communist leaders (mostly Stalin) and large red banners with Communist slogans. A good example of these slogans: "Thank you great Stalin for our happy childhood!" which made me want to puke; "Long live Soviet-German friendship!" and "Down with the capitalist warmongers!" Even without holidays, banners and portraits of Stalin were everywhere, in every classroom, office, and store, and in the home of every Communist.

Then there were innumerable books and pamphlets by and about Stalin, Lenin, Marx, and Engels in the library and in the bookstore, where they gathered dust unless their paper was good for rolling cigarettes.

There were also countless songs, particularly in praise of Stalin. When in the midst of mass arrests, Stalin made a speech in which he proclaimed: "Comrades, life has become better, life has become more joyful!" there immediately appeared a song saying: "The whole country with a single voice wishes to shout to Stalin: thank you our dearest, may you live long in good health; life became better, life became more joyful!" Of course, I did not sing such sickening words in our weekly singing class, but, being conscious at all times of my "enemy" status, I moved my lips so as not to be conspicuous.

The difference between what we were told and what we saw with our own eyes was so immense that it made one wonder who was out of his mind. We were told that the Revolution had been fought to bring people freedom, but everywhere we looked we saw the gray quilted jackets of prisoners. We were told that before the Revolution people did not have enough to eat, but after it Communist goon squads took away all the grain from the peasants in order to force them into *kolkhozes*, and some five million of them died of starvation. Slogans everywhere proclaimed that all people are equal, but there were special stores, called "closed distribution centers," full of all kinds of goods that were for members of the party only. In spite of all this, many wanted to believe in the Revolution, particularly those who had fought for it and believed that all the evil deeds were committed by people surrounding Stalin and that he did not know about them. I did not believe this because, as he was supposed to be omniscient and omnipotent like God himself, it was impossible for him not to know what was going on.

We were forced to attend holiday parades under the threat of getting a failing grade in "behavior," but I never carried any banners. We marched in a column four abreast, the lower grades first waving red flags with a hammer and sickle, then the upper grades with portraits and slogans. We marched to the center of town, where we joined columns from the other two schools, from several factories and other organizations, perhaps two thousand strong all together, and for a couple of hours we had to listen to boring speeches by various officials. They all urged everyone to fulfill and overfulfill the labor quotas assigned to them by the Communist Party under the leadership of Comrade Stalin, and to become Stakhanovites.

Stakhanov was a coal miner in the Don Bass coal region, where for propaganda purposes he was provided with several helpers, which presumably enabled him to overfulfill his daily quota by 1,100 percent. He became a "Hero of Socialist Labor," was given all kinds of medals, and was set as an example for everyone in the country. Now there were quotas for everything, and very soon, in spite of the danger of being overheard by the authorities, a ditty spread among us kids, which I did not dare repeat to Mother:

> They've just announced a new plan:
> To shit no less than a kilogram!
> Those who seven can afford,
> Will receive a nice reward.
> Those who shit only a pound,
> Will be beaten to the ground.

Every factory and *kolkhoz* had to have a group of Stakhanovites, usually members of the Communist Party, who presumably overfulfilled their quotas many times over. Not to have one would have meant that the management and party leadership of the factory were not doing their job of inspiring selfless devotion to communism. Therefore, the reality of this overfulfillment of quotas was very questionable. Some years later poor Stakhanov, not being used to adulation, drank himself to death. The newspapers were full of articles about distant factories and farms overfulfilling their quotas as well as criticism for the laggards. Since the quotas concerned themselves with quantity and not with quality, there appeared products in the stores that no one wanted to buy, such as shoes that were not waterproof and fell apart after having been worn only a few times.

At the beginning and end of the demonstrations, the brass band from the sugar mill played the "International," which at that time was the official anthem of the Soviet Union, and we had to stand at attention. The Red Pioneers saluted by holding their right hand vertically above their noses, soldiers and militiamen saluted, and civilians took off their hats. The words of the anthem urged us to get ready for the final and decisive battle with capitalism, when all of humanity would arise to destroy the old world and replace it with a new one where those who were nobodies before would become the rulers. Then the band marched home, striking up patriotic songs,

and the columns marched back to where they had started, except that now
the placards were swung over shoulders instead of being carried aloft.

On May Day, it was the custom to go for a picnic into the forest or to
the meadows alongside the river, where it was also the custom for the men
to get drunk. On May Day of 1941, an older friend asked me if I wanted to
join him on a picnic in the forest. He had a half-liter bottle of Zubrovka,
which is vodka with herbs that make it easy to drink. We had no food other than two sour pickles and, since we had no glasses, we passed the bottle
back and forth until it was empty. The next thing that I remember even to
this day is making my way home while the world spun and heaved under
my feet. Wherever it was possible, I held onto picket fences, and when there
was a gap or a cross street, I stood for a while estimating my chances of reaching the next fence without falling, then dashed for it. When I finally reached
home, I felt very sick and was afraid to go inside. Instead, I hid in the woodshed where we stored firewood for the winter and began throwing up all
over the place. After a while, Mother, who must have heard strange noises,
found me there. Since Father never drank except for an occasional glass of
Madeira wine at dinner, she did not recognize my symptoms and became
panicky.

"He is sick!" she shouted to the landlady, who came to see what it was
all about. "I have to get a doctor!"

The landlady took one whiff and began to laugh. "He is not sick," she
declared, "he is stinking drunk!" It took me a long time to live down this
episode, and to this day I cannot stand even the smell of Zubrovka.

Our school had a string ensemble with mandolin-like instruments in all
ranges, from piccolo to bass. I played a regular mandolin, which was tuned
like a violin, and I was very glad that this kind of instrument did not lend
itself to playing in parades. I also collected folk songs and had several notebooks full. Because of political sensitivity, there were very few anthologies
other than those of Soviet propaganda songs. There were also many songs
of and about the underworld, ballads about thieves and bank robbers, that
were passed around verbally and were popular among the young. It was not
that we admired crime, but we did secretly admire life outside the oppressive rules of this society, as well as those who dared to resist the rules. I eagerly sought out these songs and wrote them down. One was a ballad of
more than a hundred stanzas about a girl named Mourka, who joined a gang

but became bored with it, betrayed their secrets to the militia, and was killed by the gangsters.

I also copied many bawdy songs and, since in our one room there was no place to hide them, I loosened a section of lining in my overcoat and kept them there. One evening, while I was reading a book, I suddenly heard Mother laughing as I had never heard her laugh before. She was practically hysterical, her head and shoulders were shaking violently and her right arm was swinging back and forth. It did not take me long to realize that what she was clutching in her hand were my hidden songs. She had noticed the loose lining and decided to repair it. I felt like crawling into the cracks between the floor planks, but Mother was really a good sport and I never heard her tell the story to anyone.

As I understood later, the school director's complaint about my lack of patriotic fervor also had other significance. Mother had been elected by the restaurant employees to represent them in the union, which was a government organization that enforced discipline and was run by a Communist Party member. Its purpose was to squeeze out more work for less money by presumably giving the workers a forum to blow off their steam. However, Mother took her job seriously, as she did everything else. There was an elderly widow who worked in the *artel* to which the restaurant also belonged, selling candy, cookies, and apples in our school during the long, twenty-minute midday recess. I liked her poppy-seed candies, squares of compressed poppy seeds held together by sugar. She received a small salary and a small percentage of the sales. To earn more money she also sold her wares before and after school. This did not suit the *artel* management because she was making more money than some of the managers, and they refused to pay her for the additional sales. She complained to the union and Mother went to bat for her. I do not remember the details, but Mother was accused of promoting private enterprise, and this, in addition to being the wife of an "enemy" and having an unpatriotic son, endangered her job. She gave up her union position and told me to get more involved. I do not know what happened to the widow.

While private enterprise was not permitted, it did not mean that it did not exist. One could have a pair of boots made at the *artel* for a set price. But if one did not want to wait for them a long time and also to be sure that they would fit properly, they also could be had at a higher price from the same shoemaker if you visited his house after dark. The same went for tailors, upholsterers, and most other craftsmen.

In January of 1940 we received a letter from Uncle Samuel, telling us that Grisha-the-Younger had fallen under a streetcar and lost a leg. Uncle Grisha was afraid of losing three months' pay if he was late to work, and was hanging on with several other people on an icy step of the streetcar, when he slipped under it. He was the youngest and merriest of the three brothers and liked to recite funny poems. I still remember part of one about a city-bred teacher who had been assigned to a rural school after graduation. All new college graduates were assigned jobs in distant places, which they had to take, unless they had pull with the authorities. The teacher wrote home that she had become a true country girl and that at this time the potatoes were already developing nice cobs and the geese began to lay caviar.

After his wound had healed he got a wooden extension of his stump (without a foot, like the ones in pirate movies) and was able to go back to work.

CHAPTER 3

1941

On a quiet and sunny Sunday afternoon of June 22, 1941, I came home from a long hike in the Black Forest, where my friend Dima and I had gathered a basketful of mushrooms that we gave to his grandmother to inspect to make sure none were poisonous.

Upon entering the semi-dark kitchen of the house that we shared with our elderly landlord and his wife, I heard a faint but excited voice emanating from the radio point, which was a loudspeaker hooked up by wires to a central receiver at the post office. It was forbidden to own private receivers, and those who wished to hear the news rather than to read the newspapers—which were several days old by the time they reached our town—had to subscribe to a radio point.

"It's war!" the landlord, Citizen Bida, shouted to me. He was bending over the round loudspeaker cone, the size of a dinner plate, which stood on the table on a tapered base. His right hand was cupped over his ear and his left clutched the sparse white hair on the back of his head. "The Germans have crossed the border! They are bombing cities! My God, what will happen to us?"

"How can that be?" I asked incredulously. "We have a nonaggression pact with them!"

"Pact, shmact!" shouted old Bida. "It's Molotov speaking! They are coming here! My God, what will happen to us?" he repeated, looking forlornly around the room.

"We will kick them out," I responded without hesitation. After all, only a year before the Soviet Union had defeated Finland, and a year before that, Poland. And twice a week in our singing class at school we sang patriotic songs, quoting Marshal Voroshilov's promise that "we will never give up a single inch of our land!"

"Quiet! Listen!" said old Bida, unconvinced by my certainty.

I also bent over the loudspeaker until we almost rubbed noses. The volume of the radio point decreased with the distance from the post office, and we were at the edge of the town, quite far away from it. Through the crackling static, the barely audible but still very excited voice exhorted the population to burn the fields, destroy factories, and leave the invaders only bare scorched earth.

"But how will the people live?" Old Bida's hands were shaking. "What are they going to eat?"

"That's how the French were defeated in 1812," I said. "General Kutuzov burned everything in sight."

"And what did the people eat?" shouted old Bida with tears in his red-rimmed eyes, and he ran out of the kitchen.

I had no doubt that the war would be over in a few days, perhaps in a week. After all, when living with my grandfather in Zaporozhie I saw with my own eyes hundreds of bombers on exercises. The whole sky was dark with planes, and while they appeared to be rather slow, the roar of their engines projected undefeatable might.

On the other hand, I had heard and read many stories about the hardships during World War I and the civil war that followed it. The fighting had ended only about twenty years before and we were still finding bullets everywhere—in the ground, in the walls, in the bark of trees, and everyplace else, whenever one disturbed the soil or looked closely. It was every boy's pride to be able to identify the bullets—did they come from a rifle, and if so, what caliber? Were they from a ribbon-fed Maxim machine gun, or from a hand-carried one with a flat disk magazine? Were they from a pistol or a revolver, and if so, was it a Browning, Mauzer, or Nagant? We collected and traded bullets just as we collected and traded postage stamps.

Several days after the war started we began seeing airplanes that, thanks
to my air defense training, I could recognize as German. When they were
too high to distinguish their silhouettes, one could still tell that they were
German by the pulsating sound of their engines, caused, I was told, by their
Bosch fuel-injection systems, which they used instead of carburetors. They
flew around unchallenged, and we wondered what had happened to our air
force, which we had been told was invincible.

Also, columns of Soviet soldiers, tanks, and trucks began moving through
the town. Unfortunately, unlike in 1939, when the Soviet Union and Germany attacked Poland, they were moving in the wrong direction this time—
from west to east, in full retreat. We tried to find out what was happening
from the tired and dispirited soldiers, but they did not know themselves.
We had to rely either on news transmitted over the barely audible radio
point or to join hundreds of people gathered in front of the post office,
where at five o'clock every evening the news was broadcast over a huge loudspeaker. It was either in Ukrainian from Kiev, the capital of the Ukrainian
Republic, or in Russian from Moscow. I preferred the Russian broadcasts,
not because the news was any better—day after day the government bul-
letins sounded the same: "In spite of heroic resistance, such and such towns
had to be given up to the enemy"—but because the *dictor* (announcer) from
Moscow was Citizen Levitan,[1] whose clear, crisp pronunciation was considered to be the official standard of speech.

Several weeks after the beginning of the war there was another broadcast

1. There is a reason that I refer to Levitan as "Citizen." As long as Russia existed, people
addressed one another as *gospodin* for a man or *gospozha* for a woman. Ukrainians and Poles
used the words *pan* and *pani*. After the October Revolution of 1917, these greetings were forbidden; using them would imply that one was against the Communist regime, which could
mean exile or being sent to concentration camp.

The new form of address was "Comrade" for Communists and "Citizen" for common people. An "enemy of the people" had to use "Citizen" for everybody, since he would be offend-
ing a Communist by claiming to be his "comrade." A respectful way of addressing someone
whom one knew, and also for children addressing teachers, was by their first name and
patronymic. Within family or with friends, one used the first name in its many variations,
depending on the degree of familiarity—something which so confuses readers of Russian nov-
els. Thus, Ivan would be called Vania by his father and Ivanushka, Vaniusha, or Vaniushen'-
ka by his mother as terms of endearment, or Van'ka by his pals. Younger children usually referred to adults as "Aunt" or "Uncle," even when unrelated.

from the Kremlin, this time by Stalin himself. If Stalin himself was speaking, things had to be very bad, since he practically never spoke over the radio because his thickly accented Russian was atrocious. As it became known after his death in 1953, Stalin had collapsed mentally when the Germans attacked, because he did not believe it would happen, even after having been warned by his spies. He had made the nonaggression pact with Germany to safeguard the Soviet Union from German attack. In return, the Soviet Union partitioned Poland with Germany, received control over Moldovia and the Baltic countries, and agreed to supply the Nazis with about a million tons of oil and with grain which, according to rumors, was shipped in silk sacks when they ran out of burlap.

It took Stalin a couple of weeks to collect his wits and address the nation. In his speech he, like Molotov before him, exhorted the population to burn everything, to plow under the unripe fields, and to leave the Germans nothing but scorched earth. He did not say how people were to survive after they had done all that.

Every Sunday evening throngs of people promenaded up and down the central part of the main street, which was named, like almost everything else, after Stalin. Everyone wore their best clothes and there was a lot of jovial kidding around, particularly between young men and women. Soldiers from the local garrison turned out in force, and I, being rather tall for my age, hung around with them. They tolerated me because I was useful as a go-between with the girls. When one of them noticed a girl he liked, he would write her a note, which I would thrust into her hand and run away. If she wanted to meet him, she would signal me the next time we passed, and I would get a response.

I became particularly friendly with a young soldier named Ivan Makarenko, called Vania by his buddies. He had been drafted right after graduation from teacher's college and was older than most of the soldiers, who were drafted at eighteen. By coincidence, I had just finished reading a book by a writer named Makarenko, who had organized shelters for homeless children. There were hundreds of thousands of homeless children throughout the Soviet Union, and particularly in the Ukraine where, during the artificial famine created by the Communists in the early 1930s, about five million people starved to death. I remember overhearing Mother telling someone that she saw horse wagons driving through the streets every morning, picking up bodies. I asked Vania whether he was related to the writer and he said that he was a distant cousin. Vania also liked books, so we had something to talk about. He was the only adult man I could talk to and I tagged along whenever I saw him in town, probably making a nuisance of myself, but he never showed any annoyance.

When I saw Vania after Stalin's broadcast, he was very grim. "Did you hear Stalin's speech?" he asked. "They are actually burning the fields. There will be famine here; you and your family must leave immediately. There are still some trains going east and they are full of people. We will also be moving out soon and in a couple of days the bridges will be blown up. They are already being mined. There is no time to lose!"

Mother became very upset when I related Vania's advice. "Where can we go?" she asked. "They will not let us stay in Zaporozhie with my brothers. Father had some distant relatives in Voroshilovgrad in eastern Ukraine, who once spent a summer with us. But who knows if they will take us in, and how are we going to get there?"

I remembered a large man with a long white beard who, with his daughter and a grandson, had spent a month with us some years back. He told us stories about having been a red partisan during the Revolution and fighting alongside Voroshilov, who was now marshal of the army. There was a piece of metal that could be seen through his skin, embedded in his wrist. I was very impressed by it and he even let me feel it. I also remembered Mother saying that, coming from a city where food was scarce, they had eaten us out of house and home.

"Besides," said Mother, "we are not Communists, we are their enemies. The Germans will not bother us."

"And what about famine?" I asked.

"There probably will be famine everywhere," she replied in a trembling voice. "There always is during a war. At least here I may be able to keep my job in the restaurant." Her eyes filled with tears. "We have already lost everything once. How can we drop everything and go wandering somewhere with the baby?"

"Vania said we should leave immediately," I repeated. "He is a soldier;

he knows best! He said there is no time to lose because the bridges will be blown up!"

"I don't know what to do," cried Mother.

All I could think of as we spoke were the stories about Fascist atrocities in Spain and in Abyssinia. I could practically see them as they were shown in newsreels. "I do not want to stay here with the Fascists!" I shouted. "I hate them! Perhaps I should go by myself," I said, trying to sound much braver than I felt.

Mother hesitated and then, through tears, whispered: "Perhaps you should. You look older than your thirteen years and in a couple of years you will be a man. Who knows, the Germans may force you to serve in their army or God knows what . . ."

She hugged me and cried. I did not sleep much that night and neither did Mother. Was I doing the right thing? What was I going to do all by myself? Mother always took care of me, and whatever I had read about homeless boys was rather frightening. Would I ever see Mother and Vilya again?

The next morning Mother sliced up two loaves of bread and dried the slices in the oven. She bundled them up with some other food in a pillowcase and packed my clothing into another, much larger one. She also gave me some money. All this was done while she was sobbing and I myself could barely hold back tears. The whole scene seemed unreal. I felt as if I was watching a melodramatic movie and in it was some frightened thirteen-year-old boy who in a few hours would be all alone, not knowing where he was going, where he would sleep, or what he was going to eat. I would be homeless like those children about whom I had read, but there would be no Makarenko to take me in. I was very frightened, but I did not change my mind.

"We will see you off to the train," said Mother, and we started toward the station. I carried my bundles while Mother carried Vilya. We did not talk much. It was as if, deep inside, neither of us believed that this was actually happening.

The station was way out of town and as we walked, we kept asking the passing horse-wagon drivers whether they were going in that direction and offering to pay them if they would take us there. It was not long before one of them told us to climb on top of the sacks in his wagon. In less than an hour we arrived at the station, which was a small brick building, around which was a crowd of what seemed to be hundreds of people of all ages sitting on bundles, suitcases, and sacks. Mother handed me Vilya and went into the building to find out about the trains. After a while she returned with the stationmaster, whom she knew from the restaurant. He was an energetic man of about forty, with a swarthy, gypsylike appearance.

"Raya," he said, pointing his finger at Mother, "You better get on that train with your son! It will be very bad here. Besides, he is too young to go alone."

"But I have nothing with me," exclaimed Mother. "How can I go like that with the baby?"

"No buts," he insisted. "I will send someone with you to get some things. Come, let's not waste time. There will be no train until evening."

I held my breath.

"I guess I'd better," Mother said, following him. Nothing short of Father's return could have made me happier. It felt as though a big load fell off my shoulders and a hard knot of fear dissolved in my chest. Vilya immediately began exploring the labyrinth of luggage and stared at the other children. Every now and then German planes flew over the station. Some women were beginning to get hysterical, but the planes flew high and ignored us.

In a couple of hours Mother returned with a railroad man, each of them carrying a bundle wrapped in bedsheets. She looked resigned and did not say much. Later she ran into a young waitress, Natasha, with whom she worked, and the nice woman cook who used to feed me. The cook, like us an "enemy of the people," had come to see off her seventeen-year-old son, Misha; having a bad back and not feeling well, she decided to stay.

In the evening, a freight train pulled up to the platform spouting steam and soot. I used to like the smell of burning coal and the hissing and puffing of steam locomotives, particularly when we were changing trains in the middle of the night on the way to Odessa for a vacation. There was no time now, however, to think about past trips. As soon as the train stopped, everyone rushed into the gaping, sliding doors of two empty box cars and, after a lot of pushing and shoving, we all squeezed in. The energetic stationmaster helped us with the bundles and wished us good luck. I learned later that he was killed the following week, when the Germans bombed the station.

There was no light in the car and, in the dark, people and bundles were packed into a solid mass. Little by little, everyone staked out a place, first by sitting down on the floor, then by stretching out, until we were shoulder to shoulder, like sardines in a can. Then Vilya needed to pee and we had to use a ceramic mug for a chamber pot. After an hour or so, the locomotive blew its whistle and we were on our way. We had no idea where the train was going. All we knew was that it was headed east.

No one spoke, and the silence was interrupted only by an occasional deep sigh and the clickety-clack of wheels. I soon fell asleep; when I woke up, we were standing still and gray light was seeping in through the two small windows, each about two feet wide and a foot and a half high. I was squeezed in between a hefty woman and Vilya. Mother was sleeping on the other side of him, tightly pressed against our bundles. Then someone slid open the door and jumped down to the ground. I carefully made my way to the door, trying not to step on anyone, and also jumped down. We were in an open field; there were trains ahead of us and behind us as far as I could see. People jumped from the cars and crawled under them to the other side, where they were relieving themselves in the field, men and women, a few feet from one another. The rail bed sloped steeply away from the rails, and the older people had to be lowered down and pulled back up with a great deal of effort.

Right behind our car were two platform cars carrying a disassembled German twin-engine bomber, a Junkers 88. It was not damaged and must have made an emergency landing. I was fascinated. I had never seen a military plane this close. Even with its wings separated from its fuselage it looked menacing, with a twin machine gun protruding from the cabin and sinister black crosses on its sides and on the wings. Behind the plane and also ahead of our cars were several freight cars like ours, carrying soldiers. We asked them where we were going but they did not know any more than we did.

After several hours the trains ahead of us began to move. Then our train blew its whistle and followed the solid string of trains, which moved so slowly that I probably could have run alongside and kept up.

We ate some of the dry bread that I had in my bundle and drank some water from a teakettle that Mother had brought. A teakettle was an absolute necessity when traveling by train. Every railroad station had a spigot with hot water to enable passengers to make tea. Unfortunately, we did not stop anywhere near a station.

Our eighty or so passengers were quite a mixed lot. About half were women of all ages, about a dozen were men; the rest were children, also of all ages. Most of the men were middle-aged or elderly, but several were young students from the Polish side of the border. One of them spent most of the time holding hands with a young girl student. Another wore short britches, buttoned just below the knee, a garment I had seen only once before, when I spotted a small, frightened man in similar attire, with his hands clasped behind his head, followed by a huge, growling police dog. The dog was straining the leash that was held by a lanky, long-nosed militia detective named Grizhgorin, who must have thought that he had caught a German spy.

We moved in starts and stops most of the day until we finally halted at a station, where the locomotive and all the teakettles, bottles, and pots were filled with water. Then we slowly moved on again until we stopped for the night somewhere in an open field between stations.

I was awakened by a deafening popping sound. It sounded as if a giant bottle had been dipped into boiling water and cracked. Then another crack from the direction of the locomotive, then another and another farther up, receding into the distance.

"Bombs!" someone shouted in the pitch darkness. "Open the door!"

"They are gone," said a male voice. "There is no point in running."

"They are probably trying to destroy the airplane," shouted someone else. "They will come back! Let's get out of here!" He slid the door open. Outside, soldiers were milling around and the commanding officer, a major, came up to the door and told us that there was no damage but warned us not to light matches or cigarettes.

"I don't think they will come back," he said. "There are hundreds of trains ahead of us that they can bomb. I just hope that they don't damage the tracks."

The next day this process repeated itself: we moved for about an hour and stood still for about an hour, spilling outside into the fields whenever we heard German planes.

At one of these stops, as I lay on my back trying to identify the model of the airplane, I suddenly heard someone shouting, "Halt or I will shoot!"

Then a shot rang out, then another, followed by a lot of shouting and commotion. I sat up and near the train saw a soldier on one knee, taking aim and firing at a soldier and a woman who were running perhaps a hundred yards away. The man fell and the woman stopped, clutching her arm. The soldiers ran toward them and I was about to do the same, when I heard Mother screaming at me to stay. I stood up and watched a group of soldiers approach the fallen man. They looked at him from all sides, then an officer took out his pistol and shot the man in the head. We were later told that these were local thieves. The man, wearing a military uniform, had entered one of the cars and stolen something. He was too severely wounded to survive, so the officer put him out of his misery. The woman was only lightly wounded in the arm; they let her go.

At another stop, I was sitting on the grass talking to an army captain, who said that I reminded him of his son, who was about my age. I asked him to show me his revolver and, after removing the bullets, he let me hold it. I was aiming it at something in the field, when I heard the major yelling at the captain to take it away from me. "There are enough deaths already," he shouted. "We do not need any more by accident."

That night I was awakened by a piercing scream. "She is dead!" screamed the woman next to me. Everybody jumped up. "Who is dead? Where?" Someone lit a match. The mother of my neighbor, a wrinkled, frail woman who had to be gently lowered from the car at every stop to relieve herself, lay still on the floor. Her daughter and a granddaughter sobbed hysterically. I spent the rest of the night sitting on our bundles and was glad when the rectangles of the windows turned gray and grew lighter by the minute.

The old lady was wrapped into a bedsheet and as soon as we stopped at a station to take on water, men lowered her body onto the platform and her daughter and granddaughter got off with their luggage, in the hope of finding a way to bury her.

We had finished our dried bread. At every station we tried to buy some fresh bread from the peasant women on the platform, but both Mother and I were small and light, and we were easily pushed away by bigger, heavier people. Fortunately Misha, the cook's son, fought his way through the crowd and managed to get a loaf of fresh dark bread, which he shared with us and with Natasha. No bread ever tasted so good.

We had been on the way for three days but had traveled only about 450 kilometers, or around 300 miles. We were afraid that the bridges over the wide River Dnieper might be bombed out and were greatly relieved when we finally crossed one of them near a city called Cherkassy. Once on the other side, it was believed almost unanimously that the Germans would never be able to cross the Dnieper and that it might be safe to remain there, particularly since we did not know where the train was going or when it would get there. It would be good to get some real food instead of just bread and water, against which Vilya was beginning to rebel.

When we stopped at a station on the fourth day, someone on the platform called out Natasha's name. It turned out to be her fiancé, a party functionary, who had been looking for her all these days, following the trains in a truck. It was indeed a miracle that he found her. They were heading for the Russian Republic and offered to drop us off on the way, wherever we wished.

We decided to go somewhat farther away from the river, but to remain in the Ukraine. After half a day on the open back of the truck, we reached the city of Poltava and stopped at a militia station to see if there were any accommodations for refugees, but were told to move on. After another hour of bouncing on the cobblestone road, we stopped in a small town called Karlovka. Here we were told that we could stay, and a refugee agency helped us to find a room. It was not actually a room but a windowless clay cabin with a clay floor, in a building with a thatched roof that contained several such cabins. They were intended for rent to summer vacationers, like those that we had rented on the shore of the Black Sea.

I was rather excited to be there since I knew that this was the hometown of the famous academician Trofim Ivanovich Lysenko, about whom we had learned in school. He was a biologist, and his theory was that some acquired traits are transmitted from one generation to the next. Stalin liked this idea because it agreed with something written by Friedrich Engels, an associate of Karl Marx, the founder of communism. Stalin's support gave Lysenko a great deal of power; he denounced the science of genetics, which contradicted his ideas, as being a capitalist invention. Many geneticists were then arrested for advocating capitalist ideas and sentenced to long prison terms or Siberian exile. Some perished there for being politically incorrect; I think of them every time I hear the words "political correctness."

There were many refugees in town and our compound was full. They were mostly women and children, among whom was a girl about my age who looked very much like Lusia, except that instead of two braids, she had a single one in the back. She also liked to read, and we explored the local library together. The town authorities organized a soup kitchen and also gave us bread ration cards so that we did not go hungry, even though the soup did not compare with Mother's by a long shot.

Two weeks went by but Mother was still unable to find a job. Then, in the stillness of an early morning, we heard a series of distant explosions that lasted for more than an hour: the Germans were bombing the city of Poltava. It was time to move on. Also, it was the end of August; we hoped to settle somewhere by September so that I could start school on time.

The next natural barriers that we thought the Germans would not be able to cross were the Don River in the southeast and the Volga in the east, both in the Russian Republic. We knew that beyond the Volga the steppes extended all the way to Siberia, which made us think of cold winters and Gulag concentration camps. Therefore we decided to go south, where it should be warmer. To be on the safe side, we decided to go beyond not only the Don but also the next river, the Kuban', which flowed from east to west just north of the Caucasus Mountains.

Again Mother dried some bread, and the next morning we tied up our bundles and headed for the railroad station, which was not very far. In order to go south, we first had to go to the railroad center of Kharkov, which was about a hundred miles east. We got onto the first train going in that direction. It was a familiar freight train packed with refugees, who had to squeeze back to make room for us near the door. While there was some rumbling in the back, the fact that we had a baby and were only going as far as Kharkov helped a great deal.

We arrived in Kharkov in the early afternoon and joined hundreds of families like ourselves, sitting on their bundles, waiting for a train south and hoping that the station would not be bombed. We were told that there might be a train in the evening, and I went outside to look at the big city. At the streetcar stop right outside the station, there was a sign saying that this streetcar went to the zoo. I asked someone how far it was, and was told that it should not take more than twenty minutes. At that moment the streetcar arrived and, never having been to a zoo, I got on.

We did not get very far when the air-raid sirens began to wail and passengers were herded into the nearest building. Only then did it occur to me that Mother did not know where I was, that the railroad station might be bombed and that we might miss the train. We could hear the planes making low passes over the city, but there were no explosions. As soon as the "all clear" signal was given and streetcars began to circulate again, I rushed back to the station.

Naturally, Mother was frantic and furious, and I was very embarrassed and contrite. After scolding me with tears in her eyes, she said, "You know, I depend on you as the man of the family and sometimes forget that you are still a child." That really hurt, but I had to admit to myself that she was right.

Fortunately we were not bombed. Toward evening an empty freight train pulled up to the platform and we were on our way south. After crossing the River Don, we entered the region of the Cossacks. While we were now in the Russian Republic, people here spoke mostly Ukrainian, since the Cossacks were descendants of runaway Ukrainian serfs. Before they were freed, the serfs had belonged to their masters and could not leave their villages. The runaways had settled on the southern fringe of the Russian Empire, which was something like the western frontier in the United States, except that instead of Indians, they fought the Chechens and other native Muslim tribes, becoming known as fearless horsemen and eventually being incorporated into the czar's cavalry.

On the second day, the train crossed the River Kuban' and crawled into a station called Nevinnomysk, where we were told to disembark. Several horse wagons from neighboring collective farms were waiting for us. Since harvest time was approaching and many men were in the army, the farms needed all the help they could get. The wagons had slanted sides, wooden wheels with iron rims, no springs, and were pulled by a team of two horses. The young farmers were dressed like farmers in the Ukraine, with patched-up trousers, old boots, and shirts with stand-up collars that were buttoned not in the middle, but somewhere in line with the left ear, the buttons running down in a straight line. I asked them if they were real Cossacks, since for some reason I had imagined that Cossacks always wore the uniforms one saw in the movies—knee-length black jackets with a row of cartridge pockets on each side of the lapels. Our driver, a boy somewhat older than I, explained that those clothes were worn only in parades. (Interestingly enough, the design of these uniforms was borrowed from the native tribes, whom the Cossacks had fought for centuries.)

After several hours of bouncing over bumpy dirt roads, we arrived at the collective farm, called Stanitsa Otradnaya. (*Stanitsa* is a Cossack word for village and *otradnaya* means "joyful.") While it was a large village of several hundred families and was tidier than similar villages in Ukraine, I did not discover any signs of joy. On the dusty square in front of the *kolkhoz* office, about twenty young horsemen rode in a circle. Every so often, on command of an older man, they swung around so that they faced the tail, or slid under the belly of the horses and appeared on the opposite side. All this was done rather lethargically, at a slow pace, and neither the horsemen nor the small workhorses looked as if they were enjoying it. "They are draftees," said our driver. I had difficulty imagining them attacking German panzers.

A collective farm or *kolkhoz* was, as its name implies, a farm that was operated jointly by the villagers. People were paid according to the number of "workdays" that they had earned during the year. To earn a "workday," one had to fulfill an established quota of work for specific tasks. Certain skilled tasks, such as driving a tractor, earned more than one "workday" per day. Tasks requiring less skill, such as raking hay, earned one "workday" for raking a specified area. At the end of the year, whatever was left over, after mandatory deliveries to the government, was divided by the total number of "workdays" and distributed to the farmers in the form of grain and money. While in theory this sounded fair and just, and was supposed to inspire the best effort on everyone's part, in practice it did not. Since no one owned anything specific, no one saw why they should work harder than someone else to maintain the common property or take good care of commonly owned animals. Everything was done just to "get by." The one area in which the system was efficient was in extracting as much as possible for the state. In fact, as I found out later, the Germans retained the collective farms in the occupied areas for this purpose. Also, as had been true during serfdom, the peasants could not move away from the farms without special permission.

The soil was very fertile, and Stanitsa Otradnaya appeared more prosperous than the *kolkhoz* I'd seen in Derazhnya. Even though the houses were
of the same construction in both places, here they were neatly whitewashed
and their thatched roofs appeared to be in good repair. Our caravan of half
a dozen wagons halted at the office building, which was distinguished by a
red tin roof; here the chairman of the Communist Party made a brief speech.
He welcomed us and told us how important it was for the war effort that
we pitch in with the farm work. He then assigned us to different homes. We
were sent to a distant hamlet called "Fruitful" that consisted of about thirty houses, and were deposited at the house of an elderly widow who lived
alone.

The house consisted of a single room and a kitchen, with space for only
a table and a bench. The one place where the three of us could sleep was in
the niche over the baking oven. For those who have not seen such a setup,
it is difficult to imagine how one could sleep on top of an oven, but it is
very simple. The oven is located along one wall in the corner of the kitchen.
The hearth is about waist-high and about three feet wide and six feet long,
with a vaulted ceiling about a foot and a half high. The outside surface of
the hearth ceiling is flat and is the floor of the niche, which was about four
feet by four feet, into which we had to climb from a bench. It was quite
tight up there, and when we stretched out, our feet dangled in midair.

The old woman was very talkative and in no time we knew everything
about everyone in the hamlet. Of course, we told her that Father was dead.
Her only son had been drafted, and she was glad to have someone to talk
to. She also told us that the Communists had executed all of the Cossack
officers and—just as they did in the Ukraine—exiled the most prosperous
farmers, those who had hired help and saw no reason for joining the *kolkhoz*.
As in Ukraine, these farmers were called *kulaks* and were declared "enemies
of the people." Many were killed to set an example; those who were spared
were robbed of their land and livestock and exiled to Siberia or Kazakhstan.
When the peasants protested, Lenin sent the following telegram to the Central Executive Committee of the region on August 10, 1918:

"Hang (I mean hang publicly, so that people see it) at least 100 *kulaks* . . .
Do all this so that for miles around people see it all, understand it, tremble,
and tell themselves that we are killing the bloodthirsty *kulaks* and that we

will continue to do so. Reply, saying that you have received and carried out these instructions. Yours, Lenin."[2]

Mother was assigned to work in the day care center, where she could be with Vilya, and I was told that I could help an older boy, Sasha, with whatever he was doing. This suited me fine because I was interested in learning as much as possible about farm work. Sasha was a pale, phlegmatic boy who knew farm work but never overworked himself. His job was to pitch in wherever there was a need, so that we never spent too much time on a task to be bored. Thus one day, when the cowherd got sick, we took the cows to pasture in the foothills. We collected them early in the morning, as soon as they were milked, and herded them along the dirt path to the hills. Several times Sasha warned me to make sure that the fifty or so cows under our care did not get into the clover fields, because their stomachs would be distended by gas to the point where they might burst. Dry clover was fed to them in winter mixed with hay.

The morning was fresh and clear and we walked alongside the cows, keeping them on the path with our sticks. As we reached the top of a hill, I froze in place—in the distance before me, shimmering in the morning sun from one end of the horizon to the other, extended a chain of snow-capped mountains. I had never seen mountains before, let alone snow-capped ones, and their majesty left me breathless. It was a colossal, jagged, irregular picket fence separating Europe from Asia.

Another time, Sasha and I drove a team of horses to Cherkessy in the Karachai Republic, which was only about twenty-five miles away, to deliver grain. The Karachai are one of the native tribes who had resisted the Russian expansion in the last century. Cossacks referred to them and to other natives as "the Asiatics."

On the Karachai side of the invisible border the villages were called *auls* instead of *stanitsas,* and people had dark complexions and somewhat slanted eyes. Many men wore voluminous sheepskin hats, even in the heat of the summer, and now and then we saw a man riding on a donkey, which to me was very exotic. It took us about half a day to get there, bouncing in our springless wagon on deeply rutted dirt roads, and facing the tail ends of two

2. Stephane Courtois et al., *The Black Book of Communism: Crimes, Terror, Repression* (Cambridge, Mass.: Harvard University Press, 1999), 72.

horses, who calmly went about their business of passing gas, raising their tails and defecating or, being female, sprinkling us with urine. Sasha had been there before and knew where to get water for the horses in the yard of the government grain-receiving station. While he went inside, I gave the horses water from a bucket and attached their feedbag to the shaft of the wagon.

After some time Sasha returned with an inspector in a white lab coat who, with a long tube, took a sample of the grain from deep inside, and went away. After a long wait, the inspector came out and told us to take the grain back where we got it, because it contained too many weed seeds. Sasha was very unhappy about this turn of events, but there was no appealing the inspector's decision. We had hoped that with an empty wagon we could get back while it was still daylight, but with a full one we did not make it until midnight, groping our way in total darkness on barely distinguishable dirt roads, which to me looked all alike. Mother got very worried.

Otradnaya had only an elementary school, with students through the fourth grade. Beyond that, the children had to go to a boarding school in Armavir, but with the war going on I was probably the only person who worried about missing a school year. The news from the front lines was getting worse and worse. By October the German armies had taken over most of Ukraine and were pushing toward Rostov on the River Don, which was only about two hundred miles away. Again, it was time for us to go.

We packed our bundles, said good-bye to the nice landlady, and hitched a ride on the next wagon going to Nevinnomysk, a fairly large town on the railroad to the Caucasus. The authorities here wanted us to move on, but Mother went to see them with Vilya, and they could not refuse bread to a child. They gave us food ration coupons and Mother found a room. She decided to look for a job here and to wait and see whether the Germans would actually cross the Don before we fled farther.

Our room was in a two-story house on a hill overlooking the railroad tracks, not very far from the station. One afternoon, as I opened the door to go outside, I heard the familiar, loud popping sound. I looked up and saw two German planes, just about at my eye level and about five hundred yards away, slowly flying over the tracks and dropping bombs one after the other, like giant birds dropping their excrement in flight. These were ground-attack planes rather than bombers, and the bombs did not appear to be large. I could practically distinguish the pilots in the cockpits. While the bombs were popping below, I saw in the distance two Soviet fighter planes circling at high altitude, apparently totally unaware of what was going on. I felt like shouting at them to look down.

By the time the air-raid sirens began to wail, the Germans were gone, leaving behind them billowing clouds of smoke. We decided to stay until the next morning, hoping that by then the fires would be put out and the tracks repaired. Also, this time we decided not to depend on rivers to stop the Germans, but to try to cross the Caspian Sea into Turkmenistan. We were afraid to keep going south to Georgia, Armenia, or Azerbaijan because if the Germans were to conquer the mountains, there would be no place for us to run.

On the next morning we again dragged our bundles to the railroad station. The station was not badly damaged, and trains were running from the direction of Rostov toward Makhachkala, which was a Caspian seaport. There was no question of any schedule; the trains came as soon as the rails had been cleared. After several hours of apprehensive waiting on a crowded open platform, listening for the cranelike sound of German planes, we piled into a passenger train that was already full. There were people and bundles in the aisles and on the platforms between the cars; no one asked us for tickets.

After several hours of starts and stops, we pulled through a cloud of smoke into the station called the "Mineral Waters," a resort town in the foothills of the Caucasus Mountains. The station had been bombed only two hours before and, according to rumor, about two hundred people who, like us, had been waiting on the platform were killed. There were fire hoses everywhere washing down the platform and pouring water into the station building. As soon as we stopped, hordes of people appeared from the ruins and, not being able to get inside, climbed onto the roofs, handing up bundles and children and suitcases. We felt lucky to be inside.

As the train pulled away from the station, an army officer, who looked like a native of the Caucasus, was pushing his way through the aisle. I don't know whether he was drunk, but he was shouting at the top of his voice: "So, the Germans bombed here? Good for them! That son-of-a-bitch Stalin has killed the best people in the Caucasus! I hope they help us to get rid

of him!" I looked at Mother and she looked at me. People had been executed for much less than that. "Don't you dare ever repeat this," she said,
but there was a faint smile on her face.

On the next day we reached Makhachkala, a port city on the Caspian
Sea and the capital of the Dagestan Autonomous Region, and were ordered
to leave the train.

Outside the station was a large square, every inch of which was covered
with people. There must have been several thousand women, children, babies, and old men sitting on their suitcases, sacks, and bundles of all shapes
and sizes under the open skies, which were fortunately cloudless. We found
a few square feet of space on the sidewalk across the road from the station
and began asking questions. Some of the people had been here for a week,
since the small freighters going across the sea to Krasnovodsk could take
only a few people at a time. You had to register and wait for your turn. The
authorities gave ration coupons for bread, and there were hot and cold
drinking-water taps at the station. Those who were pushy enough even
managed to get some thin noodle soup at the station kiosk. There were no
toilets that could accommodate the crowd, so one had to go behind a parked
freight train, where there was some space between it and a wall, or else stand
in endless lines at the station. The Germans had not bombed Makhachkala
yet, but the streetlights did not go on at night and window shades were
drawn in the buildings. If you were not in your place by nightfall, you might
not be able to find it in the dark.

The climate here was close to subtropical, with palm trees and other exotic plants that I had not seen before and found very interesting. On three
sides the city was surrounded by mountains and, outside of the square, had
the airy and clean appearance of a resort town. The people in the city were
mostly Russian; only occasionally would one see a native mountaineer in a
long coat, with a tall, fur-trimmed hat and the ubiquitous dagger in his belt,
riding a horse or a donkey. It was late October but the temperature was quite
pleasant during the day and not too cold at night.

Every inch of the square not covered by people was covered with litter,
but this was nothing in comparison to what we saw one morning. During
the night, the freight train, the space behind which served as a latrine, had
gone, exposing a frightful mess only about a hundred feet away from the

square. Fortunately, we were on the far end of it, but that did not prevent swarms of flies from reaching us, and there was fear of disease. Also it was now impossible to find a relatively private spot among the railroad cars, which greatly upset Mother.

I had read that many people in India sleep on the sidewalks and now knew how they must feel. There was no place to wash, and those who wanted to take a bath at the public bathhouse had to stand in line for at least twenty-four hours. We slept on our bundles fully dressed and woke up shivering in the morning chill, hoping that it would not rain. Upon getting up I usually ran to get in a bread line before the store opened, and by noon returned to our nest, all the way fighting the urge to pinch pieces of the warm bread, a kilo of which had to sustain all three of us through the day.

In the afternoons I wandered about the town looking at the exotic vegetation and the unfamiliar architecture, or watching huge cranes loading and unloading the cargo ships in the port. During one of my wanderings I stumbled upon a monument that was surrounded by flowers and discovered that this was the grave of Suleyman Stalski, a Dagestani poet, whose verses we had to memorize and whose songs we had to sing at school. Stalski was his pen name, which was about as close as he could make it to Stalin. He had received all kinds of medals and honors for being an obsequious court flatterer, like those of whom I had read in stories about Middle Eastern pashas. There is a Russian word for something that is sickeningly sweet—*pritorny*—and just as one remembers something outstandingly pleasant or beautiful, one also remembers something outstandingly unpleasant or ugly, even after more than sixty years:

> Comrades, let us sing a song
> About the greatest man on earth,
> About the most wise and majestic being,
> A song about Comrade Stalin!
> He led our struggle against enemies
> In battle for happiness and fortune,
> He lit the bright spring stars
> Above our humble dwellings.
> So Comrades, let us sing a song
> About the greatest genius in the world,

About the most beloved and dearest,
A song about Comrade Stalin!

No wonder Stalin loved him and showered him with decorations.

On the fourth or the fifth day I returned to our spot to find that Mother was not there and Vilya was sitting with neighbors. He looked frightened but was not crying. "Don't be alarmed," said the woman before I had a chance to say anything, "but your mother was taken to the hospital. She was bleeding." "Yes" said Vilya, "an ambulance came with two horses."

I gave Vilya the bread, told him that I would be back soon, and hurried as fast as I could to the hospital, chased by frightful scenarios running through my head. The hospital was on the edge of town, in the foothills of the mountains, and it took me more than half an hour to get there. Mother was very pale.

"How is Vilya, is he very frightened?" she asked as soon as I entered the large room holding about ten bedridden women. "I am very sorry for doing this to you," she whispered, with tears in her eyes. "They promised to discharge me tomorrow afternoon. Come and get me at two o'clock." Not having known what to expect, I was relieved to see her as she was.

It was strange and frightening not to have Mother with us and I slept very little. Mother was very weak when I came for her, and I had to support her as we very slowly made our way "home." "They wanted me to stay another day," she said, "but I was afraid that we may miss our boat." She had saved some cookies for us, which Vilya and I immediately devoured.

Two days later it was our turn to leave. We dragged our bundles up the gangway of a small, dirty freighter and found a place on the deck, which was just as crowded as the square. There were about a hundred of us. The ship did not look like a seagoing vessel. We sailed after dark without lights, following the shimmering streak of moonlight on the water.

"Let's hope the German planes do not find us," someone said in the darkness. "We would be like sitting ducks to them."

"Amen," came a woman's voice from somewhere.

CHAPTER 4

1942

We sailed all night and all day without seeing or hearing any airplanes. This was very fortunate because there was no place to hide. The ship was not equipped to carry passengers and there was no food for us. We were given only water, which had a metallic taste and was tepid. This may have been for the better because many passengers were seasick. Even though the waves were not large, the boat rocked up and down and rolled from side to side. People were leaning over the rails, gagging and throwing up everything they must have eaten for the last week. We were not allowed below deck. There was only one toilet that we could use, and instead of standing in line, men urinated overboard.

As the distance from the European shore increased, we felt safer, as if an invisible line somewhere in the Caspian Sea dividing Asia from Europe had the magic power of preventing the Germans from crossing it. We ate some bread, which was the only food we had, and took turns holding onto Vilya, who was anxious to look overboard and explore the coils of rope and the winches at each lid of the ship's hold. The deck was packed solid with people shivering in the cold breeze, trying to protect themselves against the salty spray. But to me this spray was invigorating and, in spite of my empty stomach, I felt good. This was my first voyage on a ship, and it was an adventure. I tried to figure out the purpose and functions of all the pulleys, cables, and machinery, and the steadfast throbbing of the diesel engines was both exciting and reassuring.

Sometime during the second night we arrived in Krasnovodsk on the Asian shore of the Caspian Sea in the Soviet Socialist Republic of Turkmenistan. As the sun rose that morning, we were tied up at a dirty dock full of bales, crates, and barrels. There were several other small ships and several oil tankers, which must have been transporting oil across the sea from the Baku oil fields in Azerbaijan. The tankers were anchored offshore and were surrounded by large oil slicks that shimmered in the sunlight with all the colors of the rainbow. Thick black hoses ran from the tankers to platforms full of huge valves, while big fat pipes ran from these platforms to storage tanks on shore. A strong smell of crude oil overpowered the occasional whiffs of salt air.

There were some warehouses with red tin roofs, and not far from the port was the railroad station, where we were told to go and await a train that would take us somewhere inland to be settled. We joined several hundred other people who were already camped around the small station building that had the usual hot and cold water spigots on the outside wall. This was the beginning of the Turkestan-Siberian railroad that crossed the Central Asian republics of Turkmenistan, Uzbekistan, and Kazakhstan, with a branch to Kirgizia, and eventually joined the Trans-Siberian railroad in Novosibirsk.[1]

The town of Krasnovodsk, which means Red Waters, consisted of single-story barracklike buildings with rusty tin roofs, scattered around the port and the railroad station. To the north were extensive salt flats—layers of salt left after shallow ponds of salt water evaporated in the sun. The salt was being gathered into large mounds by people with wooden shovels. To the east stretched Kara-Kum, the Black Desert, an endless emptiness spotted here and there with small, dried-out prickly bushes and an occasional tuft of grass. I was very interested in the unfamiliar plants, which had long spikes and small leaves to decrease evaporation of water. Beyond the Black Desert was Kyzyl-Kum, the Red Desert, stretching all the way to Kazakhstan. We had no idea where we were going to be settled.

The sky was clear and blue, and as the sun climbed higher it became very hot; even the occasional breeze was hot and dry. When a two-humped camel

1. I spell the names of the regions, places, rivers, and cities the way they were spelled then, which was as they were pronounced in Russian. When the republics became independent countries, the spelling was changed to conform to pronunciation in the native tongues.

passed by, we all ran to take a close look, never having seen one before. It was loaded with sacks and was led by a boy in a quilted caftan, which we thought was strange in this heat, but we later saw that most Turkmen wore similar caftans. They also wore round caps called *feskas,* very much like those we wore back home, which Mother insisted we had to wear to prevent sunstroke. Then a man riding an ox came down the road. He sat in a wooden saddle and his reins consisted of a rope tied to the nose ring of the beast. To me this looked very funny because, in Russian, when something is grossly inappropriate, we say that it fits like a saddle on a cow.

At noon we lined up at the station's food counter and bought three camel-burgers and a loaf of bread, which was all that was available. The meat did not have any particular flavor and was tough and dry. In the evening it became very cold and we bundled up in everything we had. Before falling asleep I watched the stars, which were much brighter than they had been at home.

Among the waiting refugees, Mother recognized Eva Rokhberg, the wife of the much-hated restaurant manager, who had made the lives of his personnel miserable and even begrudged them leftover food. I had seen her several times at the restaurant. She was disliked as well, partly perhaps because of her husband and partly because she behaved as if she owned the place and walked with her nose high in the air. She was about Mother's age, but short and practically spherical, and she usually wore an expensive leather coat. Now she looked haggard, with sagging cheeks and wandering eyes, as if she did not quite comprehend what was going on. She was with two children, a boy of about nine and a girl of about six who whined ceaselessly and whom she carried all the time.

On the next day, a freight train backed into the station and we were packed into it as before, with no room to spare. We headed southeast along the edge of the desert, where occasional stretches of sand dunes alternated with arid expanses of semi-desert, covered with dry, prickly bushes. Every now and then we stopped at a small station where everybody lined up at either the water spigots, the latrine, or the food counter, where usually one could buy only bread and occasionally some raisins. The setting was exotic: camels, donkeys, incomprehensible language, parched soil on the left, and mountains in the distance on the right, behind which lay Iran. The railroad had only one track, and every so often our train pulled over into a short siding and waited until the train going in the opposite direction went by.

During the night Vilya awoke crying and said that he had to go potty immediately. The only vessel on hand was the mug that we had used for his chamber pot. He had severe diarrhea. A little while later Mother suffered stomach cramps and had to use the same vessel right in the midst of the people. In the morning we saw that both of them were passing blood and guessed that they had dysentery. Several other people came down with the same problem, but there was no doctor on the train or at the small stations. After a while the air in the car became unbearable even though the sliding door was kept fully open. Some of those who were not afflicted complained, but did not offer any solution. After a while, they quieted down. It was impossible to empty the chamber pots out of the door because the stuff would fly into the open door of the next car. Eventually someone found a hole in the floor in the middle of the car, which had been covered by a metal cover and must have served for cleaning the car after it had carried cattle. This resolved the problem except for those who had to sit next to it.

On the following day we halted in Ashkhabad, the capital of Turkmenistan, but again there was no doctor at the station and we were afraid to go look for one in the city, not knowing how long the train would remain. Someone had suggested that walnut shells steeped in hot water might be of help, and I ran around at every station looking for them. Unfortunately, the slanted-eyed women in colorful long dresses at the small bazaars sold all kinds of fruit, but no walnuts.

Mother and Vilya could not eat anything and were becoming very weak. Finally, when we stopped in Samarkand, the ancient capital of Tamerlane's empire in present-day Uzbekistan, I found walnuts at a crowded fruit stand. People were pushing and shoving but I fought my way to the counter, all the time wondering whether I was going to miss the train. We were never told how long the train would remain at a station and I knew that it could leave any minute for an unknown destination, but I had to have those walnuts.

As I ran back clutching the walnuts wrapped in an old newspaper, I saw the train beginning to move. Unfortunately the doors were on the opposite side of the train where there was no platform, and I had to wait until the last car passed before I could cross the track and start running. The doors were at the level of my chest, so that it was not easy to climb in even when the train was standing still. Our car was near the end and I began catching up with it even though the train was constantly picking up speed, but there was no way that I could jump into the door, particularly since in one hand I was clutching the walnuts. Then, to my horror, I saw that there was a manual rail switch right in front of me and I knew that if I tried to run around it, I would fall behind, but there wasn't enough room between the switch mechanism and the train for me to squeeze by without falling under the wheels. I had only a split second to decide what to do. At that moment, strong arms lifted me off the ground and pulled me in through the door with my legs barely missing the switch. Two men at the door had noticed my plight and snatched me up at the last second. In the meantime, Mother was becoming hysterical.

The walnut shells worked; both Mother and Vilya felt better the very next day and were able to retain some bread and noodle soup that I managed to buy at the station in Tashkent, the capital of the Uzbek Soviet Socialist Republic. Tashkent was surrounded by orchards and cultivated fields, and the people looked well fed. Most men and many women wore embroidered *feskas* and the women wore their coal-black hair in long braids. I remembered a book I had read sometime earlier entitled *Tashkent, the City of Bread,* which described an inrush of refugees from the starving cities in the west right after the Revolution, because there were rumors abroad that there was bread in Tashkent. Those trains must have been even more packed than ours, because the hero of the book rode on the roof. Again, there was something to be thankful for.

As we proceeded toward the northeast, the temperature began to drop, and when we reached the town of Dzhambul in Kazakhstan there were occasional snow flurries. The name "Dzhambul" was familiar to me because Dzhambul Dzhabayev was another one of those court flatterers who glorified Stalin and who made a good living from doing so. We had to memorize his poems, and the one that I still remember went something like this:

> Fly, my song, from village to village,
> Let the steppes hear the bard Dzhambul.

During my life I had known many laws.
The moon was made dark by these laws,
The back was bent from these laws,
Tears flowed from these laws,
And the brow was deeply furrowed by these laws.
Now, steppes, listen to happy songs!
The songs about Stalin's Constitution!

For such stuff he was awarded the Lenin Prize, given a large house, and honored by having not only the town but the whole province named after him.

We still did not have any idea where we were being taken, and as we were leaving the warm climate, we began to worry that we might wind up in Siberia, which was the very last place we wanted to go.

Finally, the train stopped at a station called Lougovaya, which was at a fork of the railroad tracks, with one branch going to Frunze, the capital of Kyrgizia, and the other continuing to Alma-Ata, the capital of Kazakhstan, and then on to Siberia. We were wondering which way we would continue when a uniformed railroad official climbed aboard and told us that we had arrived and would be distributed among several local collective farms the next morning.

I got some hot water from the spigot at the station and, after standing in a long line, some soup at a small window, where I handed in money and an enameled cylindrical canister that Mother had enough foresight to bring with us. Without a vessel for food we would have been lost, since there was nothing available in stores and the prices at the bazaars were beyond our means. The soup consisted of murky hot water with a few strands of gray noodles and even fewer tiny yellow discs of some unidentifiable fat floating on its surface. Still, it was hot, and it warmed us up.

The night was very cold; we put on everything we had and waited for morning. When it became light, we saw that it was sleeting and everything was covered with ice and mushy snow. The wagons did not arrive until noon. There were five of them. They had just delivered a load of sugar beets and were full of mud, into which we had to put our bundles. Mother and

Vilya climbed on top of the bundles with Eva and her children and another woman with children. There was no room for me, but after sitting on bundles all these days, I was glad to walk.

Each wagon was pulled by two oxen, which plodded at a snail's pace. The Kazakh drivers were well prepared for this weather. They wore gray quilted jackets and trousers and had fur-lined hats with earflaps tied under their chins. They sat at the front of the wagons and urged the oxen on with long sticks. The oxen were not harnessed to the wagon like horses but pulled it by means of a wooden yoke. The driver spoke broken Russian, but did not always understand our questions and did not show any interest in us.

A few hundred yards from the station we turned off the cobblestone road onto a soggy dirt road with deep ruts. Most of the time I was able to walk on the side of the road, out of the mud, but every now and then the road went through narrow passages between hills; then I had to wade through mud more than ankle-deep. My boots were leaking and it did not take long for my feet to become soaking wet. After a while the people in the wagons were covered with wet snow and some took turns walking and riding. Vilya and Eva's children were too small to keep up and lay on the bundles shivering and crying. The pace of the oxen did not change. Our driver, a man of an indeterminate age, told us that the *kolkhoz* was about fifteen kilometers (ten miles) away but, not having a watch, he had no idea how long it would take us to get there at this pace.

The road led through endless empty areas of a semi-desert without trees or houses or any signs of habitation. The skies were leaden, with low clouds and sleet alternating with snow flurries. After about two hours we entered a settlement, consisting of surprisingly trim, large houses with red tin roofs, neatly arranged in several rows on each side of the road. I did not expect to see anything so orderly in this wilderness.

"This is a Russian *sovkhoz,*" said the driver. "We are about halfway to our *kolkhoz.*"

"Can we stop here to warm up somewhere?" asked Mother, her teeth chattering.

"No," said the driver. "There is no place to warm up."

The *sovkhozes,* an abbreviation for "Soviet Enterprises," were state farms where people worked for wages, as in factories. In the *kolkhozes* or "Collective Enterprises," they received shares of the harvest and theoretically jointly owned the farms. When the *kulaks* were exiled to these areas from Ukraine, Belarus, and Russia, they were dropped off in the middle of nowhere and ordered to build *sovkhoz* farms. Being hard-working and knowledgeable, they managed not only to survive but also, after about ten years, to rebuild their lives. Some even became relatively well-off. By not giving them any ownership in the farms the Communist government hoped that their capitalist ways of thinking would eventually die out.

Mother tried to walk for a while but she was still too weak from dysentery and had to climb back on the wagon, where she could shield whimpering Vilya with her body. I was drenched to the skin, but walking kept me reasonably warm, except when strong gusts of wind attacked us with freezing rain. The oxen walked at a constant crawl and every now and then I walked ahead to the first of the five wagons, but eventually I figured out that walking behind the wagons gave me some protection from the wind. At one point we walked along a stream overgrown with reeds and crossed a small bridge. Otherwise there was absolutely nothing to be seen anywhere, only slush-covered desert on all sides. It took about two hours more before we reached three rows of clay huts with thatched roofs and tiny windows. There were no fences or vegetation of any kind; neither trees nor bushes nor any indication of gardens, just huts sticking out of the barren ground like sore thumbs. The women and children on the wagons were now frozen stiff, and the rest of us were thoroughly wet and exhausted.

When we stopped near a hut that was twice the size of the rest, a tall, middle-aged man wearing a sheepskin coat and a round karakul hat came out of the door.

"I am the *kolkhoz's* bookkeeper," he said in heavily accented but fluent Russian. "We will drop you off at your *kibitkas* and later I will visit all of you to explain some things."

"Where is the toilet here?" asked Mother, stiffly climbing off the wagon. "I must go to the toilet!"

An amused grin spread over his face. "Toilet?" he asked. "There is no such thing here; you go outside the *kibitka* and do this . . ." He removed his coat, crouched down, and put the coat over his head. "And we pour water from a pitcher into our left hand to wash up. Remember: only left hand, and we eat only with our right hand. I repeat: wash only with left hand and eat only with right hand!"

We continued, dropping off people on the way, one or two families per *kibitka,* depending on the number of people. We and Eva with her children were dropped off at a single-room *kibitka,* which one entered from a small hallway. The room had a clay floor and whitewashed walls. There were two bunks, one at each wall, a small window in the third wall, and something resembling a low brick stove in the corner. There was nothing else, except on top of the stove, where there was a small glass jar with a short metal tube in its lid, from which protruded a wick. I figured that this was some kind of lamp, but we did not have any matches to light it.

We untied our bundles and sat shivering in semi-darkness awaiting the bookkeeper. When he finally came, he lit the lamp with a match and a feeble yellow flame produced a gloomy light that threw long shadows. Black soot streamed up toward the ceiling. This contraption was appropriately called a *coptilka* or "soot-maker."

"There are some reeds in the hallway for making fire," said the bookkeeper. "You have to make it last until the weather improves, then you will go to the stream and cut some yourself. I will give you a sickle. Or you can pick dry weeds outside the *aul* [village]. Tomorrow come to see me and we will give you a ration of flour." He looked at us for a moment and said to me, "Come with me to get some food." He did not have to say it twice—all we had had to eat that day was a slice of bread in the morning and another at noon.

Shivering, I trotted after the bookkeeper through ankle-deep slush down the muddy street of the hamlet. It was getting dark and I worried that on the way back I might not be able to find our *kibitka,* since they all looked alike.

"Remember, don't touch any food with your left hand," admonished the bookkeeper. We entered the dark hallway of a *kibitka* very much like ours, and then a room where seven or eight men of all ages were sitting cross-legged on a carpet. The older men had white, wispy beards and wore *feskas.* Several women were puttering around the stove in the corner. Other than a bed and a wooden chest, there was no furniture. The room was permeated with the odor of lamb fat and tobacco smoke, which made me slightly nauseous.

The bookkeeper shook hands with all the men, who took his hand with both of theirs and spoke to him in a very respectful manner. I mumbled greetings in Russian but they just looked at me without responding. There were no smiles and I did not feel very welcome, but this did not seem to bother the bookkeeper at all. "Sit down next to me," he said.

They made room for us on the carpet and I sat down, trying to cross my legs like they. A young woman with long braids brought a brass water pitcher with a long, curved neck and a brass basin. She poured water over our right hands and let us dry them with a towel. Then two older women brought a large platter heaped with fat chunks of lamb and another one full of pieces of flat, round bread. Everyone took turns taking a piece of each with his right hand, the oldest person first. "Eat!" said the bookkeeper, winking at me after every man had had his turn. "It is our custom to feed the stranger!" He did not have to repeat this. I had never had lamb before. It was hot and fatty, but it tasted great. It was also slippery, and several times I was about to raise my left hand to get a better grip, but caught myself in time. I was sorely tempted to pick up a piece of bread to eat together with the meat, but there was no way this could be done without using my left hand. So I ate the meat, put the bone into a common dish, then ate a piece of bread. Everyone had several helpings and I did not worry about being polite. When the food was gone, women brought cups of steaming green tea and I finally felt warm. The women did not eat with us.

After the meal, the bookkeeper said something and a woman brought me a whole flat bread about ten inches in diameter, thin in the middle with about an inch-thick rim. There was nothing in which to wrap it so I placed it against my body and buttoned my coat over it. It felt nice and warm against my chest. The men laughed and the bookkeeper patted me on the shoulder.

I managed to find our *kibitka*, where a fire was burning in the stove and a pot of water boiling. Clothing was spread around to dry and everyone was now thawed out sufficiently to wolf down their piece of bread.

The next morning the bookkeeper came to formalize our membership in the *kolkhoz*, which was called Kzyl Charva, *kzyl* meaning "red" and *charva* someone who is neither rich nor poor. In Russian, the peasants were classified into the *bedniaks*, or the poor (who presumably did not exist any more under the Soviets), the *seredniaks,* or those who were neither rich nor poor, which now presumably included everyone, and the well-to-do *kulaks,* who were the enemies of the people. The word "red" of course meant Communist, as opposed to "white," which meant royalist or anti-Communist.

Our *kolkhoz* consisted of about seventy *kibitkas* arranged in three rows, one on each side of a dirt road and the third about two hundred yards away, running parallel to railroad tracks. There were a dozen refugee families, officially called "evacuees," whom the bookkeeper insisted on calling "evacupees," which in a way made some sense, since we were evacuated from an occupied territory. Membership in the *kolkhoz* entitled us to a daily ration of about three-quarters of a pound of flour for an adult and half that amount for a child. This was considered to be an advance against our future earnings, and we were not allowed to leave the *kolkhoz* without official permission.

The bookkeeper lived in the *kibitka* next to us. He was an Uzbek, a race in appearance close to the Iranian, with oval heads and straight noses, while his wife was a Kazakh, a Mongolian race with round heads and flat noses, but both languages are very similar to Turkish. They had one daughter of about five, who was given to them by the wife's sister because they did not have children of their own, and the sister had several. We were told that this was a common custom.

The fire in the stove the night before must have been too much for it and it fell apart. I mixed some clay with bits of reeds and put the bricks back where they belonged, hoping that they would dry and stay together.

Mother went over to the bookkeeper's house and offered to help his wife, who spoke only a few words of Russian, to clean her house. For this she received some food, which she shared with Eva and her children. Eva's boy, Shoura, was about nine and looked a lot like his father, the party organizer at the restaurant who had begrudged my eating there. He had the same blank stare and mumbling way of speaking. The girl, Nina, was about six, a mousy, whiny child with a hairless patch surrounded by scabs on the back of her head. Later I found out that it was mange, which is contagious. She whined continuously. To shut her up, Eva let her suckle her breast.

Mother made some "rubbed" soup from our flour ration—it got its name from the way it was made, by mixing flour with some water and rubbing the stiff dough between two hands so that the crumbs would fall into boiling water and remain separate, without sticking to one another.

The next day Mother brought from the bookkeeper a pair of round frying pans and a chunk of sourdough. To make bread, the dough was dissolved in warm water and mixed with flour. After kneading, it was left for a couple of hours to rise. In the meantime, both pans were heated in the fire and when the dough rose, a chunk of it was placed in one of the pans and squeezed around into a pancake, the rim thicker than the middle. Then it was covered by the second pan and placed back into the fire. From time to time, one slightly lifted the top pan and peeked inside. When the dough turned brown it was ready to come out. Care had to be taken that the pans were sufficiently hot, or the pancake stuck to the bottom and had to be scraped off. A piece of sourdough was saved for the next time.

Mother did not think that it made sense to go through this procedure twice, and she suggested to Eva that we pool our resources and share the food. Eva readily agreed. I did not like the idea, not only because Eva's husband did not treat Mother well in the restaurant, but also because I strongly disliked both her and her children. She was moping all the time, crying and complaining about a backache. I did not think she was going to do her share and told Mother what I thought. She responded that we were in this situation together and that we could not eat while they were not eating. As far as her husband's behavior was concerned, one had to do what one thought was right at the moment, regardless of the past, and without expectation of gratitude in the future. I did not agree with her then, but her philosophy had a great influence on my life.

It did not take very long to prove me right about Eva. In several days we ran out of reeds for fuel and had to find something to burn in the stove. Because my boots leaked, I could not walk in the slush at the stream and I had to limit myself to scrounging for dry weeds and thorn bushes outside the village. I hit the stems of the thorn bushes with a bent strip of metal to break them off and piled them up on a bed sheet. For a while Vilya helped me, but after a few times pricking himself on the thorns, he lost interest.

The bookkeeper had given us a small scythelike gadget with which one could chop the reeds that grew in a stream about a mile away. Mother, together with some other refugees, went to get them. Carrying them home was not a simple matter. A bundle of reeds about a foot and a half in diameter weighed just about what Mother was able to carry. The reeds were about ten feet long and the bundle was tied in two places by wrapping it around with a twisted pair of reeds. Then some of the reeds were partially pulled out on each side of the bundle, forming two loops. The bundle was then stood up vertically and arms were put through these loops. The bundle was carried upright, like a backpack, but it was top-heavy and difficult to carry without losing one's balance in the snow.

In the meantime Eva, whose shoes were in good shape, was lying in bed with her children, moaning and crying and waiting for Mother to prepare food. I resented this very much, but there was nothing I could do. My job was to keep the stove in working order, which meant rebuilding it almost every day because the clay did not hold even after I had added some manure to the mixture, which was supposed to have made it stickier.

Sometimes, when the fuel was not dry, I had to keep blowing at barely glowing ashes until I was out of breath. Smoke would fill the room, but in order to prepare food we had to keep trying, even if the door had to be kept open and we were freezing. This bothered Eva a great deal and every now and then I threw in a wet branch on purpose, just to annoy her.

Before the Revolution, the Kazakhs were mostly nomads, living in yurts—large, round felt tents built around portable, sectional wooden lattice frames. They were easily disassembled and transported on horse- or camel-back. The Kazakhs also raised a breed of sheep that I had never seen before—their tails consisted of a flap about six inches wide and ten inches long, which during the summer filled up with fat. Just like the hump of a camel, this tail served to nourish the animal when there was not enough food. They also had horses, goats, and camels, all of which were milked. Horse milk was fermented, making a mildly alcoholic drink called *kumys* that was supposed to be good for people sick with tuberculosis. When an area had been grazed out, they disassembled their yurts, loaded them on camels, and moved to a new location. There they tied the frame sections into a circle with homemade woolen ropes, stretched large sheets of felt over them, and wrapped them around with the same kind of very strong rope.

When the Soviets took over, nomadic life ended; the wealthier tribesmen were shot, the herds were confiscated, and collective farms were set up, usually near streams that could be used to irrigate the fields. In each *kolkhoz* they made the former hired hands Communist Party members, set up party cells, and appointed a party chief and a *kolkhoz* chairman. Just as in all other enterprises, the party chiefs reported to the county party committee and were supposed to keep an eye on the chairmen. They were also the eyes and ears of the NKVD with regard to any anti-Soviet sentiments.

Our *kolkhoz* had a chairwoman, who was middle-aged and stout and wore expensive leather coats and boots. She was always accompanied by the party chief—a big, self-assured man who carried a horsewhip with which he periodically slapped his boots. The chairwoman's *kibitka* was not far from ours; in the evenings we could hear the noisy drunken goings-on there and salivated over the aroma of lamb that was being roasted on spits over an open fire in her yard. Native customs of hospitality obviously did not apply to us. All we had to eat was our flour ration, which we stretched with bran that Mother earned by cleaning filthy *kibitkas*. Having a Caucasian servant must have given the native women a great deal of prestige and satisfaction.

The Kazakhs preferred their bread white and gave Mother the bran that they sifted out of the flour. Otherwise it would have been used to feed chickens. Some of the work that Mother did for them included resurfacing the clay floors of the *kibitkas* with fresh clay, which was backbreaking work. Eva, of course, could not do such work because of her back problems, but Mother did not seem to mind. Eva did help Mother to clean the two-room school building, but for this they were getting the *kolkhoz's* "work-day" credits rather than money or food.

The single-track railroad ran about a mile outside the village and had a bypass branch so that trains going in opposite directions could pass one another. A guard, who lived in a small shack, manned the bypass switches and the semaphores. Upon receiving the signal that trains were coming, he directed the train that came first onto the bypass track, where it waited until the oncoming train went by. Every so often the guard was found tied up and undressed by vagrant robbers, who could easily sell secondhand clothing on the black market. Since the nearest militia outpost was at the railroad station some ten miles away, they were of no help, and these robberies continued until the guards were armed with shotguns. The robbers were criminal ex-convicts who had been released from Siberian Gulags and were making their way south, hoping to find a warmer place. As far as I know, no political prisoners were released. The weather here may indeed have been warmer than in Siberia, but it was not warm. Frost frequently lasted several weeks, and several inches of snow covered the ground.

When the ground and the stream froze solid, I wrapped my boots with rags and was able to go for the reeds, which by now were several miles away, those nearby having already been cut. Obtaining fuel became our major preoccupation. The fire had to be kept going, and when we were lucky enough to find some cow or horse dung, sometimes it was still glowing in the morning. Otherwise I had to find a kibitka from whose chimney I could see rising smoke and beg for some glowing ashes. Not everyone was friendly enough to share their fire, so it was a very unpleasant task. Later I obtained a piece of flint stone and a hardened steel tooth from a horse-drawn reaper, with which I could create enough sparks to ignite a dry piece of rope or a bunch of dry grass, and that solved the problem. I believe that the reapers were manufactured in Russia under license from McCormick, an American company.

Burning dry dung is not as bad as it sounds. It did not smell any worse than burning peat moss. Natives compressed it into loaves, which they dried and used for baking and cooking. Of course, they got their manure from the *kolkhoz's* stables and barns, while we had to compete with dung beetles to pick up what was left on the road.

One day, Mother returned from the bookkeeper's very upset. Their little girl was sick with scarlet fever and the doctor, a refugee woman who converted one of the *kibitkas* into a small infirmary, did not have any medicine other than aspirin. The doctor kept vigil with the child for several days and nights but could not save her. Several other children died of the disease and the village was filled with wailing as groups of women gathered in the *kibitkas* of the deceased. I was told that the Kazakhs buried their dead in a sitting position.

We were very much afraid for Vilya, but there was no place to escape. Our friendly bookkeeper and his wife were so brokenhearted that they could not continue living in Kzyl Charva, and after they were gone, there was no one in the *kolkhoz* who would lend us a sympathetic ear or would be willing to help us.

In the spring, we were moved into a room behind the Communist Party Meeting Hall and Library. Mother and Eva were assigned to keep it clean. I was very excited when I heard the word "library," which I did not even know existed in this village, and hoped to finally have something interesting to read. The "library" turned out to be a large room with several wooden tables on which were displayed party publications, both in Russian and in Kazakh, glorifying the accomplishments of the party and giving statistics on production of sugar beets, wheat, and cattle. During the six months or so that we were living there, not a single meeting was held in the building and not a single person came in to read. Once, the party chief came in, presumably to inspect for cleanliness, but I saw him surreptitiously putting a booklet in his pocket and tearing out a page to roll a cigarette when he was outside on his horse.

The village was near the foothills of the Tien-Shan mountain range, on the other side of which was the Kirghiz Soviet Socialist Republic and, beyond that, China. A rail branch from the Lougovaya station, where we had arrived, led to Frunze, the capital of Kirgizia. It was named, to add insult to injury, after the commander of the Red Army that conquered the region in 1920. The whole of Central Asia had been part of the Russian Empire since the early 1800s, and when the Communists came to power, they reconquered it by defeating the poorly armed bands of tribal horsemen, called *basmachi,* who had declared independence in the various regions.

The mountains stretched all across the southwestern horizon, their jagged peaks reaching halfway up to the zenith, so that when the evening sun hid behind them, the sky remained bright for a long time. In the winter the ground was covered with snow, but as it became warmer, purple crocuses and tiny white flowers, whose names I do not remember, broke through the hard soil of the desert everywhere, and for a short time transformed it into a garden. After the snow melted on the mountains, huge red and yellow patches many acres in size created a colorful quilt on the otherwise monotonous gray mountainsides. These were fields of red and yellow tulips, which must have been native to this land. I found it interesting that the fields grew side by side, touching in places but not intermixing. Also, all kinds of strange creatures began appearing from their burrows. Vilya and I had a lot of fun chasing kangaroo rats that hopped on their hind legs like real kangaroos, but were too fast for us to catch them. Desert turtles of all sizes began visiting us, some large enough for Vilya to ride on. Always being hungry, we frequently thought of trying to eat them, but never did.

Then snakes appeared under the little desert bushes, called *kourai,* which later developed sharp needles and, when dried out in the fall, served as our major source of fuel. The snakes were gray, about two feet long, and were not poisonous; however, I killed those that came too close to the house anyway. One day I happened to look at one of the snakes that I had killed a few hours before and, much to my surprise, saw it moving backwards into a hole. I could not believe my eyes, and looking more closely, discovered that it was being dragged by dung beetles that had dug a hole to bury it. They lay their eggs on whatever they have buried, thus providing food for the larvae when they hatch. The dung beetles were very useful in sanitation: no sooner had one finished a bowel movement behind the house, than these beetles began flying in from downwind. They made balls about an inch in diameter from the feces, dug a hole nearby, rolled the ball into the hole, laid their eggs, and covered up the hole with dirt. This was all done in a very short time and was amusing to watch. They rolled the ball backward, pushing it with their hind legs with their heads tilted toward the ground. I don't know how they know where they are going.

We did not see any newspapers nor hear radio broadcasts, but the bad news from the front had a way of reaching us through rumors, which passed from someone who had been at the railroad station in Lougovaya to our eager and anxious ears. The Germans had besieged Leningrad, were within sight of Moscow, and had taken the northern Caucasus. Another rumor had it that the local carpenter, who was the only Russian living permanently in the *kolkhoz,* was telling his Kazakh friends to start sharpening their knives and to be ready to slit our throats as soon as the Germans won. He promised them all kinds of riches that we presumably had brought with us.

In addition to the depressing news, we began to feel the results of undernourishment and lack of vitamins. This manifested itself in boils that most of us had developed on our backs and necks. They appeared out of nowhere, starting as large pimples and growing to be about a half-inch in height and filled with pus. After some time they burst and became festering sores that lasted for weeks. I had two or three of these at a time; no sooner did one of them heal than another took its place. They were particularly uncomfortable on the behind, because they made it painful to sit down. The doctor applied some tar-smelling ointment that looked like axle grease and bandaged them with gauze, which we washed every so often and had to use over and over again.

As if this were not enough, we were being eaten alive by vermin. There were three kinds of parasites: fleas, bedbugs, and lice. The fleas hopped all over the place and must have been nesting in the reeds on which we slept, even though we changed them as often as we could. They were difficult to catch and hard to squash. One definitely did not want to squash the bedbugs because they emitted a revolting odor. They were flat, wingless insects the size of ladybugs that lived in cracks in the bunks and in the walls and came out at night to suck our blood. I tried putting the legs of the bunk into cans filled with water, but that did not deter them at all. They simply climbed up to the ceiling and, when they felt our body heat, dropped onto us from above like paratroopers!

But worst of all were the lice. They infested our hair and our clothing and it was quite common to see women, natives as well as refugees, grooming one another and their children like monkeys, squashing these disgusting insects between their thumbnails. We even rubbed our hair with kerosene and combed it with fine-tooth combs, but it was a continuous battle. When it became warm, we were able to remove our underwear, in which we slept and which began disintegrating, and squashed the lice in its seams, joking that if we laid it on the ground it would crawl away. But this did not get rid of the eggs, the nits, which could be killed only by high temperature. From time to time, when the weather was good we walked the ten miles to Lougovaya where one could take a hot shower and have all clothing baked in the delousing ovens of the communal bath.

While this brought temporary relief, it did not do our clothing any good. Our clothes disintegrated to the point that my patches had patches of their own, and the only thing that remained of my underwear were areas where the fabric was double, such as on seams and around the collar. We gave up trying to darn the socks and wrapped our feet with rags. Much of my time was spent patching my clothes and shoes, the soles of which were held on by strings. I tried to make a pair of moccasins out of raw leather that Mother managed to obtain somewhere, but they quickly fell apart after becoming wet. After a while, most of the refugees began looking like hoboes, with clothes patched in all colors of the rainbow. This did not contribute to our status with the well-fed and well-dressed natives, most of whom considered us to be nothing but freeloaders.

Among the refugees there were two boys and a girl about my age, but we did not have common interests and did not become friends. My only friend was a man in his forties who had been a bookkeeper before the war. Now he could not do office work because he had lost his glasses and was able to read only by holding the paper up against his nose. I liked to visit him, but his one-room *kibitka* was even more crowded than ours. He shared it with his old mother, a sister with a baby, and two women with two girls. As in our kibitka, the only furniture consisted of two bunks and each family sat, ate, and slept on theirs. Both he and his sister were well read and we discussed the books we had read, the war, and the *kolkhoz*. Even in this forsaken place we never talked about the government, Gulags, or party leaders. But no matter how a conversation between hungry people began, the subject inevitably turned to food. We salivated remembering what we had eaten years ago, drooled over long-ago excreted pastries and slavered in anticipation of the delicacies we were going to savor if we survived the war. I had been a rather finicky eater before the war and remember once reproaching Mother that all my life she had been feeding me chicken, which happened to be Father's favorite. Now I probably would have eaten one whole, feathers and all.

I did not have much contact with the native children, who usually made fun of my clothes. Even though they spoke Kazakh, it did not take much imagination to figure out what they were saying. The only one with whom I exchanged a few words and a few laughs was Aktamak, a girl of about fifteen who flirted with me in her broken Russian, but mostly with unmistakable gestures. Her name meant White Neck, which did not exactly describe its actual color, because the natives did not wash any more frequently than we did. Not that there was a scarcity of water—there was a well in the village and a stream nearby—but in the desert, where in the past the no-mad Kazakhs spent the summers with herds of sheep, they must have ac-quired a habit of never wasting it. I frequently saw native women doing dishes by simply wiping them with their index fingers, licking the finger, then wiping again. No water was necessary.

Aktamak lived with her uncle's family in a *kibitka* next door. I don't know what happened to her parents. One day she disappeared, and when I asked her uncle where she was, he pretended that he did not understand me. Sev-eral weeks later I was passing a *kibitka* at the edge of the hamlet when I heard her voice calling me. By then I had given up my name Etan, which had caused me so much trouble, and called myself Anatole, nicknamed Tolya. But Aktamak had trouble even with that and called me Toylya. She stood at the door wearing fancy harem pants and an embroidered jacket. I was very surprised. "What are you doing here?" I asked. "I am a married woman now," she replied with a sad smile. "My uncle sold me to an old man for some goats and sheep. I am wife number two." I had seen this old man. He was all wrinkled and, like most Kazakhs of his age, his facial hair consisted of a skimpy mustache and a thin little goatee with a small bunch of hairs growing under his lower lip.

While polygamy was officially prohibited, it was still possible with ap-propriate bribes to the party chairman, whose job it was to see that Soviet laws and regulations were upheld and that people did not openly practice their Islamic religion. The only limitation was that the two wives had to live in separate houses. It had also been a custom of the Kazakhs to marry their brother's widows and take care of their families. This practice also contin-ued unofficially.

The village had a two-room schoolhouse with classes through the fourth grade. After that, children had to go to sleep-away schools in the province capital, Dzhambul. Very few did, even though theoretically there was mandatory education to the age of sixteen.

Kazakh toddlers wore pants with a slit at the bottom, which opened up when they squatted, so that diapers were unnecessary. In the street of the hamlet I noticed several little boys who looked very much like girls. It turned out that indeed they were girls wearing boys clothing because their parents had wanted a boy. They also had boys' haircuts until they went to school. I wondered how this confusion would affect them when they grew up.

Spinning wool was the universal occupation of Kazakh women. They did it constantly, even while performing other chores and even while walking. They stretched the loose wool into a pencil-thick strand as they fed it to the twisting string, the end of which was attached to a wooden mushroom-shaped top that also served as a spool. They made the top spin in the air by rolling it against their hips, then letting it go. When the twisted string became so long that the top almost reached the ground, they spooled the yarn onto it and spun it again. The yarn was then woven into fabric on hand-looms. It was coarse but very strong and warm. They also spun heavier strands, which were then twisted or braided into very strong rope.

In the spring, after the first hay was cut, all the refugees were assigned to work in the hay fields. If I had not been undernourished and perpetually hungry, I would have enjoyed getting up with the sun, walking several miles over dew-covered paths, and raking into piles the fragrant grass that had been cut by a horse-driven reaper several days before and was already dry. Whenever I smell cut grass, the picture of those fields appears in my mind's eye.

Each one of us was assigned an area to rake. At the end of the day a young, tall Kazakh wearing a snazzy felt hat with a feather arrived on his horse to measure the raked area with an *arshin*—two sticks joined at one end, with the tips of the legs three yards apart. He swung the *arshin* from one leg to the other as he walked around the raked field and recorded the area that had been raked. We nicknamed him "Foka," which in Russian slang means a sort of dandy.

Each job was rated according to a quota called a "workday"—a theoretical unit, which was presumably the amount of work an unskilled person could complete in a day. Of course, we were given no training and were assigned only the lowest-rated work. I usually earned only about three-quarters of a "workday" per day, even though I worked very hard.

The desert in the spring was full of life. Prairie dogs were popping up from one burrow and disappearing into another; land turtles grazed on blades of new vegetation, and snakes lay in coils all over the place. In addition to the small gray snakes, there were large yellow ones, about five feet long and two inches thick, which I was told were actually legless lizards. They were harmless and it was considered bad luck to hurt them. Once, when one of our refugees had killed one out of sheer stupidity, a group of Kazakhs buried it and became very upset and hostile to us.

While at work, I met some Kazakh boys who were my age, some of whom spoke Russian and were curious about life where I had come from. Since it was hot, I wore less clothing with fewer patches and did not look so much like a hobo. One of the boys, whose family had been wealthy before the Revolution, told me about their nomadic past, when they did not have to work in the fields and were free to move from pasture to pasture with their flocks. Whatever they needed they obtained through barter with the neighboring Uzbeks, who were farmers, or by selling their sheep and wool. He also told me that, according to Kazakh custom, if one praised an object in someone's house, the owner would give it to him. Then the recipient had to hide his valuables, because the giver might come over and praise something in his house. Of course, without telephones, such visits were unannounced.

I also began compiling a Kazakh-Russian dictionary for myself, and after a while I was able to ask simple questions in Kazakh and to understand simple answers. I also learned to ride oxen, but some of the animals sensed my insecurity and did not go where I wanted them to go.

Raking hay had its own dangers, namely poisonous spiders. There were two kinds—the one called *shayan* had a sinister-looking gray speckled body about an inch wide and two inches long. With its legs spread out, it was about five inches across. Its web was usually stretched between branches of bushes not far from the ground and was strong enough to capture large grasshoppers and beetles. The other spider was about an inch across, with a milky white body and a bright red head. They were everywhere, but I was bitten only once, by the white one. I walked several miles to the doctor's office, all the while sucking at the bite and spitting. My finger swelled up and became red and painful, but the doctor told me that there was nothing she could do and that it would be over in three days, which it was. There were also huge tarantulas dashing all over the place, with their menacing antennae pointing upward and forward, but I managed to avoid them.

Another danger came from the blazing sun. Because the air was dry, it was quite comfortable in the shade, but in the sun one could have fried eggs, if we had had them, on the bare ground. Once I fell asleep in the shade of a haystack at our lunch break. I wore a cap, but it must have fallen off, and as the sun moved, my head became exposed. I woke up with the most excruciating headache, which lasted for more than a week. It was an acute sunstroke, and I felt as if my brain was boiling and trying to burst out of my skull. No amount of aspirin was able to alleviate the pain.

Most of the time the hay fields were near streams that flowed from the mountains and from which we drank, even though we knew that animals might be wading in them and drinking somewhere upstream from us. Other fields were not near streams, and in the immense heat a bottle of water that we brought with us did not last very long. We had to wait for the horse-drawn water barrel, which frequently did not show up. Once, when the barrel did not arrive, we had to walk about a mile to a yurt where they had *kvass*, which was a watery drink made with flour and water and allowed to ferment. It had a sour taste and was quite refreshing. Everyone drank from the same tin cup, which one dipped into the barrel and, on having drunk, passed on to the next person. There was no water to rinse it, nor anything with which to wipe it. When the Kazakh behind whom I stood in line turned to pass me the cup, I saw that he had no nose. Instead, there was just a raw- looking black hole. I had seen several noseless people in the village. We were not sure whether they were lepers or syphilitics. I froze with the cup in my hand, but there were people in line behind me and I did not have time to decide whether to drink or not. I was very thirsty and there was nothing else to drink, so I dipped the cup into the barrel and drank, trying not to touch it with my lips. I felt sick the rest of the day and many days afterwards whenever I thought of it.

I did not catch anything from the noseless Kazakh, but I did catch malaria from the mosquitoes that bred in the stream. I woke up one night shaking, with clattering teeth. Fortunately our doctor had some synthetic quinine and I recovered after about a week, but the attacks kept reoccurring every few months.

One day we were told in the usual pompous Communist manner that a political and cultural event would take place on the following Sunday af-

ternoon. Sunday turned out to be a pleasant day, and most of the population gathered in front of the schoolhouse and sat on the ground. Only the
chairwoman of the *kolkhoz* and the party chairman sat on chairs, like a roy-
al couple. The party chairman addressed the audience in Kazakh for about
fifteen minutes, of which I understood only references to Stalin and communism. The Kazakhs gravely nodded their heads and at the end politely
applauded. Then several musicians appeared from the schoolhouse and
played some unfamiliar instruments, one of which looked like a violin but
was held vertically on the knee, like a miniature cello.

The music sounded harsh and repetitive. After that, several women sang
some upbeat songs, which frequently contained the word *kzyl* and the
phrase *kzyl asker,* which means "red soldier." Several dancers in costumes
then twirled around to the music and we all politely applauded. The performance lasted about an hour, by which time people began to talk to one
another and it appeared that everyone had had enough. The party chairman
made another speech and a young man explained to us in Russian that the
Communist Party cared very much about culture and had sent these wonderful performers to propagate it to the masses.

As soon as the desert dried out and it became easier to walk along the
dirt road to the Lougovaya railroad station, Mother began going there on
Sundays to see if there was not a way to improve our situation. Sometimes
she did not get back until after dark, frequently walking alone. This did not
seem to bother her, even though we continually heard of people being held
up and robbed. For long stretches of the way there was no one around and
the road led alongside a stream overgrown with reeds. But Mother appeared
to be fearless. Once, coming home after dark from a visit to another *kibitka,* she passed something that she did not remember having been there
before, and approached it to investigate. Much to her embarrassment, it
turned out to be a Kazakh neighbor with his coat over his head, relieving
himself.

After several trips she met a black-marketer by the name of Bronson, who
entrusted her with some green tea and tobacco to sell in our *aul.* Since
Mother already knew the wealthier Kazakhs for whom she had done clean-

ing, she had no trouble selling everything he gave her. The green tea, which was a favorite of the Kazakhs, was in the form of round cakes about six inches in diameter and an inch thick, compressed from ground leaves. There was always demand for tobacco. She went back, paid for the merchandise, and got more. Soon she was able to buy some clothing and food for us, which she still shared with Eva and her children, in spite of the fact that nothing prevented Eva from earning her own money doing the same. However, there were still many days when we did not have enough to eat, or the food consisted of patties made of pure wheat bran without any flour, which gave me a terrible heartburn.

In the summer, wearing more presentable clothing, I went to the *sovkhoz* and registered for the seventh grade in their Russian school. Since I had started school a year earlier than usual, the loss of a year did not really set me back—being in the seventh grade at fourteen was normal. I also registered two other boys, also refugees from Ukraine, who had expressed interest in going to school. On the wall of the school office was a map of the Soviet Union, and I figured out that we were approximately four thousand kilometers, or about twenty-six hundred miles, away from home.

There was a tremendous difference between the appearance of our *kolkhoz* and the *sovkhoz*. Even though here the buildings were also made of adobe, they were taller and larger, with good doors and windows, and there were trees near the houses and flowers in window boxes. The village was surrounded by vegetable gardens crisscrossed with irrigation ditches, which brought water from a stream that flowed from the mountains. The barns were large and clean and everything had been neatly whitewashed. The people here were the *kulaks,* exiled from the European part of Soviet Union, and it was obvious that they knew what they were doing—the place was much tidier than any farm I had seen in the areas from which they had been exiled. While they were not particularly friendly to us, neither were they hostile; I liked just being here in a Russian environment.

While the weather was good in September, walking the six miles to school with the boys was good exercise. But when the weather became bad in October, the boys lost their zeal for education and I was left to walk the lonely road all by myself. I frequently met all kinds of hoboes on the road and, as we approached one another, had to decide whether to hide in the reeds, which I had done many times, or face them. As the days grew short-

er, I walked home at dusk and became somewhat apprehensive, particularly when approaching clear stretches of the road where there was no place to
hide. I had to judge whether, if I were to see someone suspicious approaching, I would still be able to escape. Occasionally, in places where the road
curved among the reeds, I would find myself face to face with people coming the other way. However, since even my better clothing did not look as
though someone would pay money for it and did not create the impression
that I might have something of value, I did not have any problems. Once I
saw a man in the distance and noticed that there was smoke rising over him.
As he came near, I saw that he had a thick rope hanging over his neck, one
end of which was smoldering so that he could have fire whenever he wanted to smoke.

The teachers at our school were mostly evacuees and were quite good.
The men were invalids of one kind or another: the math teacher had a glass
eye and the geography teacher a clubfoot. Only the German teacher was all
in one piece; he had not been drafted because the government did not trust
ethnic Germans, even though they had been in Russia as colonists for two
hundred years, since the time of Catherine the Great, and many were members of the Communist Party. I remember him telling us how important it
was to learn German and giving us as an example a cock-and-bull story of
a soldier who crawled up to the German officer's tent and overheard their
plans.

Our big problem was a lack of textbooks and notebooks. There was nothing we could do about the textbooks, but we solved the notebook problem
by making them out of newspapers, which we were able to buy occasionally at the railroad station. This was not a very good solution because the ink
spread on the porous paper; also one had to write in large letters. But these
notebooks were better than nothing.

When the weather was really bad I did not go to school, but I did not
have a problem making up missed lessons. Trouble came when the weather became bad during the day. Then I had to walk in blinding snowstorms
or in freezing rain. My clothing was not up to this. The soles of my new
canvas boots were made of unprocessed leather that quickly disintegrated
and, in addition to wrapping my feet in rags, I also had to wrap rags on the
outside of the boots. It was a real miracle that we did not suffer from peren-
nial colds, but this hard life seemed to increase our immunity.

At some point we heard that two hundred Spanish children were in a *sovkhoz* nearby. During the Spanish Civil War the Soviet army supported the pro-Communist Republican government. When the Republicans were defeated by the rebels led by General Francisco Franco with the help of Germans and Italians, the Soviets brought several thousand Spanish children as well as all Spanish government gold to the Soviet Union. General Franco was called a Fascist; however, after the war it became known that he had saved about 250,000 Jews by granting them transit visas through Spain, at a time when some democratic governments were turning back ships with refugees, thus condemning them to death. According to the Soviet newspapers, the Spanish children were presumably urchins and were being saved. However, according to rumors, they were kidnapped to be raised as Communists, like the puppies in George Orwell's *Animal Farm,* in order to be used later as Soviet agents in Spain.

In the late fall of 1942 more refugees arrived in the village from Uzbekistan. We had envied them because the climate there was much warmer, but that year the *kolkhozes* in Uzbekistan were ordered to plant cotton, which was needed for gunpowder, instead of wheat. They were promised that they would be supplied with food from somewhere else, but the food never came and there was mass starvation. A middle-aged couple with a boy of about ten was settled with us and slept on the floor between our bunks. Now there were nine of us in a room no larger than about twenty by twenty feet. The new family was from Kishinev, the capital of Moldavia, where Father was from, and said that they knew my father's family. They told us that in Uzbekistan they were in the same town with my aunt and grandparents, who had all died there of typhoid fever. They also told us that Father's sister's husband and their two children were killed when the Germans bombed the railroad station in Kishinev.

Their boy was unable to walk because all his toes had been amputated due to frostbite. When his bandages were being changed, I saw white maggots crawling in his wounds, which emitted a horrible stench. Our doctor did not have any medication to eliminate the maggots, which the boy said made his wound itch continuously. Most of the time he sat in the corner of the room looking around with huge dark eyes and whining, which drove his parents and us to desperation. The man himself suffered from malaria and an excessive dosage of synthetic quinine made him lose his hearing. After about a month the situation became unbearable. As sorry as we felt for them, we could not stand it and moved out into the first *kibitka* that became available. Unfortunately, Eva moved with us.

One day our school was ordered to send its older students to a neighboring Kazakh *kolkhoz* for a week, to help them harvest sugar beets. The whole seventh grade, about twenty boys and girls, piled into a truck and were transported to the *kolkhoz*, where we were put up in a meeting hall. We were fed some sort of watery soup and slept all in a row on the clay floor on blankets, without undressing. Our leader was the physical education teacher, a young, thin, stuttering former soldier who had been shell-shocked on the front. He was from Moscow and, like most Muscovites, considered himself to be superior to the provincials.

In the morning we were taken into the fields. Our job was to gather sugar beets that had been turned up from the ground by a plow, chop off their leaves, and pile them up into mounds that were later collected by ox wagons. It was late fall and a cold wind chilled us to the bones. Then it began to drizzle and we got soaked.

When a warmly dressed Kazakh, who was in charge of the beet harvest, came galloping up on his horse to see what we had accomplished, our teacher asked him to take us back until the rain stopped. The Kazakh said that it was not raining hard and that we should proceed. Our teacher, who had a very short fuse, told him where to go in language not commonly used in front of children, especially girls. The Kazakh galloped away and returned with the local party chairman. Both men began shouting at our teacher, who was getting more and more excited. He told them that he was a wounded veteran and was not about to take any insults from lousy draft dodgers. The Kazakhs became furious because the ethnic slur Russians used for Kazakhs was "kalbit," which, I was told, means "lousy." As they were screaming at one another and waving their arms, our teacher turned pale and suddenly fell to the ground in an epileptic fit. He was shaking and foaming at the mouth; his eyes rolled up into their sockets so that only their whites were visible, and we thought he was going to die.

We all began shouting at the Kazakhs, demanding that they get a doctor and immediately take us home. When our teacher calmed down somewhat, and his arms and legs stopped twitching, we carried him back to the meeting hall, which was quite a distance away. I can still see in my mind's eye the procession of boys and girls walking single file on a narrow, muddy path in the misty drizzle, with four boys carrying the spasmodically jerking body of our teacher on a dirty blanket.

Sometime later, two horse wagons came to the meeting hall. We wrapped the teacher in some of the blankets that were given us to sleep on, and piled into the wagons. We were driven back to our school, the Kazakh drivers cursing us all the way for forcing them to be out in the rain. By that time I knew most of the curses—the Kazakh language is infinitely richer in them than Russian, which is quite an accomplishment because, in this respect, Russian outshines all other European languages with which I am familiar. It was obvious that the Kazakhs had never accepted the presence of Russians in their midst and that the arrival of refugees had not improved the situation.

We struggled through the winter trying to keep warm. While Mother was doing enough business to keep us from starving, we still had to worry about keeping from freezing and having fuel for cooking. Finding some dry cow patties made Vilya very proud. He also learned to squash lice as well as any of us and he never complained.

During the winter the Germans were for the second time stopped on the outskirts of Moscow, and a counterattack in the northwest permitted evacuation of some people from Leningrad, which had been besieged for more than a year. They escaped over frozen rivers and lakes, and several families were brought to our *kolkhoz*. Among them was a girl about my age, named Carolina, which was an unusual name in Russia and sounded very exotic. All these people looked like walking skeletons. Carolina told me that Leningrad had so little food that all its dogs and cats, and even its mice and rats, had been eaten. There were cases of cannibalism too, when people would cut off whatever flesh there was on the buttocks of frozen corpses lying in the streets. Carolina's pregnant sister, who looked as if she had some flesh on her, disappeared one day and was never found.

I remembered having read that in some cultures, it is feared that curses can harm or even kill people. However, Hitler and Stalin, who were cursed by hundreds of millions every single day, did not seem to be any the worse for it.

I graduated from the seventh grade with good grades and suggested to Mother that perhaps I should go to a technical school to become an aircraft technician, as I had discussed with my friend Ben back home. In this way I would begin to earn money in three years instead of seven, as would be the case if I completed tenth grade and then embarked on four years of college—assuming I could get in, which was very doubtful since I was the son of an "enemy of the people."

"Don't even think of it," Mother said in a tone that did not brook contradiction. "You are going to go to college and will become an engineer, even if I have to scrub floors until you graduate!" There was nothing I could say to that.

We were surviving thanks to Mother's business, and eventually Kazakhs began dropping in to buy tea or tobacco. One night we were awakened by loud banging on the door. It was a drunken Kazakh demanding that we let him in and sell him some tobacco. When we told him to come back in the morning, he began throwing himself against the flimsy door, shouting that he would kill us all. We thought the door hinges would give way at any moment and, remembering the rumors about the carpenter telling the Kazakhs to sharpen their knives, were very frightened. The children and Eva began to scream and Mother shouted at him to go away. I grabbed my hay-loading pitchfork and held it with the handle on the floor against my foot and the sharp points toward the door, so that if the door gave, he would impale himself. Fortunately, the noise attracted other people who took him away.

We decided then and there that we had to escape from the *kolkhoz,* and on the very next Sunday Mother began looking for a job and a place to live in Lougovaya. However, being members of the *kolkhoz,* we could not just leave. Theoretically we were like serfs and had to have special permission, which we did not think we could obtain. But we also knew that the Kazakhs would be glad to get rid of us, and if we left inconspicuously they would not go chasing after us.

Several weeks later, Mother returned from Lougovaya and told us that a horse wagon would come for us at midnight. We tied everything into bundles and, when the wagon arrived, it took us only a few minutes to load the bundles, the sleepy children, and Eva. A bearded old man who, without management's knowledge, borrowed the wagon from a cooperative to make some money on the side, led the horses. Mother walked behind the wagon and I walked alongside. It was a moonless night and there was very little contrast between the dirt road and the ground alongside it, so that we practically had to feel our way just to stay on the road. I did not notice that at one point the road ran between two hillocks and was so narrow that there was no room for me alongside the wagon. As I tried to scramble up the incline, my foot slipped in the mud and the rear wheel of the wagon rolled over my shin. Fortunately nothing was broken and I managed to proceed without anyone being aware of what had happened.

CHAPTER 5

1943

After groping in the dark for a couple of hours, we came to Lougovaya. I knew the area around the railroad station and the delousing bathhouse, but we turned onto an unpaved side street and Mother went from house to house trying to find the right place in the dark. She finally found a sort of double *kibitka* and knocked on the window to the right of the door. A feeble light appeared in the window and we entered a small, windowless hallway with a door on the right side. In the wobbly light of a soot-maker we saw three sleepy-eyed, unshaven young men, probably in their late twenties, in a room about ten feet wide and fifteen feet long. I do not know how Mother managed to talk them into sharing this already overcrowded place with the six of us until we could find a place to live.

Along the wall to the left of the door was a cot about two feet wide consisting of boards on sawhorses, where one of the men slept. Along the opposite wall was a similar cot, but about three feet wide, on which slept the other two men. They told us to make ourselves as comfortable as possible. Eva with her brood spread their rags on the clay floor between the cots; the only place left for Mother, me, and Vilya was either on a crude table under the window in the corner opposite the door, or under it. We decided to sleep on it and shoved our bundles under it. With a crumbling stove occupying the corner next to the door, there was not more than a couple of square feet of free space left.

In the morning, the men had to slide out of the ends of their cots (because there was no room to step down on the side) to go to work. Since everyone slept in their clothes, there was no problem with lack of privacy, and since breakfast consisted only of bread and water, the lack of space did not create a problem in preparing meals either. In winter, when it was so cold that water froze in the room, Mother's overcoat, which we used for a blanket, frequently froze to the windowpanes and had to be chiseled away.

The reason these men were not in the army, like all other young men, was because they had been Polish prisoners of war and had been released only recently from prisoner-of-war camps; they were not Soviet citizens. They were taken prisoners when, after the 1939 Nazi-Soviet Pact, Germany attacked Poland from the west on September 1, and then the Soviets attacked it from the east several days later.

Since most Soviet able-bodied men were away in the army, some of these guys had a choice of jobs where there was food, such as unloading sacks of flour in the bakery, or work in warehouses. Such jobs presented opportunities to siphon off valuable foodstuffs, usually with the knowledge of management, who received a share of the proceeds when these goods were sold on the black market.

Mother had lined up jobs for herself and for Eva as cleaning women at the local *artel*. The pay was low but it assured a permit to live in town and to receive bread-ration cards: 400 grams (less than a pound) for adults and 300 grams for children. The bread was dark and mushy, with embedded wet pieces of salt the size of beans; most days it was all we had to eat. It was my job to stand in the bread line at the store, and it took a superhuman effort to refrain from pinching off more than my share on the way home. Vilya, who by then was six years old, frequently waited for me several streets from the house and, upon seeing me, ran shouting, "Bread! Bread! Give me some bread!" When occasionally the bakery did not receive flour on time or some equipment broke down, there was no bread for a day and sometimes for several days.

While our situation was unenviable, in comparison with some other people's it was not the worst. On warm evenings we usually ate outside, sitting on the ground. I had built a sort of fireplace in which we burned weeds that

Vilya and I gathered beyond the outskirts of town and, if we were lucky, horse or cow manure. When we had flour or potatoes Mother made soup, which we ate out of tin cans. Inevitably, whenever we ate outside, two ghosts silently appeared a few feet away from us. One was a boy about nine years old, the other was his sister of about seven. Both were living skeletons, with knobby knees and large, staring eyes above their sunken cheeks. They never said anything, never begged; they just stood there with outstretched hands and stared at us until we gave them a little bit of whatever we were eating. They quickly devoured this and disappeared as silently as they came. I knew that people were dying by the millions in the war and in concentration camps, but I could not visualize them. These two children, however, were perishing right before my eyes. They still haunt me whenever I think of those days.

As the time went on and Mother was still unable to find another place to live, the young men remained understanding and patient. They came home late in the evening totally exhausted and just wanted to go to sleep. We did not always have kerosene for the soot-maker and sometimes, sitting in the dark, they told us about their lives back home and in the Siberian POW camps. Sometimes they sang plaintive Polish songs that brought tears to their eyes. One of the men, whose last name was Mislobodski, was tall and blond with an upturned mustache and a pleasant tenor voice. It was usually he who began to sing and the others would then join in. The songs were about a soldier asking his officer for permission to go home to visit his girl; a maiden encountering soldiers of whom she was afraid; Gypsies dancing around their campfire. The songs were sad and nostalgic, and listening to them we yearned to be back home, where there were orchards and gardens and food.

On the other side of the little hallway in our *kibitka* were two rooms in which also lived a family of refugees. The man repaired sewing machines at the *artel* and, clandestinely, for private customers, so that they were much better off than we. They were able to buy food at the market, where peasants sold milk, cheese, and butter at prices that we could not afford, and where old women sold tobacco and salt by the glass.

Our yard was completely bare, with only a few weeds growing along the edges. It was surrounded by a three-foot-high adobe-brick wall. There was a roofless and doorless adobe outhouse in one corner and a garbage pit in the other. On the other side of the back wall stood a prosperous-looking house with a tin roof and a barn that housed a cow, several pigs, and many chickens. It belonged to a former *kulak* family that had been exiled to Lougovaya in the 1930s and worked themselves up to a point where, back home, they would have been considered *kulaks* all over again.

Until school started, I got myself a job at the *artel* as an apprentice in the harness-making shop. The objective of this job was to create loops at the ends of thick ropes. This was accomplished by untwisting one end about five inches, inserting into the rope a wooden wedge about fifteen inches from the end, so that it separated the strands, then threading one of the untwisted strands through the hole. This was done several times for all the strands, so that when the loop was attached to a wagon, the tighter the rope was pulled the more it squeezed the strands, preventing them from slipping.

As a worker, I was entitled to the adult ration of 400 grams of bread a day, which made the job really worthwhile. Bread for workers was distributed by an energetic red-haired woman right at the *artel*. She carried sacks of loaves from the bread factory on her back and weighed out our rations on a balance scale. She did not have a complete set of weights and used pieces of bricks, which presumably corresponded to the missing weights. I cannot say that they did not, but she was always rather well dressed, which by our standards meant that her clothes were not patched and her boots looked solid, implying an additional source of income.

There were nine of us in the shop including the manager—a white-bearded old man, who enjoyed teaching us the tricks of the trade. There were two more summer workers, Taissa, a pimply girl of about sixteen, and Abrasha, a son of the chairman of the *artel*, Comrade Marderer. He had been a harness-maker back in the Ukraine, and his only qualification for chairmanship was the fact that he was a party member. All members of the *artel* were refugees; there was not a single Kazakh in the whole place. In addition to the harness shop, there was a shoe-repair shop, a sewing department, a watchmaker, and a *kvass* maker. *Kvass,* the fermented sour drink made with water and flour, was sold from a kiosk at the railroad station.

Abrasha (Abram) was in the tenth grade, but he looked much older and his cheeks and chin were black from heavy stubble, in spite of him having shaved every day. Rumor had it that his father kept buying deferments from the draft by getting him new birth certificates. Since eighteen-year-old boys were drafted, he had remained seventeen for the past several years.

Abrasha had read much more than I, and while working on the ropes, we talked endlessly about books until someone mentioned food, either citing from a book a description of a meal, or because of the sucking feeling in our stomachs. Then, for the rest of the day, the subject remained food. Abrasha did not indulge in small talk and was the only one who did not like talking about food, probably because unlike the rest of us, he had never experienced hunger.

Like his father, Abrasha was an ardent believer in communism and, again according to rumor, was opposed to the buying of deferments. However, his only sibling had drowned in a swimming accident before the war, and his parents' wishes prevailed.

One day Abrasha asked me what I knew about philosophy. I did not know much about philosophy, but I knew where the question came from. I had read a book entitled *How Steel Was Tempered* by Nikolai Ostrovsky, about the Revolution and the ensuing Civil War. Ostrovsky had been a Communist guerrilla but now was paralyzed by some horrible disease. I can still remember his picture in a magazine, his cadaverous face with huge eyes, topped by lots of curly hair. In this book a commissar, the political leader who was present in every unit, asked a peasant recruit what he knew about philosophy, and then proceeded to enlighten him on the scientific inevitability of the triumph of communism, based on Karl Marx's philosophy, the dialectic materialism.

Abrasha proceeded to enlighten me in the same way. He explained that Karl Marx had combined the dialectical ideas of the German philosopher Hegel, according to which all change arises from the conflict of opposite forces (as in class struggle), with the materialistic ideas of another German philosopher, Ludwig Feuerbach, who taught that everything is based on physical processes. I did not know enough to argue with Abrasha then, but history shows that in real life most people from the less affluent classes want to join the more affluent ones, rather than fight them.

Naturally, I did not tell Abrasha about my father. I just told him that he was in the army and that we had not heard from him. But my skeptical ques-

tions probing discrepancies between propaganda and reality must have
made him ever more eager to convince me that, when true communism arrived, everyone would receive everything according to his needs and contribute according to his ability. This was the standard propaganda line that
called for sacrifices now, so that future generations would live in an ideal society. In the meantime, we were living under socialism, which is the first
phase of communism. It eliminated the rich and presumably made everyone equal.

One day the concept of equality under the Socialist system was illustrated to me very vividly. It was the third day that no bread had been available
and we had not had anything to eat. That evening Abrasha invited me to
his house to look at a book he had somehow managed to obtain. As I entered the kitchen, the breath was knocked out of me by an overpowering
smell of cookies, which were cooling on a metal tray while his mother took
another full tray out of the baking oven. I stopped as if paralyzed, unable to
take a breath or to speak. His mother looked at me questioningly and, after a while, I caught my breath, said good evening, and proceeded to the
next room, all the time hoping that she would call me back and offer me a
cookie. She did not. I was unable to concentrate on what Abrasha was telling
me, and later, when his mother finally gave me a small cookie, I was careful to take the smallest possible bites in order to make it last. I did not let
them know that I had not eaten in three days. Afterwards, I often thought
how difficult or even impossible it is for those who have food to imagine
that someone may have none. It is like imagining that someone may not
have air to breathe or water to drink.

As I discovered many years later, there actually was no need for us to go
hungry. The desert was literally crawling with food: desert turtles and snakes
were there just for the taking. The fact that people starved to death rather
than eat them is another proof that materialism, dialectical or of any other
kind, does not prevail in real life and that ideas and taboos are more powerful than even the instinct to survive.

After several months, the three young men saw that we were unable to
find another place to live and one by one moved out. I do not know how

they had voluntarily accepted two families with three small, cranky children in a place where there was not even enough room for all to stand at the same time. This took an extraordinary amount of kindness and empathy on their part. They were always cheerful and occasionally shared with us the American powdered eggs or powdered milk that they received from the agency that helped Polish refugees. There was no agency to help us, refugees from the western Soviet Union. The Soviet Red Cross was supposed to help refugees to find one another, but my inquiries about the whereabouts of our relatives went unanswered.

In September, I started the eighth grade. Our school was in a two-story building, the first floor of which was occupied by the Polish army that was being formed by General Wladyslaw Anders from the Polish POWs recently released from the camps. Somehow Anders had escaped the fate of the many thousands of Polish officers who had been executed by the NKVD in the Katyn Forest soon after their capture in 1939. The Soviet government wanted the new Polish army to fight side by side with the Red Army, but Anders refused, and the army instead was equipped by the British and brought to Africa through Iran and Palestine. They fought in Libya at Tobruk, and a very large number of them died in Italy where, according to survivors, they were used as cannon fodder by American General Mark Clark in the battle for Monte Cassino.

After the Polish army departed, the first floor was taken over by a military flight school for fighter pilots. We often watched their acrobatics and mock fights in the sky as they tried to get above and behind one another, which is the best position for shooting down the enemy. Some of them got into trouble for landing their two-seater trainers in the desert to pick up their girlfriends for a ride.

Because our school had only one floor of the building, it had to operate in two shifts. Our classes began at seven in the morning, which was all right so long as it was already daylight and it was possible to judge the time, since we did not have a watch or a clock. While the weather was warm, I slept outside on a goatskin and, not having to get dressed or brush my teeth, or have breakfast—other than some bread and water—I was always on time for school. When it grew colder I obtained a second goatskin, with which I covered myself. A small sack stuffed with hay served as my pillow.

The problem was in the winter, when it was impossible to judge the time.

Several times on moonlit nights I walked the two miles to school only to find it closed because I had arrived at 3 or 4 a.m. It took me very little time to get going—all I had to do was to put on my boots and jacket, which I used as a blanket. Frequently, the water in the bucket was frozen so that there was no drinking or washing up. Walking around town in the dark was not safe: there were frequent "undressings" in which robbers stole their victims' clothing. I did not think that anyone would want mine, but I still walked in the middle of the road so that no one could grab me from an ambush, and was always ready to run.

The winter was very cold; unlike in the *kolkhoz,* there were no reeds nearby for fuel and the weeds had either all been picked or were covered with snow. I cut off a beam that was protruding from the end of the roof, but it did not last us very long. Even the manure that had been dropped into the slush on the street was unusable. The only place where we could warm up was in the hot shower at the communal bath, while our clothes were being deloused, but to get in there one had to stand in a long line in the cold.

Most of our teachers were refugees, and some were very good. I particularly liked the physics teacher, a woman of gypsy origin, whose brilliant, half-gypsy son was advanced from the middle of the eighth grade into the tenth. And he did it in spite of the fact that he was so nearsighted that, in order to read, he had to rub his nose on the books. His skipping a year gave me an idea of how to make up for my lost year, and when Abrasha gave me his ninth-grade textbooks, I began to study them every day in addition to doing my eighth-grade work. The only problem I had was with math. In order to understand trigonometry, one had to know geometry and algebra from the eighth grade. Other subjects I could manage by referring to the eighth-grade books.

Another school friend of mine, whose last name was Safronchik, had one kidney removed because of some disease. But even with that, he was still more athletic than I and managed to go over the top on the stand-up swing of the flight school, while I became disoriented as soon as I was upside-down near the top. He was well fed and well dressed because his father worked at the railroad station, selling soup to passengers. One day, an undercover inspector found that his father was charging more for the soup than he was supposed to. He was arrested, sentenced to several years of hard labor, and died within a few months at a construction job, chipping out a railroad tunnel with a pick and a shovel somewhere in the Pamir Mountains.

Our worst teacher was Ivan Kirilovich, who taught gym and military education. He was exempt from the army because of a large white cataract on his left eye, which made him look like an alien from another planet. He was also semiliterate and a malaprop. The standard Soviet military rifle was model 1897, called a "three-rifle gun" because it had three spiraling grooves or riflings, which made the bullet spin as it traveled through the barrel so that it would fly straight and not tumble. But, according to Ivan Kirilovich, the reason for this name was that exactly three matches fit into the muzzle opening. In colloquial Russian one could say, instead of exactly, that "accurately" three matches fitted there or, incorrectly, it could even be abbreviated to "accurat" three matches, but he was saying "kakurat," and so his name became Kakurat Kirilovich. He was also mean and, for the slightest infraction of discipline (such as whispering while in formation) forced us to do push-ups, sometimes in the mud, until we were completely exhausted.

Nevertheless, totally unintentionally, one day I made Kakurat Kirilovich very happy. Since there was some space in our room after the three Polish men left, we let a couple of fellow refugees stay with us for a few days when they came from a distant kolkhoz to sell some tobacco leaves on the market. I had run an errand for them and for this they gave me some dried tobacco leaves, which I crushed and kept in my pocket because there was no place to hide them from the kids in the house. We were not permitted to smoke either in or out of school, but this was not a problem since no one could afford tobacco, which was sold in the market by the glass at astronomical prices. When I showed up at school with a pocketful of tobacco, it instantly made me very popular with all the boys. At our noontime recess we crowded ourselves into the outhouse and rolled cigarettes with the thinnest newspaper that we could find.

At that very moment Kakurat Kirilovich appeared at the door. We threw away the cigarettes, but this was not enough. He threatened to punish us all unless the owner of the tobacco was found. I did not want to get my friends in trouble and sheepishly admitted my guilt. Kakurat Kirilovich then gripped my arm and marched me to the office of the assistant principal, who ordered me to turn my pockets inside out over his desk. My pocket was too full to be turned inside out and I began unloading it a handful at a time. After the second handful, I noticed that both of them were grinning and drooling. As if in a hypnotic trance, they stared at the growing mound of tobacco. They probably had not seen so much of it since before the war. By the time I finished, they were both panting and told me to get out and never do it again. As I saw them fall on the tobacco before I was out of the door, I thought they really wished I would do it every week.

When we had some money, I went to the railroad station and stood in line for noodle soup, which was sold only when a passenger train was at the platform. There were very few noodles in this soup, and even fewer tiny circles of fat, but it was hot and I sipped some of it on the way home to keep warm. We invented a little ditty about this soup that rhymed in Russian: "Whether you eat it or drink it, it is still only water, and you will never have a bowel movement."

While waiting in the soup line, I often saw freight trains packed with people who were exiled from the Northern Caucasus. There were Chechens, Kabardins, Balkars, Ingushes, and Karachai, all accused of aiding the Germans. They were being dispersed throughout Central Asia and Siberia. Frequently they were sitting in open platform cars on top of loads of coal or gravel. Pelted by rain and sleet, men, women, and children huddled together under blankets. I could not imagine how these wretches had aided the Germans, and felt a great deal of solidarity and compassion for their suffering. I would have liked to give them some soup, or just to talk to them, but as soon as their train stopped it was surrounded by armed guards who kept everyone away.

There was a library near the railroad station, from which I was finally able to get some good books. One of them was *The Grapes of Wrath* by John Steinbeck, which describes the drought of the early 1930s in the American Midwest and the migration of impoverished farmers to California. I could not compare our plight to theirs because the circumstances were so different, but I had difficulty understanding how these people could be poor if they had their own trucks—something that in the Soviet Union was unimaginable. The young woman librarian let us into the stacks, and I saw many books being stolen by rednecks, who intimidated her when she dared to protest. They usually sought out books with thin, nonglossy paper that could be used for rolling cigarettes.

Lougovaya was so far out of the way that no one bothered to remove from the library forbidden books by authors declared enemies of the people. The *Small Soviet Encyclopedia* still listed party leaders and generals who had been executed, describing their heroic deeds on behalf of the Revolution. Since even their names became unmentionable, it was as if they had never existed; they became nonpersons. Possession of this encyclopedia in other places would have created a lot of problems. In his book *1984*, George Orwell explains the reason for such falsification of history: "Those who control the past control the future, those who control the present, control the past."

I still remember a passage from a book by a Western writer named Leon Feuchtwanger, who wrote about his visit to the Soviet Union. The book was published, but then immediately withdrawn and outlawed. He had asked Stalin why his pictures were displayed everywhere, to which Stalin replied that the Russian people were used to having pictures of the czar and were displaying his pictures only out of habit, which he would not force them to abandon.

I also stumbled upon the complete proceedings of the Moscow show trials. Reading them made me wonder how these old revolutionaries could perform so many acts of sabotage and espionage without having been discovered earlier. Also, if they were not guilty, why were they so eager to confess, knowing that the previous group that had confessed had been executed?

Under Abrasha's influence I tackled Karl Marx's *Das Kapital*, the Bible of Communist economics, in which Marx "proves" the "scientific and historic inevitability" of the capitalist system's collapse. In his view, just as the feudal system was replaced by newly emerged capitalism, it is "historically inevitable" that, in turn, capitalists will be replaced by the proletariat, which they themselves had created. Marx predicted that this revolution would begin in the most industrialized country, such as Germany, from where it would spread all over the world. This prediction was modified by Lenin, according to whom the revolution would more likely start in a less-developed country, such as Russia, where capitalists were not yet strong enough to suppress it.

Upon its victory, the proletariat would establish a dictatorship that would destroy "rotten bourgeois" values and replace them with scientifically established values. However, since the proletariat was uneducated, it would be led by "working intelligentsia" who, under the guidance of the Communist Party, would know what is good for everyone. And, since the Communist Party represents the people, anyone who opposed it opposed the will of the people and must be eliminated.

But it was not Karl Marx but Feodor Dostoyevski who described this kind of dictatorship in simple words. In his book *The Brothers Karamazov* he describes an imaginary scene in which Jesus returns to earth in the 1500s and is brought before the Grand Inquisitor because his message of freedom disagrees with the Church's teachings. The Grand Inquisitor tells Jesus: "We shall convince the people that they will only become free when they resign their freedom to us . . . and we will decide all things, and they will joyfully believe our decision, because it will deliver them from their great care and their present terrible torments of personal and free decision." No wonder the Communists had banned Dostoyevski's books.

In my attempt to understand *Das Kapital,* I managed to follow the calculation of "surplus values" but got lost toward the middle of the book and decided to give up and live with this gap in my education. The same thing happened with Engels's *Dialectics of Nature,* the Bible of Communist science. From this book I remember only the idea of "quantity turning into quality," illustrated by the boiling of water; when the quantity of heat reaches a certain value, it changes the quality of water by turning it into steam. Engels claimed that society operates in the same way, where accumulated quantity of discontent leads to a revolution that changes the quality of society. While in the West Engels is relatively unknown, in the Communist pantheon he was one of four gods: Marx, Engels, Lenin, and Stalin. Engels was a wealthy German who had supported Marx financially and in every other way, even to the point that, to save the married Marx from embarrassment he, being single, assumed paternity of the child Marx had sired with his maid!

In the library, I frequently saw a tall, elderly man with snow-white hair, including eyebrows and eyelashes, and kindly blue eyes that sparkled when he smiled. If he had had a long beard and a fat belly, he would have been a perfect "Grandfather Frost," as they called the secular Santa Claus, who appeared on New Year's days in the Soviet Union after Christmas was outlawed. I got to talk to him and we became friends, if one can say that considering the difference in our ages. His name was Dimitri Petrovich and he had been exiled here from the capital of Georgia, Tbilisi. The reason for his exile was rather bizarre. While many people, like my father, were arrested for having contact with foreign countries, he was arrested for not having contact with his brother in Iran. This brother, an engineer, had worked on construction of the railroad to the Iranian city of Tabriz and remained there after the Revolution. Another brother, who lived in Russia, corresponded with the one in Iran, so that Dimitri Petrovich had no need to do it himself. He had been sentenced to twenty years of exile because, since he had no open contact with his brother, the NKVD suspected that he must have had a clandestine one. His wife, who had been a concert pianist, had to sell her piano so that she could send him food parcels.

I enjoyed visiting him on long winter evenings and discussing the books that we had just read. He lived in a small, one-room house not far from us, which he shared with the landlady and another man who recently had been released from a Siberian concentration camp and was in very poor health. In spite of the overcrowding, we sat on his cot and, in the light of the ubiquitous soot-maker, read interesting passages from books, totally oblivious of the others.

One cold winter evening when I went to visit Dimitri Petrovich I stumbled on something while entering the dark hallway. It was too dark to see what it was, and I backed up and opened the entrance door wide. In the weak light of the moon I could barely distinguish the legs of a corpse. My heart skipped a beat at the thought that it might be Dimitri Petrovich, but there was nothing to do but step over these legs and enter the room. I was happy to see Dimitri Petrovich alive and well, and to learn that it was the unfortunate roommate, who had died during the previous night. They were waiting for the militia, who picked up corpses and carried them away stacked like cordwood on their wagon—a sight I encountered almost every day on the way from school.

Dimitri Petrovich had introduced me to a man named Ivan Ivanovich, whose daughter was doing very poorly in the seventh grade. I began tutoring her two nights a week for a small payment and dinner with the family. Ivan Ivanovich worked for a government agency involved in meat supplies and had not been drafted because he suffered from brucellosis, which, as I understood it, was a disease one could catch from milk that had not been boiled. His wife was a quiet, kindly woman who was very much worried about her daughter, their only child.

I had a very hard time explaining algebraic equations to this girl; not only was she not very bright, but she had only boys on her mind. But the dinners were wonderful, usually consisting of a vegetable soup and some meat with potatoes or cabbage. It was better than anything I'd eaten in years, and sometimes the kind woman gave me some leftovers for Vilya and Mother.

In the corner of their entrance hall they kept a huge hog that one could smell throughout the house. But after a while I got used to it, and it certainly did not affect my appetite. To the contrary, this was a smell of prosperity.

One day Ivan Ivanovich asked me if I would come early on Saturday morning to help them butcher the hog. When I arrived, the beast had already been scrubbed clean and, with a muzzle over its snout, was hoisted up by a hand-winch and suspended by its front legs from a hook in the hall ceiling. It was so huge that while its front hoofs touched the ceiling, the hind ones were close to the floor, where a large pan had been set to catch the blood. Ivan Ivanovich stuck a knife into the pig's armpit and I immediately understood the meaning of the expression to squeal "like a stuck pig." Even with a muzzle, the squeal was piercing, and we were afraid that one of the neighbors might hear it, because Ivan Ivanovich had no intention of giving the skin to the government, as required by law, even though he could have been heavily fined if found out.

The squealing subsided as the pig bled to death. Ivan Ivanovich knew what he was doing, and in a few hours the hair of the pig had been singed off, its internal organs were removed into a washtub, and the fat cut up in pieces and stored with layers of salt in a barrel. The skin remained on the fat, which was in places four fingers thick. I had never seen so much meat at any one time. Other than the contents of the intestines, nothing was discarded. I was paid with some meat and blood which, when cooked, tasted almost like liver, but gave me a terrible heartburn.

By fall of 1943, our luck had changed. Mother finally saw that Eva did not do her share and separated from her, finding a room for us in the Kazakh section of town. Most refugees were afraid to live among the Kazakhs, but after our sojourn in the *kolkhoz,* we were used to living with them and knew that—just as among any other people—there were good and bad ones.

For me, getting rid of Eva and her brood was like removing a nasty splinter that had been irritating me for more than two years. Vilya was in a nursery school, and I finally was able to read and study in peace and quiet, which I needed very badly, since I was trying to complete two years' study in a single year.

Mother got a new job at the *artel,* selling *kvass* from a tiny kiosk in a small park enclosed by a picket fence across from the railroad station. The park must have been recently planted, for its scraggly, sickly trees were only about eight feet tall. In the park, there were usually some men in ragged Gulag uniforms—gray quilted jackets and pants, from the holes of which protruded dirty wads of cotton. They were freed inmates who had come south in search of a warmer climate and did not go any farther because it was known that, in the warmer regions, such as Uzbekistan, cotton had been planted instead of wheat and there was nothing to eat. There were always between ten and twenty of these former prisoners lying in the park—some alive, some dead, and some dying. When it was warm, most of those alive sat there stripped to the waist, intensely hunting for lice in their shirts, or rather rags that used to be shirts. Some of those who were dying of dysentery had taken off their pants soiled with blood and feces, turned them inside out, and hung them on the picket fence to dry. Of course, the flies had a field day spreading the disease among the town inhabitants. Every day the police wagon came to pick up the dead while the train from Novosibirsk brought in more semi-dead inmates.

I went there every day to help Mother, and every day walked among the bodies, hoping to find Father alive and dreading to find him among the dead or dying.

It was *kvass* that saved us. It sold for a ruble a cup, and every morning a full barrel of it was delivered to the kiosk. *Kvass* was measured with a tin cup with a handle, which was dipped into the barrel and poured into one of several tin cans, which were served to those customers who did not have their own vessels. The cans were then rinsed in a bucket of water that was replaced twice a day. As the level of *kvass* in the barrel dropped, Mother surreptitiously added a bucket of water that I brought from the station. At the end of the day the stuff was pretty thin, but buyers did not expect anything better for one ruble and did not complain. I stood in for Mother very often and once, while she was away, I was distracted by a man while his accomplice snatched Mother's pocketbook in which we kept the money. I tried to give chase but he was faster than I. After that I began putting the money in my pocket and, when no one looked, transferred it into a box, which I hid under the counter.

Remembering what had happened to my friend Safronchik's father, we were careful not to overcharge anyone, but the added water produced some money every day and we did not starve any longer. I strongly suspect that Mother got this job on the condition that she would share the gains with someone in management, but she never mentioned it to me.

One day, as I was studying at home alone, someone banged forcefully on the door. When I opened it, two big captains of the militia pushed their way into the room, followed by our Kazakh landlady. Captain of the militia was a very high rank, just below the chief, and I was very frightened, not knowing what crime I could have committed that required such high-level action.

"Where is the goat meat?" asked one of the captains menacingly.

"What goat meat?" I stammered.

"From the goat you have stolen!" growled the other captain.

"I have not stolen anything, I don't know what this is all about!"

"Yes you did, where is it?" He was losing patience.

After I said that they could search the place, he told the landlady to show me the bones, and she showed me an animal's vertebra that she had found on the trash heap in front of the house.

"Do you think that if I had stolen a goat I would throw the bones in front of the house so that they could be found?" I asked the policemen. "These are pig bones that someone gave us. Here, I have some left over," and I showed them another bone with some meat on it that a friend of Mother's had given us the day before. I hoped I would not have to name this friend because the pig was probably slaughtered illegally, but the men did not press the point.

"That's my baby goat!" shouted the landlady.

"Its pig!" I shouted. "You can have it analyzed."

The landlady's Russian was very poor and she switched to Kazakh.

"It is *chushka* (pig)!" I shouted. *"Yeshke* (goat)!" she shouted.

"Chushka!" "Yeshke!" "Chushka!" "Yeshke."

Then I had an idea. I knew that Muslims did not eat pork.

"If it is goat, here eat some!" I said, extending the bone to her. She shied away.

"Yeshke!" she shouted again.

"Why don't you eat it then?" which in Kazakh is: *"Negge jemeisyn?"*

"Yeshke!" "Negge jemeisyn?" "Yeshke!" "Negge jemeisyn?"

We had another few more rounds of this, until the captains got tired of it. Finally one of them ordered her to bring them some *airan* (yogurt). Where there are goats there must be yogurt, which was probably why the two officers came in the first place. If there was no goat meat to be confiscated, at least they could have some yogurt.

As they were walking out, one of them looked at me very sternly and, shaking his finger, said, "You may be getting away with it this time, but if it happens again, you will be in real trouble." The woman brought them two drinking bowls, called *pialkas,* full of yogurt, which the Kazakhs kept in flexible bags made of cow stomachs. The officers drank it and went away with the landlady running after them.

Peace and quiet did not last very long. Mother allowed three refugees from Moldavia who had also escaped from a *kolkhoz* to move in with us until they could find a place to live. They were an old, wizened, toothless mother and her two daughters in their late twenties. One of the daughters made her living sewing all day long on a hand-cranked sewing machine, which made studying very difficult and did not produce in me much goodwill toward them. However, Mother thought that letting them in was the right thing to do.

They slept on the floor next to our cot, but there still was a little bit more space on the floor next to the oven and, since Mother could not stand not having it used by someone in need, other refugees appeared for various periods of time. Once there was a bearded former rabbi from Odessa with his sickly son, who had bright red hair and whose face was completely covered with freckles. This was the first time that I had encountered a rabbi or, for that matter, any cleric. Having been a member of the "Union of Militant Atheists," I was pleasantly surprised to find the rabbi to be a soft-spoken, obviously very learned person. He did not appear at all to be an avaricious parasite who would entrap gullible people in his web of superstition and, like a spider, suck their blood, as we were taught all clerics had to be. The rabbi's son must have been in his thirties; he was very serious and hardly ever smiled. Before the war he had taught English and German. We talked about books, and once he said to me that it was a pity I did not know English, because he had Theodore Dreiser's wonderful novel, *The Titan,* which he carried with him from Odessa and which was his most prized possession. I admired him for his love of books. The casual way in which he mentioned knowledge of foreign languages made me think that perhaps someday I also could master them. I had picked up several hundred Kazakh words with ease and had no difficulties with German in school.

Since even corresponding with someone abroad was a crime, it was too much to hope that someday I could travel to the West. According to Abrasha, Western countries had a higher standard of living than we, but it was only temporarily so. Once the war was over, there would be another great depression that would lead to a revolution, after which communism would rule the world and usher in peace and prosperity forever.

I had no way of judging the prospects of a postwar depression, but I saw the American military jeeps and trucks (which we called Willises and Studebakers) and heard from soldiers that, while Soviet-made copies were falling apart, the American-made vehicles lasted a long time. There were also American dried and condensed milk, powdered eggs, and canned meat and fish sold on the black market, which we could occasionally afford these days. I could not believe that all these goods were produced by a system that was about to collapse. Also, Mother remembered that right after the Civil War in the Ukraine, there were distribution centers flying the American flag and handing out food to the starving population. She even knew that it was President Herbert Hoover (since there is no "h" sound in Russian, it was pronounced "Kherbert Khoover") who had organized this assistance. The name "America" meant hope. Many people had emigrated to America before World War I and in the early 1930s some of them came back to visit their relatives with their children, telling them of a life that we could not even imagine. However, there were two aspects of American behavior that were said to be very peculiar: they were said to frequently put their feet on the table, and they would not sit down to eat without having their shirts on.

Soviet propaganda depicted life in America as one endless unemployment line, one depression succeeding another. To prove this they published books by such American writers as Upton Sinclair, John Steinbeck, and Sinclair Lewis, who wrote about the problems of life in coal mines, on farms, and in small towns.

However, the propagandists usually tripped over their own feet, as in a book by Soviet correspondents Ilya Ilf and Evgeny Petrov entitled *The Single-Story America*. The point these writers were making was that while American skyscrapers are well known, most people lived in single-story tract houses, so monotonously similar to one another that an inebriated person could only tell that he was in his own house by the newspaper on his fireplace mantelpiece. I could not understand for the life of me how living in a house with a fireplace, even if it was similar to other houses, was worse than living in the hovels that the vast majority of Soviet citizens lived in. And I began to dream of someday seeing this land of skyscrapers and monotonous tract houses for myself.

While I admired America in spite of such propaganda, an article in the newspaper made me wonder about some of its leaders. According to this article, the American vice president, Henry Wallace, and the president of the Far Eastern Institute, Owen Lattimore, traveled in Siberia and visited a Gulag concentration camp. Upon returning to the United States, they reported that these Gulag camps were actually rehabilitation centers whose inmates were healthy, well-fed, slept in clean beds with white sheets, and worked with great enthusiasm. One of them, I believe it was Henry Wallace, said that he had the privilege of shaking the hand of the greatest industrialist in the world, the head of the Far Eastern Gulags!

I had assumed that most educated people in the world knew from history about the Potemkin villages, but these two obviously did not. Potemkin was chief minister to Catherine the Great. To prevent her from seeing how people really lived, he built prosperous-looking houses along the highway that he knew she would travel, but these houses were only facades, with nothing behind their front walls. Henry Wallace ran for president on a Progressive Party ticket in 1948 and received 1,157,172 votes, as compared to 24,105,812 for Harry Truman. Many years later, I was coming home from the airport on the Connecticut Limousine when the driver announced that we had the honor of having with us Mr. Wallace, the former vice president. Some people applauded, but I thought that honor rather dubious.

    As soon as the Moldavian women began to feel at home, they brought in a young woman of about eighteen, also from Moldavia. She was scrawny, had a long, pointed nose, and reminded me of a chicken. Her name was Ester. She had an aggressive manner of speaking in a high-pitched, penetrating voice; I immediately disliked her. Mother, however, felt sorry for her, fed her, and after a while and against my violent objections and reminders of Eva, took her into our family. She said that helping an orphan was the right thing to do. This meant that, as in utopian communism, Ester could take whatever she needed and contribute whatever she wished to contribute. She contributed very little. I think that because Father was from Moldavia, Mother had a soft spot for people who came from there, even though, as a group, they had a reputation for self-centeredness. By that time we had food to spare, mostly in the form of flour, which we kept in a sack. Since there was nowhere to lock anything up, the sack was always kept sewn up, and every time we took some flour out of it, we sewed it up again with a needle and thread kept just for that purpose.

    One day, I came home from school earlier than usual and caught the old crone helping herself to flour from our sack while Ester looked on. When I asked what she was doing, the old woman said that Ester had told her to take as much as she wanted. The situation in the house became totally intolerable. Mother was very hurt when she heard the story and told all of them to get out. They did not show any intention of doing so and the atmosphere in the room, where seven of us lived practically shoulder to shoulder, was sizzling, but there was nothing that we could do to get rid of them. We did not talk to them, but their presence gritted on our nerves. Eventually it would have come to blows if we had not found out that Eva had moved somewhere and our old room was available. We moved right in, and

Mother promised she would never again take anyone into the family against my will, no matter how sorry she might feel for them.

There were new neighbors across the hallway, a family with five children ranging from two years to about twelve. Their last name was Oumanski; the man was the manager of the sewing department in the *artel,* which meant that they had plenty to eat and had good clothing. The woman was very kind and became Mother's friend, but her husband was rough and loud and had to have everything his way. In addition to being a real tyrant, he also had a peculiarity of which I had never heard before: every night he forced one of his sons to scratch his heels until he fell asleep. If the boy thought that his father was already asleep and stopped, he received a strong kick and had to continue, with tears running down his face. Except for an occasional slap on the behind when I was small, my parents never spanked me, and I could not even imagine that a situation like this could exist.

One cold winter morning a militiaman checked to see who was living in the house. Seeing the empty hallway between the rooms, he brought in a Karachai family from the northern Caucasus that the government had decided to settle in Lougovaya. This family consisted of an old stooped woman and her son, with his wife and three children. They were squeezed into the unheated, windowless hallway, about fifteen feet deep and twelve feet wide, between the doorways to our room and to our neighbors. The outside door was not sealed and the temperature in the hallway was almost the same as outside. The family had a couple of carpets and slept on one of them, all in a row, while covering themselves with the other. The old woman did not speak any Russian and the younger ones spoke very little. There were a number of families like this in Lougovaya under the supervision of a young Karachai, who arranged jobs and ration cards for them and helped them in other ways as well. I got to speak to this young man one day and he told me that he had been a member of the Komsomol, the Communist youth organization, but that did not make any difference: every Karachai was exiled, including members of the Communist Party. They were taken from wherever they happened to be—adults from work, children from schools, and old people from homes. They were frequently shipped in separate trains and

many did not know where the rest of their family was. They could take with
them only whatever they could carry. When I asked him whether it was true
that they had collaborated with the Germans, he smiled sadly and said that
perhaps some nationalists did, but that the great majority was suffering only
for being Karachai.

I was at home when several months later two husky militiamen appeared
at the house. The old woman was alone. The militiamen told her that she
had fifteen minutes to pack. She did not understand and one of them
showed her the position of the hands on his watch and motioned for her to
pile their belongings together. She gesticulated wildly, indicating that she
was alone, but they just continued pointing to the watch. Tears ran down
her cheeks as she piled everything on one of the carpets, barely able to tie
its ends together. The bundle was almost as large as she was. I tried to help
her to hoist it on her back, but it was too heavy. The militiamen stood outside the door, smoking and impatiently looking at their watches. The neighbor woman from across the hall, who was very pregnant and could not be
of much help, brought out a bench, and the three of us somehow managed
to get the bundle onto the bench and finally hoisted it onto the old woman's
back. The militiamen just watched. In my mind's eye I can still see this old
woman, doubled over under the huge bundle, flanked by the husky policemen as she shuffled toward the railroad station, which was about a mile
away. I don't know whether her son, daughter-in-law, and grandchildren
managed to join her or were sent to Siberia separately.

Thanks to the diluted *kvass,* our lot continued to improve. We even
bought a nanny goat and a baby goat. It was my job to milk the goat, which
in Kazakhstan is done from behind, rather than from the side. The goat had
a large udder and every night gave almost a quart of milk. The kid goat was
old enough to graze and, to make sure that it did not get at the milk, was
tied to its mother's neck with a rope long enough to permit grazing but not
to reach the udder. Unlike its mother, who was gray with a white stomach,
the male kid was black and white and was very playful; Vilya and I had a
lot of fun butting heads with it. Since the goats would be stolen if left outside, we brought them into the house at night, and the baby goat frequent-

ly slept at my feet on the cot. Cleaning up their droppings was not a problem since they left solid pellets, but to absorb the urine we had to gather hay, sand, sawdust, or whatever else we could find to cover the floor near the stove where the goat was tied up. The nanny goat had to be tied up for the night because it would devour everything it could reach, including clothing.

Every morning I took the goats down the street, where they joined a herd that was taken to pasture by a goatherd. In the evenings I picked them up at the same place, but after a week the nanny goat knew her own way home. When the Karachai family was gone we were able to keep the goats in the hallway, and the neighbors with five children bought a cow, which they also kept there.

We also bought some decent clothing. I had a warm Soviet military long-coat and a dark green Estonian officer's tunic that had brass buttons with three lions, which had been offered to Mother at the *kvass* booth by a freed prisoner.[1] The tunic did not have lapels and its buttons ran all the way up to the neck, so that it was very warm. It looked like new and fit me as if it were tailor-made. I liked it so much that, when it became worn, I had a tailor take it apart and turn the fabric inside out so that it looked like new again.

While it was good to be decently clothed, this kind of clothing also created a problem. The railroad station was patrolled by military policemen looking for army deserters, and because I looked like a soldier, I had to carry my birth certificate everywhere I went. There was no photograph on the birth certificate and after some time it began falling apart. A friend of mine, Sasha, had lost his birth certificate and went to the militia station where he was issued a "Certificate on the Loss of a Certificate," which served him just as well. When I turned sixteen on April 24, 1944, I was issued an internal passport, with a photograph showing me with hollow cheeks, which had to be carried at all times.

Having turned sixteen, I had to go for a weeklong pre-draft training camp during the spring break at school. The camp was near the capital of

1. The Baltic countries of Estonia, Latvia, and Lithuania were occupied by the Soviet Union in 1940 as a result of the division of Eastern Europe by the Nazi-Soviet pact. There, like in the rest of the Soviet Union, the potential "enemies of the people" were either executed, imprisoned, or exiled.

Kazakhstan, Alma-Ata, and we were issued permits to travel there and given train tickets. We trained with military rifles instead of the .22 caliber ones that we had at school, and by the end of the week we felt like real soldiers. On the train back we sang soldier's songs, and a passing woman crossed herself and exclaimed, "My God, now they are drafting children!" This deflated our bravado to some extent, but we continued to sing. At that time the Germans were already being driven out of Ukraine and Belarus. There was optimism in the air and it looked as if by the time we might be drafted at age eighteen, the war might be over. I was not eager to go to the front—I hated Stalin just as much as I hated Hitler. In addition to the dying prisoners, who were victims of Stalin, our town was full of war invalids missing an arm or a leg, or disfigured by severe burns—victims of Hitler.

At Mother's *artel* everyone had to take turns as a night watchman at a shop a mile out of town, in the middle of nowhere. With all the holdups and robberies in town this was not a safe thing to do, particularly for a woman, and I got a friend of mine, Grisha, to do it with me. We armed ourselves with a pitchfork and a kitchen knife and went there before sunset. The shop was an adobe building with a flat roof and, after some deliberation, we climbed onto the roof. There was not much that we could have done against an armed robber or against several men, so we decided that discretion was the better part of valor and pulled up the ladder onto the roof. The night was moonless; we lay on our backs and looked at the bright stars. We did not get much sleep, waking up at the slightest noise, and were glad to finally see the sun rising over the desert.

Grisha and I often went to the movie house near the station. Most of the films shown there were about the war; some had good love songs or songs about the lives and courage of soldiers at the front lines, but others were the same old idolization of Stalin, such as:

> In the expanse of our wonderful fatherland,
> While being hardened in battle and in labor,
> We have composed a happy song
> About our great friend and leader.
> > Stalin is our battle glory,
> > Stalin is the soaring of our youth.
> > With this song we conquer the enemies;
> > Singing this song, we follow Stalin!

Anatole at age sixteen in Kazakhstan, internal passport photo, 1944.

Once I saw a movie there entitled *Nasredin in Bukhara*. Nasredin is a folk hero in Central Asia and the Middle East, something like Gioufa in Italy or Ivan the Fool in Russia. He is a simpleton who winds up outsmarting everybody. The villain in the movie was the ruler of Bukhara, who is surrounded by court flatterers (very much like the Soviet poets) who sing his praises and kiss his shoes. The hero is Nasredin, who had organized a revolt against the king. When Nasredin and his followers are imprisoned, a mob assembles around the prison and people shake their fists and shout: "Free the prisoners! Free the prisoners!" I caught myself just in time before raising my fist and shouting "Free the prisoners!" The allegory was so obvious that I wondered how this movie managed to slip by the censor.

We also went to dances a few times, where a disc jockey played tangos, foxtrots, and waltzes on an old wind-up gramophone. Grisha knew how to dance but I did not; most of the time I just watched, only daring to ask girls to dance whom I knew from school, if they happened to be there. As we were leaving after one of the dances, two drunken sailors attacked us for no apparent reason. They had been a year ahead of us in school but had been drafted into the navy. The taller one was hitting Grisha while the other was punching me; both were shouting "Kill the damned Jews!" I never had anything to do with either of them and was so taken by surprise that all I could do was to cover my face with my arms and keep repeating, "What is this for? What did I ever do to you?" After a few minutes we managed to escape, and they were too drunk to pursue us. I was not hurt but Grisha, who had fought back, had a bleeding nose.

My idea of being Jewish was that one either believed in the Jewish religion or was brought up in the Jewish tradition. My only exposure to religion was during the year that I lived with Grandfather and he mysteriously disappeared for a few hours on Friday nights. My parents never mentioned religion or practiced anything traditional. According to Father's sister Ida, whom I met after the war, when Father was a boy he used to run away from religious education classes, until his parents stopped sending him there. Mother grew up without her mother and, as far as I knew, never learned the rituals, which in any case could not be practiced before the war. During the war, Stalin allowed some religious freedom and ordered churches to collect money for the war effort. Enough was collected to equip a tank division, which was appropriately named after St. George the Victorious.

Religion did not matter to me even without the Communist teaching that it was "opium of the masses." I could not imagine how a presumably just and omnipotent God could allow the suffering of innocents. I had Ukrainian, Jewish, Russian, and Polish friends, enjoyed books by writers of various nationalities, including Russian and Ukrainian translations from Yiddish, and knew that there were both good people and villains among all of them. I had even written a poem on the subject, proclaiming that I was a human being only, not a member of a tribe. I could not understand how some people could be proud of belonging to one nationality or another, since this was not something that they themselves had accomplished or even elected. It is like being proud that one's eyes are a certain color. While I knew that many outstanding people were of Jewish origin, I also knew that so were many Communists.

By the summer of 1944 the Germans had been chased out of Ukraine and we and our neighbors across the hall, the Oumanskis, decided that it was time to return home. We believed that because a second front had been opened in Europe on D-Day, there was no chance that the Germans could return. We obtained a permit to travel as repatriates, but one could not yet buy railroad tickets to Ukraine because not all railroad lines had been restored. We settled for Kuybyshev, a city in central Russia that had been a temporary capital of the Soviet Union when the Germans were attacking Moscow. This time we traveled on a passenger train, which was packed to the hilt. We did not have much luggage, but the seven Oumanskis, with children ranging from one year to teenagers, had to bribe the conductor for enough space to accommodate them. Needless to say, we did not feel bad about leaving Kazakhstan, Lougovaya, and the adobe hut.

At the station called Arys in Kazakhstan, I saw a cattle train like the one that had brought us over in 1941. There were people milling all over the platform, and I struck up a conversation with a young man and a woman of about my age. They were ethnic Greeks who were being exiled from the Crimea, which in ancient times had been part of Greece. The NKVD had told them that they were being deported to Greece through Iran and the Middle East. They were very happy about it and it broke my heart to tell them that the turn-off to Iran was about a thousand miles back in Ashkabad, and that they were on the road to Kazakhstan or Siberia instead. They did not believe me, but I knew that I was right.

We traveled north along the River Syr-Darya, which, together with Amu-Darya, flows into the landlocked Aral Sea. If its water had been fresh, the Aral Sea probably would have been called a lake. Between the two rivers is the semi-desert of Kyzyl-Kum, which was being irrigated by the diverted waters of these rivers in order to grow cotton that was needed for gunpowder. Unfortunately, the water continued to be diverted even after the war, until the Aral Sea, due to evaporation, was diminished to about half its original size and its salinity increased so much that all the fish died. Then the salt flats, left after the water had evaporated, cracked in the sun and created salt dust, which the wind carried to the cotton plantations, killing the cotton plants. Many years later I saw a television interview with the Communist Party chief who had been in charge of this disaster. He said that his assignment had been to deliver an ever-increasing quota of cotton, as was required by the central planners in Moscow; it was not his job to worry about what would happen to the Aral Sea.

There were mountains of salt next to the railroad station in Aralsk, near where the seashore used to be. Not knowing whether salt would be available in the Ukraine, we bought two chunks of it that were bigger than soccer balls. While all this salt was sitting here, only a few hundred miles away salt was being sold on the black market by the glass. Since the people in charge of food supplies were getting paid the same amount whether they were doing anything or not, there was no incentive to distribute it through official channels. However, the railroad employees—there was a conductor in each railroad car—bought it here and supplied black marketers all along the railroad.

Mother decided that instead of going back to Khmelnik, we would go with the Oumanskis to their city of Kremenchug, which was much larger and might offer better employment opportunities. There were no passenger trains going there from Kuybyshev, so we climbed onto a freight car of a train going to Ukraine. We had just settled on our bundles in a corner when a woman with a couple of children plunked herself right on top of us and refused to move. Mother, who must have been very much on edge in view of the insecurity of our situation, screamed at her as I had never heard her scream before. I was just climbing into the car when this happened and heard someone asking what was going on and someone else's reply that they were finishing off the unfinished. Both Oumanski and I rushed to Mother's aid, and the woman retreated to the opposite corner.

As soon as we crossed the River Don, we entered the area that had been occupied by the Germans, and all that could be seen from the train were ruins of buildings. Not a single railroad station, no matter how small, had been left undamaged. The train stopped in Kharkov, where we found another freight train that finally took us to Kremenchug.

Kremenchug was only partially destroyed, and Oumanski found a three-room apartment, of which we took one room. The town was on the Dnieper, not very far from Zaporozhie, but we did not know whether Grandfather and our uncles had returned there, or even whether they were still alive. I had written to the militia in Zaporozhie, where everyone had to register, inquiring about them, but I never received a reply and so we saw no point in going there.

Kremenchug was about four times the size of Khmelnik, but about a quarter of it had been destroyed and there were no job openings in the few government-operated canteens, which could not even be called restaurants. Neither was there any work in the government stores, which Mother would also have liked. Most commercial activity was taking place at the bazaar, where peasants sold vegetables from their gardens, eggs, chicken, milk, and whatever else they produced, at exorbitant prices. This was also a flea market where one could buy secondhand clothing, both civilian and military, and other things that people had to sell in order to eat. One day I bought two cans of fish. They looked somewhat swollen, but the soldier who was selling them assured me that they were perfectly good. However, as soon as I pierced one of them, I knew that I had been taken. The stench was as horrible as that of the decomposing cats or dogs, which in this part of the world no one had any incentive to bury unless they were near one's house. We kids watched these dead animals turn into skeletons as we passed by holding our noses. For a time I considered selling the second can of fish to someone as stupid as I, but my conscience did not permit it.

Once, when I went to the market to buy milk, I suddenly heard someone shouting "Raid! Raid!" Dozens of people, mostly in military uniforms, ran in all directions, pushing and shoving and stepping on wares spread out

on the ground. It was total pandemonium. The marketplace was surrounded by military police. As their ring continued closing in, we were herded
into one area, from which people were let out one at a time, after showing
their passports or military identifications. I had seen military policemen in
the past, roaming throughout the marketplace and checking men who
could be deserters, but this was something new. People were led away at
gunpoint and loaded onto trucks. Some were trying to hide in the few stalls
or under piles of old clothing. When my turn came, the policemen eyed my
Estonian tunic and its lion buttons with great suspicion and began asking
me who I was. I just handed them my passport, and after comparing my
face with the photograph several times they let me go. I did not stay around
to see how it all ended.

After several weeks, it became apparent that there was nothing for us in
Kremenchug and we decided to go back to Khmelnik. Without wasting
much time, we got onto a train going in that general direction. I carefully
studied the railroad network to make sure that we changed trains at the right
places, but there was no assurance that all lines had been restored and actually functioned. Because some lines had not yet been repaired, we had to
change trains several times, and instead of going south we wound up somewhere near Kiev. One night, while we were sitting in the ruins of the Fas-
tov station, waiting for a train that would take us closer to Vinnitsa, which
was the nearest large town to Khmelnik, we heard shooting outside and saw
soldiers running in all directions and crawling under trains. It turned out
that someone in military uniform had stabbed an officer while attempting
to rob him. Soon afterward we heard soldiers systematically going through
the station checking identifications.

"Take off the coat!" said Mother, with panic in her voice. In a situation
like this, soldiers could act as judges, jury, and executioners on the spot. I
quickly took off my military long coat, and when the soldiers eyed my Estonian jacket with suspicion, showed them my passport. Mother assured
them that I had been sitting there all night, and they passed on.

On the fourth day of what normally would have been a one-day trip, we
finally came to Vinnitsa, from where we took an antique narrow-gauge train

to Khmelnik. The wide-gauge tracks laid by Gulag prisoners before the war had not yet been restored. The station building in Khmelnik had been leveled, but there were several peasants with horse wagons awaiting the train in the hope of making some money.

Among the passengers was a woman whom Mother had known before the war. She was returning from Vinnitsa, where she had testified in court against a Ukrainian policeman who had served the Germans. She had a room, which she was renting to two women, but she thought it was large enough to accommodate us also. Mother agreed to give this a try until we could find something else, and we all piled onto a wagon.

CHAPTER 6

1944‒1945

We rode into Khmelnik on a cobblestone road, and except for the area around the station everything looked almost the same as it had three years earlier. There were, however, some signs of neglect. There were huge pot-holes in the road, and many of the houses were pockmarked with bullet holes. But when we entered the old section of town, we saw that the once noisy, smelly, lively area inhabited mostly by Jews had become a ghost town. There was not a single house with any sign of life. Not a single house had a roof, or a ceiling, or a door, or a window—there were only crumbling walls, stripped of every piece of wood or glass or metal for which the peasants could find use somewhere else. It was much grimmer than areas that had been bombed or burned. There one could somehow comprehend and ac-cept the total annihilation, horrific as it was, but here the walls were intact but dead; they stood silently like monuments in a cemetery.

We turned off the main road just before the bridge over the river and halted at the ruins of a house that I recognized because one of my classmates had lived in it. I stood where once had been the front door and looked into the former living room. Now there were just walls. Even the wooden floors had been removed and the rooms, which I remembered having visited, were being used as latrines. A small part in the back of the house remained in-tact; it contained a small room, a tiny kitchen, and one larger room. The landlady, Frieda, who had worked with Mother at the restaurant before the war, lived in the kitchen. In the tiny room lived a retired colonel who had

been wounded in both legs and stayed in bed most of the time. We were to
share the larger room with an old woman and her middle-aged daughter.

I asked Frieda about my classmate who had lived in this house. We had
not been close friends, but since his nickname was Tunchik and mine was
Tanchik, we had both been mercilessly teased and in our misery had developed a sense of solidarity. Frieda told me that he and his family, together
with most of the Jewish population, had been killed by the Nazis. She and
a few others remained alive by managing to escape to the part of Ukraine
that was occupied by the Romanians rather than the Germans. They had
returned only several months before, after the Germans were driven out.

Romania had been allied with Germany and its army had controlled the
southwestern part of Ukraine. The Romanian zone began only about forty
miles south of Khmelnik, at the railroad center called Zhmerinka, but getting there was not a simple matter. The Ukrainian police, organized by the
Germans, knew that the escapees carried whatever valuables they might
possess and, since the policemen could kill them on the spot without any
questions asked, it gave them an incentive to track down the poor souls.
However, some Jews managed to get through with the help of a sort of "underground railroad" run by Ukrainians who, for an appropriate amount of
money, smuggled them across.

Once there, the refugees were confined in labor camps, where most of
them survived. While the Romanian Fascist "Iron Guard" Party of General Ion Antonescu had its equivalent of the Gestapo, called the *Sigurantsa,*
and had persecuted Jews in Romania and killed tens of thousands of Jews
upon retaking Moldavia, the Romanian army in the Ukraine was more interested in an adequate labor force along its supply lines.

As soon as we had deposited our bundles in the corner of the room that
was assigned to us, I went outside. The house was on the edge of what had
been a beautiful park with ancient trees, across the river from the Gulag castle. While the castle was now empty, memories still made its gray stone walls
and towers menacing. The park had belonged to the castle and was surrounded by a high stone wall with a stone tower on each corner. Its Polish
owners obviously did not want anyone to peek in. Now the walls were just

rubble and there was not a single tree in sight—all had been cut down by the Germans, who may have intended to make a stand in the castle. My best friend Ben had lived on the other side of the park. I ran to his house, but there too were only crumbling walls. I found out later that after the Germans came, Ben went to stay with Ukrainian friends of the family in a nearby village. They kept him until harboring Jews became a capital offense, and then he had to leave. As he walked through the fields toward the town, a policeman spotted him and shot him dead.

The next day I wandered through the streets, searching in vain for familiar faces. Looking through the window of a bicycle repair shop, I recognized one of my classmates, Abrasha Elzon. It seemed that he had not grown during the three years since I had last seen him; indeed, while we had been of about equal height, now he was about a head shorter. I remembered him being very talkative, but now I had to pull the words out of him, and he did not look at me as he spoke. He told me that out of a dozen Jewish kids in our class, he was the sole survivor. He would not talk about himself or his family, who had lived in one of those pre-Revolutionary inns, like that of old Berkovich in Gorodok. He told me only about one boy, Tsula Lozovski, who was passing by our school, which was being used by German troops, as a group of soldiers were picnicking on the grass. They set their German shepherd on him, and it tore him to pieces as they laughed and ate their food.

I was told later that Abrasha's father had been appointed by the Germans to be the headman of the ghetto in the old part of town where all Jews were forced to move. This was a very precarious position, which some Jews took because there was need of some kind of organization in dealing with the Germans, while others took it in the hope of saving themselves and their families. However, for Abrasha's family this did not work: his father and mother were marched together with the rest of the Jews into the forest where I used to gather mushrooms, and were shot in a ditch. Peasants later told that the earth over the ditch moved for several days because not all of the buried people were dead. Lusia, the girl on whom I had a crush in the sixth grade, was among the victims. Abrasha also had an older sister who, after being raped by soldiers, drowned herself in the river.

A boy I knew, whose father was not Jewish, survived because as they were being marched to be shot, his mother screamed that he was not Jewish; she made him drop his pants to prove that he had not been circumcised, and a policeman let him go.

The Jewish population was not all shot at once, but rather in periodic pogroms of several hundred at a time. The Jewish headman had to provide names of those to be shot next, and the police then rounded them up. Small children were in the first group, torn from the arms of their mothers and thrown into the ditch alive. The order to exterminate the children was issued by the Ukrainian authorities and signed by Dr. Mazuruk, the pediatrician who years ago I had seen secretly praying before icons. The so-called justification was presumably to prevent the spread of a nonexisting epidemic. When the Germans retreated, Dr. Mazuruk took poison.

When the Germans entered the town, they were welcomed with the traditional bread and salt by a group of people who thought that they were being liberated from the Communists. They sang the forbidden Ukrainian national anthem, "Ukraine Has Not Died," expecting that Ukraine would now become an independent country and that land would be given back to the peasants. The Germans, however, had something else in mind. They kept the *kolkhozes* as they were, since they presented a good way of appropriating local products for the army and for shipment to Germany without having to deal with individual peasants. The Germans appointed a local administration and created a local police, which did most of the dirty work for them. There was no shortage of volunteers for such jobs because most people hated the Communists and it looked as though the Germans were winning the war and would remain forever.

After a while, the Germans demanded that the administration send young people to Germany to work on farms. At first they tried to entice volunteers through propaganda, and, since there was no work at home, many went. When they ran out of volunteers, they set monthly quotas, which the administration had to fulfill. The man in charge of sending people to Germany was our school music teacher, Ivan Ostapovich, a bald-headed, rotund, middle-aged man whom I had never seen smile. I was told that one group of people he had packed into a freight car destined for Germany had pulled him in and beaten him within an inch of his life. They then escaped and joined the Ukrainian nationalist partisans of Ostap Bendera, who were organized after the Nationalists figured out that the last thing the Germans wanted was an independent Ukraine. What they did want was *Lebensraum,* or "Living Space," into which they could expand.

While the Nazis considered Jews and Gypsies *Untermenschen* or subhumans destined to be exterminated, the Slavs, such as Ukrainians, Russians, Poles, and others, were *Mindervertige* or inferior; they were destined to serve the German *Herrenrasse* or the Aryan Master Race. (While Negroes were also classified as subhumans, I do not think that Hitler had any plans for their extermination as long as they remained in Africa.) This racial theory was promoted by Nazi scientists and was believed by many in and outside Germany. The ideal Aryan was supposed to be blond, tall, trim, and blue-eyed. This led to a joke in Germany that a true Aryan was as blond as Hitler, who had dark hair, as tall as Goebbels, the minister of propaganda, who was puny and had a club foot, and as trim as Goering, head of the Luftwaffe or German Air Force, who was obese.

Hitler was so sure of Aryan superiority that he agreed to personally congratulate the winner of the most gold medals in the 1936 Olympics in Berlin. However, when it became apparent that an *Untermensch*—black American athlete Jesse Owens—was going to be the winner with four gold medals, Hitler left the games.

Once it became clear that the Germans had not come as liberators, Ukrainian society split four ways. Collaborators served in the local government and in the police. Nationalists wanted Ukrainian independence and resisted the Germans. They also fought with the third group—Red Partisans or Communist guerrillas, who harassed the Germans behind the front lines. One of our upperclassmen, Vova Popov, became a leader of the local Communist guerrilla band, but while living in a dugout in the forest for three years he caught tuberculosis, and when I saw him he looked cadaverous, his yellow skin predicting he was not long for this world. Jews who managed to escape into the forests were turned away or killed by the Nationalists, and those who survived had no choice but to join the Red Partisans. The fourth group—the majority—were Ukrainian people who just wanted to live in peace and raise their families.

While some Germans were being welcomed at the edge of town on the road from the east, others also approached it from the west. When two German soldiers climbed onto the ruins of the bridge that had been blown up by the retreating Red Army, machine-gun fire from across the river killed one of them and wounded the other. While the Red Army had abandoned the town, a local soldier had barricaded himself in one of the cement bunkers that was hidden under a building overlooking the river; he fought off the Germans until he ran out of ammunition and was blown up, together with the bunker.

Immediately after the Germans arrived, the population received a foretaste of what was to come. The streets of the town were deserted except for the town idiot, Berele, who approached a German staff car. He was shot dead on the spot and his body lay in the street for several days until some Jews were permitted to bury him.

I went to the house where we had lived when the war began, on the edge of the Jewish section, where both Ukrainians and Jews lived side by side for many years. But while the houses of the Ukrainians stood as before, of Bida's house there remained only dirty walls, without doors, window frames, or floorboards. I wandered from room to room, looking for at least a shred of paper or a torn photograph—anything that could testify that this place had once been inhabited by living, breathing, and feeling human beings. But there was nothing, not a trace of me, my family, or of the old Bidas. Again I had the feeling as though I were wandering among gravestones in a cemetery. It was just as quiet, as lifeless, and as sad. Even the birds seemed to shun it, and there were no swallows' or sparrows' nests. Neither was there an attic, from whose rafters bats, hanging upside down, could contemplate this upside-down world, trying to make sense of it. It certainly did not make sense to me, and I could not decide who I hated more, the Nazis or the Communists.

Wandering through the ruins, I thought of the pious landlord Bida and his kindly wife. Honoring the Sabbath by not turning on the lights had not done them much good. The God of the Jews did not protect His children. Christianity did not have the answer either. After all, Germany had been Christian for at least a thousand years. Also, I had seen with my own eyes the monstrous pediatrician Mazuruk taking chances to worship his God, who preached universal love. Was it science and culture that had the power to make humans human? I had to doubt this also. Had not Germany been one of the most advanced countries in both?

I went to the house of my friend Dima, with whom I used to gather mushrooms, and saw his younger brother Vitya. He told me that Dima had lied about his age and joined the Red Army when they liberated the town. Later, I found out that his mother had worked for the Germans. Dima was probably trying to expiate her sins. One of the two granddaughters of Dr. Mazuruk did the same thing. I also stopped by the house where we had lived for a year before we moved to the Bidas' and saw a man with a long white beard standing on a ladder and fixing something on the roof. I asked whether the Korol family was still living there, and he replied that that was his name. Only then did I recognize him as our landlord. He told me that he had grown the beard to fool the Germans into thinking that he was very old, so that they would not check his documents every time they saw him. His son, Kolya, who was older than me, was drafted into the Red Army as it swept through the town on its way to Poland.

While the town began regaining some functions of Soviet normalcy with its NKVD and party offices, there was no work to be had that Mother could do, since the restaurant and food stores had not yet reopened. The cooperative *artel* had reopened and was busy repairing shoes and sewing clothing. I probably could have gotten a job as an apprentice, but Mother would not even hear of this. My job was to become an engineer, and the school year was about to begin.

The bakery was also functioning, and while our ration cards included coupons for fat and meat, the ration of bread was only 400 grams per person. The only place where one could obtain other food was at the bazaar, where peasants sold produce from their backyard gardens and war invalids in tattered uniforms sold pencils and paper, needles and thread, tobacco and matches, plus almost anything else essential for life. Many of these invalids lacked an arm or a leg and hobbled along on crutches or wooden legs. Some had disfigured faces, having been caught in a burning tank or hit by shrapnel.

To me they were heroes, but to the militiamen they were "speculators," a very derogatory term in Soviet society, applied to people who sold things at higher prices than they had paid for them. Before the war this was a criminal offense, but now the militiamen were afraid to tackle the veterans, who did not hesitate to use their crutches to protect their means of earning a living. There was a great deal of solidarity among them and when the militia tried to arrest one of them, it usually resulted in a riot, as they all ran or crawled, depending on their wounds, to the rescue, swinging their crutches. Their response to any interference was, "I shed my blood for you, you s.o.b. How do you dare tell me what to do?" They were frequently drunk and were virtually untouchable, traveling on trains without permits or tickets and bringing merchandise from distant places, where it was sold to them by intermediaries of corrupt factory managers, thieving warehouse workers, or *kolkhoz* managers who wanted to make some money on the side.

Mother exhibited a commercial ability that neither she nor I had suspected she possessed. After unsuccessfully looking for a job for a couple of weeks, she studied the prices at the bazaar and decided to go to a larger city to see if she could buy something at a price that would bring a profit. She bribed a train conductor, who let her ride without a permit or a ticket to Zhitomir, a city of about 100,000 people that was also a rail center. Several days later she returned carrying twenty liters (about five gallons) of sunflower-seed oil, which she sold at the bazaar at a good profit. Sunflower oil was the best edible oil available, the only other kind being rapeseed oil, which had an unpleasant taste. Having been successful the first time, Mother went to Zhitomir again and again, every couple of weeks, and soon was making enough money not just to survive but also to buy good shoes and better clothing for all of us.

The room we shared with the two women contained two beds, a small table, and two chairs. Mother and Vilya slept in one bed and I slept on a straw mattress on the floor. Kerosene for the lamp was very expensive and so were beeswax candles. I made a "soot-maker" like the one we used in Kazakhstan, but our landlady did not like the soot stain it created on the ceiling, so our only choice was either to sit in the dark or to go to sleep at sundown.

There were small ceramic insulators on the ceilings of the rooms, indicating that at one time there had been electricity in the house. From somewhere I scrounged a roll of plastic-coated wire, which I twisted together and strung between the insulators. The wire looked rather thin, but it was the only thing available. I also found a couple of lightbulb sockets and suspended one from the ceiling of each room. I then ran the ends of the wires through the outside wall and twisted together one wire from each socket. Frieda found some lightbulbs. Now all that was missing was electricity. There was an electric pole in the street, but I did not dare climb it to connect my wires and went instead to the power plant to get an electrician. The manager of the office carefully studied my Estonian tunic and must have decided that it would be safer to help me than to deny me. The electrician, who appeared within an hour, looked at my handiwork and declared that the wires were meant for field telephones and might set the house on fire. But after I gave him a few rubles, he decided that it was worth trying, since the lightbulbs were of low wattage and would not draw much power. He ran two wires from the pole to the house and, on one of them, installed a ceramic piece with two holes. The wire from the pole went into one hole and the wire from the house into the second. He connected the ends of the two wires with a small section of wire that was thinner than the wires in the house; it would act as a fuse, burning up before the wires in the house could catch fire.

There was no electricity during the day, but when the lights went on in the evening, I became an instant hero. However, the service was very unreliable and the lights could go off at any time for an indefinite period.

Having lived in cramped conditions with strangers for several years, the situation for me was normal. I would have considered having privacy a luxury that, while desirable, was not absolutely necessary. We dressed and undressed either in the dark or under a blanket, and we washed outside with the help of a small water tank with a plunger on the bottom. The tank was attached to a post, and when one pushed the plunger upward with cupped hands, water ran into them until one stopped pushing. When it was cold or raining we washed in a small basin in the hallway. While it was still warm, we bathed in the river. When it was cold, we did not wash, and hoped that the town bathhouse would reopen soon. In any event, it felt good to be able to change one's underwear, socks, and shirts once a week again, whether they were dirty or not.

The real problem was the toilet. It bothered me every time I had to go in the rooms where people used to live. I remembered being there, and visualized their ghosts disapprovingly shaking their heads. In addition, all the floors were pretty much covered and there were no dung beetles here to clean up. Also, since there were no doors, whenever we heard footsteps, we had to cough to warn of the newcomer. The colonel talked about using his influence to get building materials for an outhouse from the town government, but it was long in coming.

The town library had been destroyed, so there was nothing to read. I hoped that when the school year started there would be books in the school library. Every now and then I found pieces of Ukrainian newspapers from the time of the occupation and eagerly read the anti-Communist diatribes. It was such a novelty and thrill to see things in print for which one could have been shot. Most of the articles blamed the Jews for creating communism. It is true that Karl Marx was of Jewish origin, but so was Jesus, whom the Ukrainians worshipped. It was also true that many Jews, who had been discriminated against and frequently persecuted during the czar's time, joined Lenin, who was not a Jew, in fomenting the Revolution. But I believe that, percentage-wise, as many Jews later became victims of the Communists as did people of any other group, and of all the anti-Communists, it was a Jewish woman, Fanya Kaplan, who had the courage to shoot Lenin and accelerate his demise.

After a while, as the colonel's legs were healing, he began appearing from the room behind the kitchen; occasionally he even talked to us, mostly condescendingly. He was a party member, which got him a job with the local party apparatus. He was assigned an empty house across the street from us, and it was being fixed up and furnished for him. When it was finished, he brought over his wife and daughter. They were big-city people, used to indoor plumbing, and did not like living in a provincial town. Their daughter was a year or two older than I and, in city fashion, used lipstick and face powder, not the fashion among provincial teenagers. Since she did not know anyone in town, she spent a great deal of time with us. When no one was home she introduced me to heavy petting, which I rather enjoyed, but she insisted on doing it also when the lights went out, sitting next to me on the bed, with the room full of people. Since the lights could go on at any moment, my heart was not in this, but she seemed to like living dangerously.

I was very glad when the school year started. There were only about fifteen students in the tenth grade, which was the senior grade at that time. Only three or four of us were of the right age, not having missed any time or, in my case, having made up for it. The others were three years older, because for them there was no school during the years of occupation. Only one of the older students was a boy, Kolya Bezsonov, who was not in the army because he had lost one arm in an accident. He also liked to read and managed to draw with one hand much better than I could with two; we became good friends.

As before, my favorite subject was Russian literature. This may also have been influenced by the fact that it was taught by Elizaveta Semyonovna, who was only in her twenties but had already lost a husband in the war. She was from a large city and, in addition to wearing lipstick and powdering her face, plucked her eyebrows into thin arches, which gave her a somewhat owlish appearance. But she was quite pretty and was courted by all the party bigwigs, which made us boys very jealous. Behind her back we called her Lizochka, a diminutive and endearing form of her name.

Vilya, who was by then seven years old, started first grade. Initially, he had some problems because he had forgotten Ukrainian, since in Kazakhstan he spoke only Russian. But it did not take him very long to recall the language. In spite of confusing some words that were similar or were pronounced only slightly differently in both languages, he managed.

When it became cold, I went to the *artel* hat maker, who made me a magnificent hat. It was called a *kubanka* because it was like the hats worn by the Cossacks who lived along the river Kuban' in the northern Caucasus. Its cylindrical sides, about five inches high, were of light-gray karakul, which is the fur of a very young lamb. It was glossy and wavy, unlike the fur of an older lamb, which is curly. The flat top of the hat was dark blue, with two narrow green strips intersecting at a right angle; at one time this may have signified a specific Cossack cavalry regiment.

The hat made me look even more like a military man, so much so that one morning our military preparedness instructor handed me a rifle and ordered me to go to the party headquarters to stand honor guard for two dead colonels who were lying there in state. One of them had a mother in a nearby village and, when passing through this area, had decided to visit her with his friend in a military jeep. They went without an escort, because the front line was several hundred miles away and there did not seem to be any danger. They probably did not know that Bendera's nationalist guerrillas remained in the forest after the Red Army had returned, because the Communists did not want it to be known that they were not in complete control. The guerrillas saw them driving through the forest and shot both of them dead. It was very tragic and ironic for a soldier to survive all the battles, only to be shot near his village, probably by his former neighbors.

There was an officer in charge of the funeral, and he scheduled me and a real soldier to alternate standing at attention at the head of the open coffins, an hour at a time. This task was made difficult by the fact that, while I had to stand at attention, I simply could not let flies crawl all over their faces, and every so often shooed them away. All local dignitaries, civilian and military, came to pay their respects. Some of them stared at my tunic, which unlike Red Army officers' jackets buttoned up all the way to the neck, and at the three lions on its buttons instead of a star, but under the circumstances no one asked for an explanation.

Because the guerrillas were supported and hidden by their families, the government began exiling all relatives of suspected guerrillas. They were packed into railroad freight cars and the doors were locked—according to rumors, the doors were not opened again until they were in Siberia or somewhere in the far-north region.

While the authorities dealt severely with nationalists, they did not seem very eager to prosecute those who had collaborated with the Germans. The bigger fish, like our former music teacher, ran away to Germany, but the smaller ones were left alone, at least for the time being. Several policemen were caught and imprisoned in Vinnitsa, the regional capital. However, when some of the surviving Jews wanted to testify against them, they were given a run-around to such an extent that many gave up trying, because travel was difficult, there was no place to stay, and they could not take that much time off from work. Our landlady, Frieda, thought that their testimony was not wanted because the crimes they had committed had been mostly against Jews.

As time went on, some of the survivors began forming families; widowers were marrying widows, bringing together children from both sides, and soon one heard laughter and jokes and music. It is a miracle of human nature that we can bury the past and continue even after the most horrible traumas.

I made friends with some of my former classmates, who now were in the seventh grade, while I was in the tenth. Some, like Abrasha Elson, the bicycle mechanic, did not come back to school, which was a pity because he had been one of the top students before the war, but he now had to work in order to survive. Completing the seventh grade had a special significance because, in the ponderous language of officialdom, it was called an "Incomplete Middle-Level Education," upon completion of which one could go to a technical school to become a technician, or to other semiprofessional schools, such as that for paramedics. After the tenth grade, or "Complete Middle-Level Education," one could apply to a university, which I hoped to do by concealing that I was the son of an "enemy of the people." I planned to tell them that my father died in the war, and in the general postwar confusion there was a chance that I could have gotten away with it. In those heady days, when victory over Germany was assured and the atmosphere was less stringent and menacing than before the war, the general hope was that in gratitude for all the sacrifices by the people, Stalin would mitigate the terror and, as the Russian expression goes, would let the people breathe more freely.

Nevertheless, I had to be careful to avoid embarrassing situations. In our class was a petite blonde girl with an angelic smile, named Olya (diminutive for Olga). I liked her very much and it seemed that she had a crush on me. She was not only pretty but also sang like an angel, accompanying herself on a guitar. But her father was the chief of the NKVD, so I never accepted an invitation to their house, even with other kids, because I was afraid that her parents might ask me about my father. Knowing how much I loved her singing, she could not understand why I always had an excuse for not going and was very hurt by it.

Frequently, the newly formed families incorporated a child who had lost both parents. This was done informally, without adoption papers. My friend Fima's family took in an orphaned girl, so that he acquired a stepsister and also an informal sister, both about our age. Since I never had a sister, I greatly enjoyed visiting them. They had a wind-up gramophone and the girls attempted to teach me to dance the waltz, foxtrot, and tango. We had as much

fun as any normal teenagers. Only now and then one of the girls would suddenly gaze into the distance and her eyes would fill with tears. In their house
I saw a shiny, nickel-plated samovar, which I recognized as having been ours,
because one of the small knobs was cracked and I remembered having broken it. I told Mother about it, but there was no point in bringing it up with
my friends. They deserved to have it.

Several times Mother went to Gorodok in the hope that Father might
have been there looking for us, or that there might be a letter from him at
the post office. But no one had heard from him and there were no letters.

The people of Gorodok suffered the same fate as those of Khmelnik. A
large part of the town became a ghost town, and every Jewish person who
had not managed to escape to the Romanian zone had been shot in a ditch
in the forest.

Mother continued her buying trips to Zhitomir. After one of them she
announced that she had met a nice man who had proposed to her. He was
from Poland and intended to return there, which meant that we might have
an opportunity to leave this cursed country. But the thought of getting out
of the Soviet Union was so unrealistic that, while I often dreamed about it,
I could not believe that it would ever be possible.

I felt I had little say about Mother's intentions. After all, she was only in
her mid-thirties, and the chance that, after more than six years of being lost,
Father would return was practically nil. Also, at around that time I had
found a newspaper article about a mass grave containing about eight hundred corpses that had been discovered in the backyard of the NKVD building in Vinnitsa. This was the place where we were told that Father had been
imprisoned. I found the article in a Ukrainian newspaper from the time of
the German occupation.

While I had difficulty visualizing Mother being married to someone other than Father, I also knew that in a few short months I would either be in
the army or perhaps in college, living away from home. Therefore I did not
think that I had the right to influence her one way or the other.

Several weeks later, upon returning from her trip, Mother said that she
was now married and that we were moving to Zhitomir. I got transfer pa-

pers from school and said good-bye to my friends. We packed our few belongings, and off we went to begin a new life in a big city.

Mother's husband's name was Solomon Steinberg. He was a Polish Jew from a town named Radomsko in the western part of Poland. He was about forty-five years old and about Mother's height. When the Germans took over that part of Poland in 1939, he managed to escape with his family to the eastern part, which the Soviets had occupied. When the Germans came in 1941, he and his family wound up in a ghetto, where his wife and a daughter were killed, while he with another daughter and a young son managed to escape and hid in the forest with the Red Partisans. During a German attack his ten-year-old son was killed, and he himself was shot through both legs. The daughter, who was twelve, found shelter with some Polish peasants until the Germans retreated. He managed to escape and was with the partisans until the Soviet army returned, when he found his daughter. He wore army clothes, including puttees, walked on crutches, and was one of those war invalids or "speculators" who were traveling without tickets and passes, buying things here and selling them there. Before the war he bought grain from peasants, had it milled, and sold the flour to bakeries.

Both he and his daughter, Ruzka, who was now thirteen, spoke very little Russian or Ukrainian, but managed somehow to get by with Polish. Ruzka was always on edge and did not hide her resentment of Mother, who tried her best to be nice to her. All five of us lived in one room that had two beds, one for Mother and Solomon and one for Ruzka, and a table with four chairs. Vilya and I slept together on a mattress on the floor. During the first night I was awakened by an almost inhuman shriek. "Wake up, Ruzka!" shouted Solomon. "She has these nightmares every night. I cannot get any sleep!" he mumbled. Indeed, Ruzka screamed every night. We eventually became used to it.

We shared the kitchen with the landlady and with another tenant family. The landlady had taken in a teenage orphan girl who had large, sad blue eyes that were often filled with tears. The landlady treated her like a servant, frequently reminding her that she was being fed and sheltered, and owed a great deal of gratitude. Neither Ruzka nor the girl went to school. Vilya also stayed home with Mother, who did the cooking. I was happy to get away from the place and did not hurry home from school.

Solomon turned out to have a vile temper, something Mother was not accustomed to, because Father had never raised his voice to her. More than once, when Solomon thought that the food was too salty or did not like it for some other reason, he would say that when something like this happened with his first wife, he would shove everything on the table onto the floor. He must have thought that this was a macho thing to do. Mother cried, and I walked out of the house. I told Mother many times that we should go back to Khmelnik, but she always replied that she could not support us alone and that she did not want me to quit school.

Between his outbursts, however, Solomon was not a bad guy. Other than buying and selling he did not have any interests, never read a book, so we did not have much to talk about. He considered himself a Socialist and may have been a member of the Jewish Bund, whose leaders Erich and Alter were executed by the Soviets, presumably for being Polish spies. This membership was Solomon's big secret, because wherever the Communists had taken over, they exterminated the Socialists first. As I understood it, the reason for this was that the Socialists were competitors for the allegiance of those who, like both parties, believed that private property should be abolished and everything should be owned and controlled by the state. The main difference between them was that the Communists believed in a "dictatorship of the proletariat." Since they claimed to represent the proletariat, they meant a dictatorship of the Communist Party with its "Supreme Leader."

The Socialists, on the other hand, believed in a democratic way of abolishing private property and allowed for more than one political party. The German "National Socialists," or Nazis, and the Italian Fascists allowed some private property, but it had to be controlled by the state. The state, in turn, was controlled by a single party and a "Supreme Leader," who had to be from their national group. As far as we were concerned, from a practical point of view, the only difference between the Communists and the Nazis was that the Nazis killed innocent people because of their ethnic affiliation, while the Communists killed innocent people because of political or class affiliations, real or imaginary.

My new school was a Russian-language "Gymnasium for Men," which was a pre-Revolutionary name for a high school for boys. The old name and separation of the sexes were considered to be a sign of possible political liberalization, because if someone had suggested a school like this before the war, he probably would have been shot as a counterrevolutionary. With the war going on, the authorities were trying to win over as many people as they could, and had even permitted reopening some churches. Since most priests had been shot, the rumor was that the new priests were actually Communist Party members, assigned to act as priests.

There were only about twenty boys in my class, and there was a lot of camaraderie. However, as much as we enjoyed all-male company, we still wanted to meet girls. Occasionally, the Women's Gymnasium held a dance where we stepped on each other's toes to the rhythms of a wind-up gramophone, but this was not the same as being with girls on a daily basis.

One of the boys in my class, Misha Volosevich, was the son of a general. Because his name sounded Polish, the general was assigned to the Polish army and wore a Polish uniform even though he did not speak Polish. Later, he was given a high position in the Polish Communist government, set up by the Soviets in the city of Lublin, with the Polish Communist named Boleslaw Bierut as president. There was also a democratically elected Polish government-in-exile in London, headed by General Wladyslaw Sikorski, and there was a big argument between Stalin on one side and Roosevelt and Churchill on the other as to which government should govern Poland after the war. In Russian, *Bierut* means "they are taking," and a secret joke among Poles was that they would have much preferred to have a president named *Dayut*, which means "they are giving."

Misha and a big, burly boy named Petya Kotikov, whom we called *Kotik,* which means kitten, became my friends. In our bull sessions we discussed all kinds of subjects, including many injustices, such as that freed Soviet prisoners of war were being sent to Siberia as traitors. I did not tell them about my father and was careful not to say anything too provocative. Misha, on the other hand, was very idealistic and outspoken. Several times I cautioned him that even as the son of a general, he should watch what he was saying. "But this is such an obvious injustice!" he would respond with indignation. "We all know that," I would say, "but we should not talk about it aloud." Kotik also never talked about his father, and I suspected that his background was similar to mine. He was more reticent than Misha to voice his opinions.

It was winter, which in that part of the world means snow on the ground from early December through February or March. My shoes were inadequate for this, and Solomon paid for a pair of high boots to be made for me by a cobbler, who measured my feet and presumably selected lasts that corresponded to them. The soles of the boots were attached to the uppers by small wooden pegs about half an inch long, with the cross section like a wooden match. To lubricate them the cobbler kept them in his mouth, pulling them out one at a time and hammering them into the holes that he made with an awl. I wondered whether he swallowed any of them when he sneezed.

Unfortunately, either because his measurements were inaccurate or he did not have the right size of lasts, the boots turned out to be too tight, and no amount of stretching on expandable lasts would make them comfortable. The boots, together with my military great coat and the *kubanka* hat, made me look even more like a military man, and I constantly had to show my passport to military police patrols that were hunting for deserters. Some policemen eyed me with a great deal of suspicion, not believing that I was only sixteen. Most of the time, seeing that I still did not shave, they accepted it without much argument. However, on one occasion my military appearance almost got me shot.

One crisp, sunny afternoon when recently fallen snow crunched agreeably underfoot, I rounded a corner, engrossed in thought and watching the ground to avoid ice patches on the sidewalk, when I heard an obviously drunken voice shouting: "There is a military patrolman! He is after us!" When I raised my eyes, I was looking into the barrel of a gun only about ten feet away. Two drunken officers were shakily supporting one another, one of them pointing a large military pistol right in my face. I froze in place numb with horror and, as in a slow-motion nightmare, watched his finger slowly pulling the trigger. There was no time to run or fall down, or to call for help. Like a bird mesmerized by a snake, I was unable to move or even think.

"No, he is not after us," I heard the other officer say as I saw him push the hand holding the pistol to the side. The shot rang out and the bullet ricocheted from the stone wall of the building behind me. I did not stay around to see what was going to happen next.

By the spring of 1945 the Germans had retreated from most of Poland, and Solomon found out that former Polish citizens who had lived in the western part of Ukraine that had belonged to Poland before the war could be repatriated to Poland, provided that they were not ethnic Ukrainians. So it appeared that my dream of getting out of this giant prison might be realized after all. We discussed this a great deal, deciding that from Poland it might be possible to get to America, where many people from Poland and Russia had emigrated before the Communist Revolution. In spite of the propaganda about all the misery in America with which we had been continuously bombarded, it was still a common belief that in America everyone had a chance to prosper. As the saying went, "The streets there are paved with gold and one only has to know how to pick it up."

I had read an interesting book by a Ukrainian writer, Vladimir Korolenko, entitled *Without a Tongue*, about a peasant who came to America not knowing a word of English. At the outset he was exploited by his former compatriots who overcharged him for room and board and, having found him a job, took part of his pay, but eventually he did find his place and some contentment. I thought that if an illiterate peasant could do it, then so could I.

I was so excited about the possibility of emigration that I foolishly put caution aside and told my friends at school about it. Much to my surprise, both Kotik and Misha, the son of a general, made me promise that I would write to them and advise them how to get to America.

Mother and Solomon went to the western Ukraine and found a place to live in a small town called Zdolbunov, where Solomon had lived after his escape from western Poland in 1939. We moved there in the spring of 1945, and I attended a Russian school, which was opened for the children of railroad workers and other functionaries who kept the railroad running after the Germans retreated. One of my classmates, Valera, was the son of the school principal, who also taught history. Valera was a spoiled brat, a member of the new generation who grew up in privileged Communist families. He was not interested in school and thought only of girls, vodka, and cigarettes. His parents were very upset about this, and his father encouraged me to visit them, in the hope that some of my eagerness to learn might rub off on Valera. We did not have much in common, however, and he was no more interested in my company than I was in his.

We lived in two rooms of a three-room house in which the rooms were in sequence, so that the landlord and his wife, who occupied the last room, had to pass through the other rooms to reach their own. I shared a bed with Vilya in the room next to the landlords and Ruzka slept in another bed in the same room. At least once every night, and frequently more than once, Ruzka's terrified screams made me jump up. At the beginning I had trouble going back to sleep, but after a while I began incorporating her screams into my own dreams, which did not make them pleasant ones.

Solomon continued his business of traveling to Kiev, the capital of the Ukrainian Republic, where he somehow procured pencils, pens, and notebooks that he resold to black market dealers who in turn sold them at the bazaar. Sometimes Mother traveled with him, and on these occasions he entrusted me with his whole fortune, which consisted of about fifty or sixty "piglets," or pre-Revolutionary ten-ruble gold coins. There was no place to hide them safely in the house; they were tied in a handkerchief, which he instructed me to carry in my pocket. So there I was, walking around with all these gold coins, for each one of which, if they only knew I possessed them, many people would have slit my throat.

The people in town were primarily Polish and Ukrainian, with a few Chech families and a few Jews who had managed to survive. Unlike Khmelnik, Zdolbunov did not have a Jewish section that had been turned into a ghost town. It did have a park with a soccer field, and its streets were relatively clean. Most Poles were planning to leave for Poland and were selling whatever they could. The land, which had been their major possession before the Soviets came in 1939, had already been confiscated.

A young Polish man whom Solomon knew from before the war asked me to witness his signature on an important document. I agreed, and one morning he picked me up in a horse carriage. We traveled a long way on dirt roads through fields that were being plowed by horse-pulled plows, until we reached a sprawling house in the forest, where we were greeted by an old man with a long gray beard. During Polish times he had been a lawyer and he had prepared a certificate, describing the land that had been owned by the man who brought me. "Someday, when the Communists are gone, I am going to claim my land back!" he said in all seriousness.

At a time when the Red Army was entering Germany, to believe that someday they would be gone seemed to me the height of absurdity. But I only smiled and signed the papers. Little did I know that fifty years later he would be proved right. We solemnized the occasion with half a glass of good moonshine, after which we munched on half-sour pickles. On our way back we encountered a funeral and, as was the custom, I took off my hat. The Polish man did not take off his. "It's only a Ukrainian," he said. "I do not take off my hat to them."

It was not very safe to travel through forests where Bendera's guerrillas were still active, but as their families were being deported, more and more of them were giving up and surrendering. I saw whole columns of them, mostly young men with lost expressions on their faces, being marched to the nearby town of Rovno, where they were "processed" and shipped off to Siberia. Often, perhaps a hundred of them would be guarded by only two militia men, but they had no place to run and their fighting spirit was gone.

It was Passover, and the few Jews in town got together to bake matzos. The process started with kneading the dough in a wooden trough that had been hollowed out from a log. Since no yeast was added, it did not have to rise and was ready immediately. Chunks of the dough were pinched off the mass and rolled with wooden rolling pins into thin, round disks about the size of a large dinner plate that were then pricked with forks all over the surface. Sprinkled with flour on both sides to prevent sticking, they were then shoved into the hot oven with large wooden shovels. The oven had been preheated by burning wood logs, and the glowing charcoals were pushed over to the sides, leaving a clear area for the baking matzos, which filled the room with a warm, sweet aroma. After a few seconds in the oven the mat-zo disks were crisp and covered with tiny brown blisters, which stood out against the white background. I was warned not to eat too much, but the crunchy warm matzo was so delicious that I did not follow this advice and wound up with a stomachache.

This was a community project including a few slugs of moonshine and a great deal of joviality. Most of the mixing and kneading was done by men, who also took turns at the hot oven, wiping their sweating brows with towels. Women did most of the rolling and stacking of the finished matzos, which were then distributed to the participants according to their contributions. They were carried away in clean pillowcases, which served as convenient carriers for all sorts of things. Mother remembered participating in similar affairs in her childhood, and she thoroughly enjoyed it, as did I.

These people spoke mostly Yiddish, an archaic form of German with some Hebrew and many Polish, Russian, and Ukrainian words. With my rudimentary high-school German I began to understand it quite well. There were two major dialects of Yiddish: that of the Baltic countries, called the Litvak dialect, and that of the rest of Eastern Europe, called the Galicianer dialect, after a province of Ukraine called Galicia in Polish. It has absolutely nothing to do with Galicia in Spain.

As an example: "What is this?" in German is *"Was* (pronounced VAS) *ist das?"* In Litvak it is *"Vos iz dos?"* and in Galicianer it would be *"Vous iz dous?"* All this is pronounced in a lilting, singsong fashion by the unschooled and crisply by the educated. There is a great deal of literature in Yiddish, some of which I had read in Ukrainian or Russian translation.

In general, at the matzo-bake, a good time was had by all, and I marveled at how these people, most of whom had lost their families and had been hunted like animals a few months earlier, could appear so normal and have such fun.

The Passover dinner, or *Seder,* was a more solemn occasion, with Solomon reading endless prayers in Hebrew that no one, including himself, understood. A door to the outside was left open so that the ghost of Elija, who, as I was told, was an ancient prophet, could come in and partake of the special food commemorating the time when God led the Jews out of Egypt. But while God was being praised for this great deed, I could not help wondering where He had been during the last several years; the observance of this ancient ritual, while interesting, did not do anything to convince me.

We had applied for repatriation to Poland with Solomon, and after three months received the appropriate papers. On May 8, 1945, we and several other families were packed into the familiar freight car and transported west, toward the new border with Poland, which was only about a hundred miles away. At the border, the train stopped for the night.

Around midnight, we were awakened by gunfire coming from all sides;

it kept on for what seemed like hours. The only explanation we could think of was that Bendera's nationalist guerrillas were storming the railroad station, which did not bode well for us. Women cried, men swore, but there was nothing we could do. We did not know where they were and it did not make sense even to try running into the darkness.

Eventually, through a crack in the door, we saw soldiers who were firing their guns, but they were firing them into the air. "What is going on?" we shouted through the din. "The war is over!" they shouted back. "Hitler *kaput!*"

The next morning several border guards entered the train. They looked as though they had giant hangovers, and their inspection was very perfunctory. As the train crossed the border, I could not believe that I was actually out of the Soviet Union. Even though the Soviet army was also on this side of the border, I was in another country.

As frequently happens to me on emotional occasions, an appropriate poem came to my mind and kept obsessively repeating itself over and over. It was by the great Russian poet Mikhail Lermontov, when he was exiled for writing a scathing poem accusing Russian society of hounding the other great poet, Aleksandr Pushkin, to his death. Freely translated, the poem that haunted me now went something like this:

> Farewell to you, unwashed Russia,
> The land of lords, the land of slaves,
> And to the uniforms of pashas,
> And population that obeys.
> Perhaps beyond the wall of mountains
> I'll find a way to disappear
> From eyes that see around corners,
> And from the all-discerning ears.

CHAPTER 7

1945–1946

Our first stop in Poland was Lublin, the seat of the government that had been set up by the Soviets in violation of the agreement struck with Roosevelt and Churchill, who insisted that Poland already had a government-in-exile in London. The Soviets had initially recognized this government, but after it protested the execution by the NKVD of thousands of captured Polish officers in the Katyn Forest, the recognition was withdrawn and the government-in-exile was accused of being composed of Fascist stooges.

On the other side of the platform at which we had halted stood another freight train full of people, but heading in the opposite direction. These were Ukrainians who were being "repatriated" from Polish territory in an exchange of populations. Former Polish citizens from western Ukraine, which before the war was part of Poland, were going to Poland, while ethnic Ukrainians living west of the new border were presumably going to be resettled in Ukraine. The new border ran along the so-called Curzon Line, along which the Soviets and Nazis had divided Poland in 1939.

The doors of the other freight cars were also open, and I could see that they were as tightly packed with people as we were.

"Hey, how about exchanging hats?" shouted a young man standing in the doorway of the car opposite us. "You will not survive very long in Poland with that Cossack hat: the NSZ will shoot you on sight!" I had no idea what the NSZ was, but found out later that these letters stood for National

Armed Forces, or Polish nationalist guerrillas, who had fought against both the Soviets and the Germans.

"I will take my chances," I shouted back. "Where are you people going?" "Just across the border, to be resettled in Ukraine," he replied.

I hesitated for a moment, not knowing whether to tell him what I knew to be the truth. "They are taking you to Siberia!" I finally said. "They will lock the doors at the border and will not open them until you get there."

"Go to hell," he shouted. "You are just trying to scare me!"

"You will see," I shouted back. "You have been warned!"

The next day we arrived in the suburb of Warsaw called Praga. Praga is on the eastern shore of the River Vistula, while the main part of Warsaw is on the western shore. The railroad bridges across the river had not yet been restored, so this was the end of the line. We got off and sat on our bundles, while Solomon hobbled away on his crutches. In a couple of hours he returned with a horse wagon driven by a peasant, which was to take us across the river over a temporary pontoon bridge, to a train station on the other side of Warsaw. There we were to take a train to the town of Radomsko, where Solomon had lived before the war.

While I had seen partially destroyed cities in Ukraine, Warsaw was something else. As far as one could see there were only crumbling walls and piles of bricks. I walked alongside the wagon clear across the city and did not see a single building that was intact—only endless rows of ruins on both sides of the road. But, in spite of its appearance, this city was not dead. People popped up from the ruins and disappeared into them like groundhogs. Here and there temporary roofs of corrugated metal or wooden planks covered parts of the space between crumbling brick walls on the lower floors of what had been multistory buildings; the remaining parts of the upper floors loomed menacingly above them.

The destruction of Warsaw had begun on the very first day of the war, September 1, 1939, when the Luftwaffe bombed the city. Poland had a ten-year nonaggression treaty with Germany that still had five years to run, but on August 23, 1939, the Ribbentrop-Molotov Pact (named after the two foreign ministers) had been signed, dividing Poland between Germany and the Soviet Union. Seven days later, the German army attacked. One would have thought that, seeing Germany break its treaty with Poland, the Soviets might have expected that their own treaty with the Nazis, which was also supposed to last ten years, could be broken as well; Stalin, however, did not seem to believe that this would happen.

The next phase of Warsaw's destruction came in April 1943, when unarmed Jews in the city's ghetto rose up and fought the Germans for three weeks, until the entire square mile containing the ghetto had been completely leveled.

The final destruction began when the Soviet army reached the Vistula in 1944. The Polish resistance movement, called the Home Army, was ordered by the government-in-exile to liberate Warsaw in the hope that this would establish them as the legitimate government of Poland. On August 1, 1944, they started an uprising. The Home Army was ordered to cooperate with the Red Army, on the assumption that the Soviets would continue their advance and would soon cross the river to join them in battle.

But Stalin was not about to let Poles beat him to Warsaw, and even though a joint action would have saved the lives of many of his soldiers, he halted his army at the Vistula's eastern shore. For two months the Soviets watched from across the river, which is only a few hundred yards wide, as the German army ground Warsaw into rubble, exterminating everyone in sight and dispatching all captives, including noncombatants, to concentration camps. The Soviets did not even interfere with the Luftwaffe planes bombing the city. The rebels fought from house to house with captured weapons, but eventually ran out of food and ammunition. The Polish government in London appealed to the Allies for help, but the distance was such that, to be effective, Western airplanes would have had to refuel at Soviet airports for the return trip, which Stalin refused to permit. In reprisal, Churchill wanted to suspend all supply shipments to the Soviets, which were being delivered at great risk and with many casualties to the port of Murmansk in the Arctic Ocean; however, Roosevelt refused to go along.

The Allies did manage to drop some supplies, flying from bases in Italy and England, but they were insufficient. Only after October 2, 1944, when

the uprising was squelched and Warsaw was completely destroyed, did the
Soviet army cross the river and enter the city.

We found the railroad station, which consisted mostly of piles of bricks
and twisted rails, among which were a few functioning platforms. Passenger trains came and went, and eventually our train pulled up to the platform. In a couple of hours, after many starts and stops, we arrived at our
destination.

Radomsko was a town of about thirty thousand and appeared to be relatively intact. Solomon hobbled away to see if he could find anyone he
knew, and was back in about an hour with two men, a big and husky one
named Itche and a short and wiry one named Berek. They were related in
some way to Solomon's deceased wife, and they helped us to carry our bundles to their apartment in a four-story building. The two men had had the
good luck to be sent to a concentration camp in Czenstochova, about thirty miles away, where they worked in a munitions factory, while most Jews
from this region were sent to the Auschwitz extermination camp, which very
few survived.

There was a furnished apartment available in this building and we rented it, even though it was on the fourth floor and, since elevators were unknown here, Solomon had problems getting up and down on his crutches.
There was cold running water, but the outhouse was in the yard.

The town itself was relatively clean, with wide, tree-lined streets and a
large central square with flowerbeds. In comparison with Soviet towns, it
appeared prosperous. I became acquainted with some of the other tenants,
one of whom, Zbyshek Kovalski, was about my age. We hung around together. One day his father obtained a bottle of pure grain alcohol from a
distillery and challenged me to join him in drinking this 196-proof spirit. It
was drunk from tiny, thimble-sized glasses. Immediately upon swallowing
the liquid fire one bit into a piece of fatback, which somewhat soothed the
burn that started at the throat and extended all the way into the stomach.
It was a stupid thing to do, and I think that the alcohol burned the lining
of my esophagus, which has bothered me ever since, but since Zbyshek
drank it, I just could not chicken out.

Solomon's relatives were tailors by trade but now ran an unofficial cloth-ing shop in their apartment. On market days they would find a peasant who wanted to buy a suit or a jacket and bring him home. Since the choice of sizes they happened to have was rather limited, the challenge was to talk the peasant (who had usually had a few drinks) into buying what they had. I had heard jokes about salespeople pulling the back of a jacket to show buy-ers how well it fits in front, but these people actually did it! Afterward, they told the stories and had a good laugh, but I am sure that this did not en-dear them to their peasant clients after they sobered up.

While I understood Polish quite well, my speech was full of Ukrainian words. The Polish language is very formal. In addressing someone other than a close relative or a child, one uses the third person and the word *Pan* for a man or *Pani* for a woman, which are equivalent to the English "lord" and "lady." It is very difficult to curse someone when referring to him as "lord," and in this respect the Polish language is way behind Russian and miles behind the Kazakh language, in which cursing is almost a form of po-etry.

Vilya, who was now eight years old and just starting to relearn Ukrai-nian, had an even harder time switching to Polish. He spoke a funny mix-ture of Russian and Ukrainian with a few Polish words in between.

After a few weeks, we moved to an apartment on the ground floor of a two-family house surrounded by a garden and a tall fence. On the other side of the fence was the morgue of the adjacent hospital, which after dark made the garden eerie and spooky. The landlords were a young Polish couple, both of whom were teachers, and they took up as a challenge the task of im-proving my Polish. They gave me daily lessons, and very soon I was able to navigate Polish grammar with most of its intricacies: I learned when the sound "zh" should be expressed by placing a dot over the letter "z" or by writing "rz," or the sound "ou" by placing an accent over the letter "o" or by using the letter "u." They also gave me some books of light fiction, which were easy to read. These were silly romances and mysteries, a genre that I did not encounter in the Soviet Union, and I very much enjoyed them.

There was a movie house in town showing mostly Soviet films. It also served as a propaganda forum for the perennially drunken janitor of our for-mer building, who was an active member of the Communist Party. He went there every day and, before the movie began, stood up and shouted: "Long

live the Soviet Union! Long live the Red Army! Long live Comrade Stalin!"
and, while his cronies applauded, everyone else laughed.

The town was run by a Soviet military commandant and had a Soviet garrison. There were rumors that the underground Home Army and the NSZ guerrillas were around, but on the surface everything appeared to be peaceful and quiet, and we did not have any sense of being in danger. As a matter of fact, without telling Mother, I went with Zbyshek to a dance that dragged on right through the night and did not break up until two drunks, arguing over a girl, pulled guns on each other and everyone scattered. At dawn I tried to sneak noiselessly into the house, but in the absolute stillness every rustle was magnified into a hammer blow. My precautions turned out to be totally unnecessary because Mother had not slept all night and was just about to go out to look for me. I felt just as stupid and embarrassed as I did in Kharkov when I went to the zoo during an air raid, but now I was much older and should have known better.

There were about fifty Jewish survivors in town, out of a population of about a thousand before the war, and now and then another one would wander in from Germany, looking for a family that most of the time did not exist any longer. One day a thin, malnourished boy of about fourteen or fifteen appeared. He had a tattooed number from a concentration camp on his forearm. Since none of his family had survived, another family took him in. He became friendly with a young man, also a concentration camp survivor, who worked for the Security Service, which was a euphemism for the Polish NKVD. This man wore civilian clothes and carried a gun in a holster under his jacket. I had met him several times, and once asked him about the rumors of guerrilla activity. He responded that the rumors were justified but, whatever might happen, he was sure that they would never take him alive. He refused to go into detail, and I found this answer very disturbing. It sounded as if the government was not in complete control, which did not bode well for us.

One afternoon, a couple of weeks after our conversation, as this man and the boy came out of the movie house with the crowd, they were both shot from behind and killed. At their funeral a detachment of the police fired a salute, and the Soviet commandant made a moving speech about the tragedy of surviving the concentration camps only to die after the war was over. Our feeling of being secure was gone, and Mother did not let me wear my Cossack hat or go out after dark.

The looming danger and the fact that Solomon could not find any gainful activity made him look for another place to live. At that time Poland was being shifted westwards. In exchange for the formerly Polish western Ukraine annexed by the Soviet Union, Poland was given the eastern part of Germany, from which ethnic Germans were being expelled. The Polish government was replacing this population with its own, and there were rumors of great opportunities in these so-called liberated territories.

The closest "liberated" area was only a few hours away, on the same rail line we had taken from Warsaw to Radomsko. It was called Silesia, the southeastern tip of prewar Germany. On the prewar map, Germany looked like the head of a fox looking eastwards at a rabbit, the rabbit being East Prussia, which was separated from Germany by the Danzig corridor that belonged to Poland. Now East Prussia was divided between Poland and the Soviet Union. Silesia was the tip of the fox's nose and is on the eastern side of the River Oder, which formed the new border between Germany and Poland. Silesia was highly industrialized and had both iron and coal mines. During the tenth century it had been part of Greater Poland, and many of its inhabitants still had Polish-sounding names and spoke a Polish dialect. They were referred to as Silesians, and, upon passing a language test and screening to prove that they had not been members of the Nazi Party, they were allowed to remain and were granted Polish citizenship.

Solomon went down to Silesia and, being an invalid, with his Soviet uniform and his crutches, was given not only an apartment in the center of the city of Gleiwitz, now called Gliwice, but also a bakery on its outskirts.

We did not lose any time moving there. Before the war, the city had been home to several hundred thousand inhabitants. Now about a third of it lay in ruins. Some of its Germans had escaped to Germany before the Soviet army approached. Left behind was the working-class population, those with Polish names, and probably those who had not been Nazis and did not think that they would be harmed. The main street and the railroad station were intact, as were most of the suburbs.

But this was a different and surreal world, with the roles of the master race and the lesser races reversed. Now it was the Germans who were the underdogs, thrown out of their homes, packed into freight trains and deported to Germany, forced to leave everything behind. And it was German prisoners of war, with hollow cheeks and in ragged uniforms, who cleared the rubble from the streets.

Poles from all over the country swarmed over the city, buying things for next to nothing from Germans, or just appropriating whatever they wanted, like the northern carpetbaggers who had descended upon the South after the American Civil War. Soviet and Polish military patrols were trying to maintain order, which was impossible to do with hordes of drunken Soviet soldiers and all kinds of armed criminals robbing stores in broad daylight; after sunset gunshots rang out all through the night.

Our apartment was on the fourth floor of a four-story building across the square from the railroad station. There were two apartments on each floor, with common toilets on staircase landings between each two floors. The previous owners had left all their furniture and kitchen utensils. There were tiled coal-burning stoves in each of the four rooms and a coal bin for each apartment in the basement. The problem was that there was no elevator and Solomon had difficulty going up and down on his bullet-ridden legs.

It did not take us long to notice that both apartments on the second floor were occupied by Germans. This did not seem right to us, and Solomon on his crutches went to the housing office of the military commandant. On the next day one of the German families was ordered to exchange apartments with us. Their apartment was much more luxurious, with higher ceilings, better furniture, a piano, and carpets on the floor. They took only their clothing and other personal belongings, and we exchanged places. A few hours after they had moved, one of the two middle-aged women who had been living there knocked on the door. When I opened it, she timidly asked me if she could have her hairbrushes, which she had forgotten on the dresser. I told her to take everything from the dresser, where there were all kinds of small containers and bottles, and anything else she might have forgotten. She thanked me profusely and I could see tears in her eyes.

My feeling about this incident was quite ambivalent—for the first time in my life I was "top dog," and the feeling was exhilarating. On the other hand, having been an underdog myself, I felt sorry for her until I remembered that the people in Khmelnik had not been sent to another apartment by her sons or brothers, but were marched into the forest to be shot.

As an aside, I have read somewhere that the expressions "top dog" and "underdog" come from medieval England. When hunting bears with dogs, some dogs were trained to jump on the bear's back, others to attack him from below. The underdogs almost never survived.

Solomon's bakery was on the outskirts of town at the end of the street-car line, but I preferred going there by bicycle. The way led across a large square at the railroad station, through wide, tree-lined streets of mostly four-story buildings, which appeared to be the norm for buildings without elevators, through an industrial section that lay in ruins and onto a four-lane highway that led to the suburbs. Perhaps because an asphalt highway was something new to me, bicycling on it after a drizzle, when steam rose eerily from its surface and the smell of tar filled my nostrils, exhilarated me. Here was I, a boy who only two years ago was starving and covered with lice, riding through the land of the enemy. Arrogant supermen scurried out of my way; if I wanted to, I could order them around or even beat them— they would not dare to resist. Of course I was aware that my power stemmed from my Estonian tunic and the Cossack hat. It was puzzling to me that, once the Germans were defeated, there were no guerrillas nor any other significant kind of resistance; they obeyed the new laws just as they had obeyed the old ones.

While this feeling of power was exhilarating, it was not in my nature to abuse it. Once, trying to find an address, I came upon an old German couple sunning themselves on a pile of bricks in front of a semi-ruined house. As I approached, they looked up at me with apprehension, but when in my most polite high-school German I asked them for directions, they smiled and went to great length to explain how to get where I wanted to go. They appeared frail and helpless, and I wondered to what extent they could be held responsible for what their children had done. Did not I say, when children teased me for being the son of an "enemy of the people," that a son is not responsible for his father? Should not the same apply to parents?

Only once did I actually take advantage of my power. The other apartment on our floor was still occupied by Germans—a middle-aged couple and an elderly woman. They did not speak much Polish, and we did not have much to do with them, other than to respond to their greeting when we met in the hallway or on line for the toilet. In spite of our preconception that there was something demonic in all Germans, we did not feel any animosity toward these people.

A small window from their pantry gave onto our balcony. Once I peered into it and saw shelves with all kinds of jars and boxes, which were of no interest to me. Then, on one of the shelves, I noticed a neatly folded flag. I saw red, pried open the window, and squeezed myself partially inside until I was able to reach the flag.

They must have heard the commotion and opened the door. I was livid. "What is this?" I shouted. They turned pale.

"It's only a flag of Germany," they stammered. "It is not a Nazi flag . . ."

"So you are expecting Germany to come back?" I threw the flag on the floor and trampled on it.

"Please, we did not mean anything by it . . ." I could practically hear their teeth clattering with fear. I slammed the window and threw the flag into the garbage pail.

Solomon's bakery was a going enterprise. He was simply given it by the military government; its previous owner, a pudgy middle-aged German, became an employee. There were about a dozen people working around the clock, mixing the dough during the day and baking rolls and rye bread for the downtown stores during the night. There was also a small retail store, where people from the neighborhood and soldiers from the Polish garrison stationed in barracks across the street bought their bread and rolls.

A distant relative of Solomon's named Abba, who was a baker, ran the operation. Most of the employees were Germans who, due to their age or because of some physical handicaps, had not been drafted. One tall, thin baker, Sasso, had been an Italian prisoner of war. A large Silesian woman, Zosia, was in charge of keeping the place clean and providing ersatz coffee for the workers. Her Polish dialect was quite easy to understand, and in talking to her I found out that although the Silesians were German citizens and served in the army, they had been looked down upon by ethnic Germans; indeed, many were glad to see Silesia become part of Poland.

The bakery was attached to the house where the previous owners had lived. The old owners were now relegated to a couple of rooms in the back. The front part of the house became an office and bedroom space for whichever of us had to be there at night or very early in the morning. My job started at around five in the morning. I counted out the fragrant, hard-crusted rolls, which were frequently so hot that they burned my hands, and placed them into baskets that were loaded onto a flat-bed horse-wagon, for delivery to stores by six or seven o'clock. Occasionally I went with the delivery wagon and counted out the orders of rolls or loaves of bread. The wagon driver, who also cared for the horse, was an elderly, taciturn German. He never spoke on his own initiative and when asked a question gave only "yes" or "no" answers. One day, a visitor from Radomsko, who had spent the war in the labor camp in the nearby city of Czenstochova, recognized this man as having been a *capo* or headman in charge of the prisoners in one of the factories that used slave labor. He had been very strict and meted out severe punishments for the slightest infractions. The visitor reported this to the commandant's office, and the driver was taken away on the very same day.

Upon getting to know the people in the bakery, I realized that, on a personal basis, most people here were not much different from people anywhere else. The local girls hung around with Polish soldiers, some of whom were Jewish, just as they must have done when the soldiers in these barracks were German. A particularly attractive blonde was living with *poruchnik* (Lieutenant) Weiner, the Jewish commander of the Polish army garrison across the street. The street criminals, for whom one had to watch out, were mostly not Germans but Russians and Poles.

Every week a truckload of flour in fifty-kilogram burlap sacks was delivered to the bakery, and every fit male was called upon to unload it and to stack the sacks in the warehouse. We folded empty sacks by inserting one corner into the other, and put them over our heads like hats so that they covered our heads, shoulders, and backs. This did not always provide sufficient protection, and we were usually covered with flour from head to toe by the time the truck was unloaded.

Occasionally, I had to go with the truck to pick up the flour in a town several hours away. To make some money on the side, the truck driver picked up hitchhikers. They were a motley crowd, consisting mostly of carpetbaggers with sacks of loot either taken from houses that had been abandoned by fleeing Germans or bought for next to nothing at the flea market.

A person of this type was called a *szabrovnik,* a word coined just to describe such people. Once, a Soviet soldier climbed on board together with other hitchhikers and I saw him open a liter bottle of vodka, put it to his lips, and not take it away until it was empty. He then collapsed on the floor of the truck and began to snore. When we reached our destination, he managed to crawl down from the truck and walk away on wobbly legs, now and then pushing himself away from walls.

Because Solomon could not walk long distances, it was Mother's job to collect money from the stores for the bread and rolls that had been delivered to them. She had a large shopping bag, which by the time she had visited the last of the dozen or so stores was pretty much filled with money. This was dangerous, because store robberies were a daily occurrence, and she could easily have been followed and robbed or even shot. It became my job to escort her, and Solomon bought me a pistol, a Browning seven-shooter, from one of the garrison soldiers. Handguns were differentiated not by their caliber, but by the number of bullets contained in their magazines. The smallest one was a six-shooter, which a woman could carry in her purse; Mother, however, did not want one. For himself Solomon got a nine-shooter—a German Luger, which was considered to be more reliable than the corresponding Soviet pistol.

Fortunately, all the stores were on the well-lit main avenue and we felt relatively safe, walking up one side of it and returning on the other side. The most dangerous spot was at the entrance to our building, which was through a rear courtyard, because the whole ground floor in front was occupied by a restaurant. To get into the courtyard we had to pass through a gate that led into a wide corridor, then through another gate that opened into the courtyard. The corridor was always dark because lightbulbs were consistently stolen, and it would have made a perfect place for an ambush. I always entered there first, with a flashlight in my left hand and the pistol, with the safety off, in my right. I don't know how much good the pistol would have done us if someone had been determined to rob us. Life was cheap in those days and they could have shot us first, but we did not think that way at the time—it was either kill or be killed.

One evening, there was a loud banging on the door and someone shouted, "Open up!" Solomon grabbed his gun and I ran into my room, where mine was hidden in the back of the piano. I crouched behind the piano, from where I could see the front door.

"Who is it?" shouted Solomon, but they did not answer and continued to bang on the door. "Get away or I will shoot!" shouted Solomon. "It's the police," they finally answered. "Give me your name and stay away until I verify it!" shouted Solomon. They gave us a name and we called the police headquarters on our recently hooked-up telephone. It was indeed the police, and we opened the door after I hid my pistol, because I did not have a permit for it. They were looking for someone who was supposed to have been in our building, but we did not know him and, after checking Solomon's gun permit, they left.

September came and I was very much afraid that I might miss another school year. Then I found out that in the neighboring city of Katowice, which had been part of Poland before the war, there was a functioning technical college. The whole southern part of Silesia was interconnected by a network of streetcars that made travel from one city to another very easy. I went to this college absolutely sure of my qualifications, but when I saw the admissions clerk wince when he heard my accent, I knew that I was in trouble. He did not waste any time telling me that my certificate testifying to completion of the tenth grade of a Soviet school was a worthless piece of paper. To be admitted to college in Poland, one had to have a *Matura,* which meant that one had graduated from a *Liceum*—a two-year school that came after six years of public school and four years of Gymnasium. The Liceums were of two kinds—humanistic and scientific—the latter being a prerequisite for admission to a technical college. The clerk generously invited me to come back upon completion of the Liceum.

Since there was nothing to be done, I began looking all over for a *Liceum.* Much to my great surprise and satisfaction, I found that an "Evening Liceum for Adults" was about to open right there in Gliwice. It was going to compress a two-year course into one year and would combine both humanistic and scientific branches.

Classes were held in a high school, where in each classroom there was a crucifix above the blackboard. Before each class began we all stood up and, led by the teacher, those who were Catholics recited the Lord's Prayer. At the end of each class we stood up again and recited a "Hail Mary." I was very much surprised by this because the government, for all practical purposes, was run by Communists. But at that time they had not yet penetrated every aspect of life and, for the time being, did not want to antagonize the Church.

Of necessity, the subjects taught were pretty much limited to overviews, except for the history of the Catholic Church and, of all things, a whole semester of the ancient Greek plays such as *Antigone* by Sophocles. The course was taught by an old-fashioned gentleman with a typically Polish handlebar mustache and white hair neatly parted in the middle. He was always impeccably dressed in a dark suit and a tie, and always had a handkerchief protruding from his breast pocket. He also taught Polish literature, of which we had only time for the Polish equivalent of Pushkin—Mickiewicz—and for the epic writer Henryk Sienkiewicz, known in the West for his novel *Quo Vadis.*

I found the old man's lectures spellbinding, but it took me a while to figure out the reason for spending so much time on ancient plays, when there was not enough time to adequately cover other subjects. Eventually it became clear to me that the situation in Poland at that time was very much analogous to the moral dilemma treated by the Antigone—namely, the conflict between what one considered to be one's duty and the accommodations one had to make in order to survive in a tyrannical state.

In the play, Antigone buries her executed brother against the orders of King Creon, who had ordered him killed and his body left to the dogs. Antigone believed that it was her sisterly duty to the family and to the gods to bury him, even at the risk of her own life. On the other hand, her sister Ismene argued that it was futile and dangerous to defy the all-powerful king.

In Poland, there was a conflict between the duty to the Polish nation and its way of life—which, while not exactly a model of democracy, still had several political parties, private property, and religion—versus submission to an all-powerful Communist dictatorship.

There were about thirty people in our class, all of whom had graduated from the Gymnasium before the war, and to whom it was very important to obtain the *Matura,* without which one not only could not be admitted to a university but also could not advance either in the bureaucracy or the army. Thus we had several officers, many officials, and a few Silesians who, having been raised as Germans, were just as curious about all aspects of Polish life as was I.

Since one of the subjects for which there was no time at the Liceum was a foreign language, I decided to study English on my own and found a private teacher. She was a middle-aged woman from Warsaw who, like thousands of others, was looking for an opportunity in a new land. She had trouble with English pronunciation and from the very first lesson tried to convince me to study French instead, in which she was more proficient. However, I persisted in the hope that, even if I never got to America, the language of the most powerful nation in the world would prove more useful than any other.

Because of my academic pursuits I did not have as much time for the bakery as before, and Mother paid a huge Polish soldier named Brenner, who used to hang out around the bakery, to escort her when she collected money from the stores. This did not sit well with Solomon, and I once overheard him saying to Mother that I intended to become an engineer by riding on his back. I never forgot that and decided then and there to earn some money on my own.

While the town was full of Russian and Polish soldiers with tremendous thirst, the government had not yet gotten around to opening a vodka store. Since selling alcohol was a government monopoly, no other stores could sell it, at least not openly. To buy a bottle one had to know someone on the black market, and the price was very high. Therefore I decided to go to Radomsko and bring a suitcase of vodka back to Gliwice.

This was easier said than done because there was no way that I could get a travel permit, without which I could not get a train ticket. As fate would have it, soon afterwards, as I was walking down the street in my Estonian tunic and wearing my Cossack hat, I was saluted by a somewhat bewildered Russian soldier who, not being certain who I was, opted to be on the safe side. I smartly returned the salute and immediately saw the solution to my problem.

I got on the train, found an empty compartment, and stretched out on the bench. Next to the bench I put a liter bottle of vodka that was only about quarter full. I lay on my back, slipped the hat over my face, and pretended to be asleep. Every now and then I heard the door of the compartment slide open and then close again after comments like: "It's a drunken Russian, let's go somewhere else . . ." or words to that effect. After the train pulled out of the station, the door opened but this time did not close right away. Peeking from under my hat, I saw legs clad in the blue uniform of the conductor. He hesitated for a moment, but when I did not respond to his coughing, he quietly went away.

At one of the stations, the door slid open with a bang, and what I surmised to be a Polish military patrol of several soldiers discussed what to do about me. "Let's wake up the drunk," said one of them. "What, do you want a fight?" asked another. "The train is full of Russians, leave him alone." His sound judgment prevailed and they slammed the door behind them.

A few stations farther on, a Soviet patrol appeared at the door. "Let's get him," said one of them. My heart stopped beating. "Wait a minute," chipped in another, "This is not a Soviet uniform. See those buttons? He must be a Polak, to hell with him." Fortunately for me, the Soviet and Polish military police did not conduct many joint patrols. While I was very apprehensive, my papers were in order and there was not much that they could have done to me. They could not have accused me of impersonating their officers, because a Cossack hat and an Estonian jacket did not go together and, in any event, the Estonian army had not existed since 1940.

I made it to Radomsko, bought two dozen bottles of vodka, which almost split the suitcase, and made it to the station only thanks to my foresight in tying the suitcase up with a rope. I was hoping to pull the same trick on the way back, but could not find an empty compartment and had to settle in one where there were two young husky Soviet soldiers. They asked about my uniform and we had a good laugh when I told them about my trip. They were Jewish boys from Eastern Poland and confided in me that they were on a week's leave and were going to the border in the hope of escaping to Germany. They had heard that in West Germany there were many refugees from Eastern Europe and believed that from there it might be possible to get to America. I was very interested.

It turned out that the train conductors did not dare to check tickets of Soviet soldiers, and the military police patrols were only checking identification papers in an attempt to catch deserters. My return trip was therefore uneventful, except that at one point we were joined by a resplendent Polish lieutenant. He wore an impeccable uniform trimmed with silver braid, and one could see the reflection of one's face in the shine of his boots. His hat was the Polish *confederatka*, with a flat, square top, one of the corners pointing forward. He was middle-aged and had watery light blue eyes and a waxed, upturned mustache that made him look as if he had stepped out of an operetta. He knew some Russian and expressed himself on the problems of the day very authoritatively and with firm gestures.

After complaining about various shortages, he said: "You know, it's the damned Jews that are creating problems for Poland all over again. They are everywhere, no matter where you turn."

"And how can you tell they are Jews?" asked one of the soldiers with a strained smile.

"Oh, I can smell them a mile away!" said the lieutenant with great conviction.

The three of us exchanged glances, which he noticed. His face turned purple and he abruptly stood up and left the compartment. I stuck my head out into the passage and saw him rushing through the door into the next car. We could not stop laughing.

When early the next morning I brought the vodka to the bakery, where I hoped to sell it to the soldiers of the Polish garrison when they came in to buy rolls, I was met with condescending smiles. When I asked what was so funny, I was told that the day before, while I was away, the government had opened several vodka stores all over town. It took me a long time to sell the stuff at cost, but I was not yet ready to give up.

My next venture was in sausages, which were not always available in the stores. Again, I took with me an almost empty liter bottle of vodka, but this time I did not pretend to be asleep. I just pretended to be taking occasional sips, which was enough for the conductor to leave me alone. I bought a backpack full of sausages and, upon my return, went to several stores trying to peddle them, but was offered less than what I had paid. Once again I brought the stuff to the bakery, but without refrigeration the sausages became moldy and I had to throw most of them away.

These mercantile disasters did not do anything to improve my standing in Solomon's eyes. When he had accumulated some money and decided to buy more gold coins, the Russian "piglets," he sent me to Warsaw with his relative, Berek, who was about to marry Solomon's daughter, Ruzka, and was also interested in buying "piglets." A man from Radomsko named Felix, who had recently returned from Russia and whom Solomon had known before the war, claimed that he had contacts in Warsaw and was going to be our guide. I did not like Felix from the very first moment I laid eyes upon him. There was something weasel-like about his slick hair, small face, and shifty eyes, even his sashaying way of walking.

We got a ride to Warsaw on the back of a truck, wandered through the ruins that were being cleared by hand by thousands of ragged and semi-starved German prisoners, and eventually found the cellar where we could stay overnight with Felix's contacts. The next morning Felix and Berek went to see the gold coin dealer. They did not take me, because dealing in gold was illegal and the dealer, presumably, did not want too many people to know about him. Several hours later they returned with very disappointed expressions on their faces, and told me that the man had only one coin and that they had decided to let me buy it. I was immediately put on guard by their generosity, the reason for which I understood as soon as I saw the coin—indeed before I even took it in my hand. It had very little resemblance to the shiny gold coins that I had seen before. It was dirty and the imprint was uneven, as if someone had made it with a homemade die and a hammer. It was not shiny and looked more like bronze than gold. I thanked them very much and said that I did not want to deprive them of the opportunity to buy the only coin available. This made both of them visibly angry.

"Solomon will be very mad at you if you return empty-handed," one of them said. "He sent you all the way to Warsaw and you should not disappoint him!"

I suggested that they should buy it themselves because, after all, they also traveled all the way to Warsaw. They tried to pressure me several more times, but I did not budge. Neither of them spoke to me on the way home.

After a few months, all Germans who did not have Polish-sounding names had been deported. The apartment next door was now occupied by an old friend of Solomon from Radomsko named Itzhack. He was a burly, middle-aged man with black curly hair and bulging red-rimmed eyes. He had survived the war in a labor camp, while his wife, together with those who did not appear to be strong enough to work, was sent to a death camp. He lived with a large and imposing woman, also from Radomsko, whose husband had not returned. She was from a well-to-do family and was very demanding, loud, and aggressive. Poor Itzhack was knocking himself out trading on the black market to keep her in expensive clothes and fancy cosmetics. Mother did not like her and we did not socialize with them.

Several months after they moved in next to us, a small, mousy woman appeared at their door. This was Itzhack's wife, who had somehow survived after all, and it had taken her some time to trace him to Gliwice. She was a complete opposite of the other woman—petite, quiet, with a voice that could barely be heard, and who dressed in gray and black. Poor Itzhack had a problem. He had to take her in, but the other woman had no intention of leaving, and the three of them had to live in the same apartment. Mother felt sorry for the wife, who spent a great deal of time sitting quietly in our apartment, sighing and occasionally uttering a few words in a barely audible, plaintive voice. In the end, her patience paid off, for after a few months the other woman could not tolerate the wife's ghostly presence and left.

There were interesting developments on the political scene that did not presage anything good. Even though the Soviets were in complete control, they still hoped to dupe the naive Western Allies into believing that they had created a democratic government in Poland, and were thus living up to some of their agreements. Therefore they allowed three parties into the government: the Communists, whose newspaper was *The Worker's Tribune,* the Socialists, whose paper was *The Public Tribune,* and the Agrarians, whose paper was *The Voice of the People.* It was a new experience for me to read their differing points of view: the Communists approved everything proposed by the Soviets; the Socialists occasionally exhibited mild disagreement; and the Agrarians, who fought to forestall or at least to limit collectivization of agriculture, expressed strong disagreement. While most ministers were Communists, including the key ones of defense and of internal affairs (which included the secret police), a few less important ones were given to the other parties.

Under pressure from Churchill, who distrusted the Soviets much more than Roosevelt did, the premier of the Polish government-in-exile, Stanislaw Mikolajczyk, was allowed to return and was given the post of minister of agriculture. His return showed clearly what the people really wanted. There were demonstrations throughout the country, with parading school-children waving Polish flags and chanting, "Long live Mikolajczyk!" This was more than the Soviets could tolerate and, after a while, they ordered his arrest. But Micolajczyk must have had friends in the secret police and man-aged to slip out of the country dressed as a woman. All the signs pointed to a complete Sovietization of the country, which meant that Solomon's bak-ery would be nationalized, together with everything else. All major enter-prises had been nationalized from the very beginning.

Some of the people who had returned from Germany went back there in the hope of being able to emigrate to America. Some were illegally going back and forth between Poland and Germany, bringing merchandise that they sold on the black market. They told stories of many thousands of refugees living in displaced persons camps set up by the United Nations Refugee Agency to keep them until they could be resettled throughout the world. Solomon's relatives Berek and Itche went back and forth several times through Czechoslovakia and were planning to go again to a camp in a town named Landsberg in Bavaria, in the American Occupation Zone.

It was early spring 1946, and while I liked studying at the *Liceum,* I was afraid that in the near future the Sovietization of the country might be com-pleted, which would mean tightly closed borders again. Therefore, I decid-ed to go to Germany with Berek and Itche, while Mother, Vilya, Ruzka, and Solomon would follow after Solomon settled his business affairs. By then Solomon had some money, but he could not turn it into gold coins that could be easily smuggled out of the country. Another way had to be found.

Fortunately for him, half a world away in Washington, D.C., there was an assistant secretary of the treasury, Harry Dexter White, who, as was re-vealed later by deciphered communications between Soviet embassies in Washington and Moscow, was a Soviet agent. White had considerable in-fluence with the secretary of the treasury, Henry Morgenthau, who in turn had a great deal of influence with President Roosevelt. In any event, White presumably was instrumental in handing to the Soviets the printing plates for German reichsmarks, which for several years remained the currency of Germany, until they were superseded by deutschmarks in 1948.

The Soviets then proceeded to print the reichsmarks, which allowed them to buy everything in the German occupation zones of the United

States, England, and France. The marks could be bought in Poland very cheaply, and Solomon bought a stack of brand-new notes two feet high. The problem was how to smuggle them into Germany.

We bought a medium-sized suitcase, arranged inch-thick stacks of money on its bottom, covered them with cardboard, and lined the whole inside of the suitcase with wallpaper, which made the false bottom look real. There were two more packets of money left; these I stuck into my boots.

With Berek, Itche, and a fourth man with the improbable name of Moyshe Milioner, who was also from Radomsko, I took a train to a small town on the border with Czechoslovakia, where we went to the house of a local family who had the right connection. They were a young couple with a baby, and he was the manager of the government liquor store that was frequented by border guards.

They told us that at night, a border guard would take us across the border and direct us to the nearest train station in Czechoslovakia. They would pay him when he presented proof that we were across the border. This proof was a tiny porcelain doll that we would give him when we were sure that we were there. They changed tokens of proof each time, and the guard did not know what it was going to be. I had read mysteries where halves of a photograph or of a currency bill were used in similar situations, but they were so obvious that a guard could put us in jail or even kill us while taking the token that would permit him to collect.

The border guard came for us at about four in the morning. We walked without saying a word along a narrow path that led across fields, into a forest. There was only a tiny sliver of a moon peeking through the branches of tall trees, and we followed the footsteps of the guard in almost total darkness. A branch knocked the hat off my head, but there was no chance of finding it and I did not even stop. It was just a regular felt hat, not my favorite Cossack hat, which I had to leave behind together with my Estonian tunic.

After walking for about an hour through the forest, the guard stopped and pointed out a distant light, which he said was a railroad station where in the morning we could catch a train to Prague. We gave him the tiny doll token and he left, wishing us good luck. Since this was the first railroad station at the border, we thought that it might be watched by Czech border guards and decided to keep on walking along the railroad tracks away from the border. By this time, my made-to-order boots, which had never prop-erly fit, began giving me trouble—the money packets must have been cut-ting down the blood circulation in my legs. Walking was becoming more and more painful and I began falling behind. Nevertheless, we bypassed the second station also, and by the time we reached the third one at daybreak, I was neither willing nor able to walk any farther.

We bought tickets to Prague and got onto the next train. Fortunately, no one asked us for identification, because all we had were small pieces of pa-per called "index cards" (exactly like the Social Security cards in the United States). They gave a name, which I do not remember, and stated that they were issued in Germany, in the American zone of occupation.

By the time we arrived in Prague, my feet had rested somewhat and I was able to walk for about half an hour to the safe house where we would stay overnight. The city had capitulated to the Germans and was not destroyed. It was already getting dark as we walked along a river, but I could still see church steeples and walls of palaces, which I wished there was an opportu-nity to visit.

When I finally took off my boots, I discovered huge, bloody blisters on my feet. Some of the blisters had burst and raw flesh could be seen behind the ragged edges of loose skin. Our hosts gave me bandages, but there was no question of my walking across the German border at night, as we had originally planned. I told my companions that I was going to take a train come what may.

After some deliberation, they decided also to go by train. The next morn-ing I had great difficulty putting on my boots, but there was no choice and, cursing the *partach* boot-maker in Zhitomir, I eventually managed it. I did not dare to put the two packets of money back into the boots, and attached them instead to the small of my back with a bandage. With a great deal of pain I made it to the railroad station, where we took a train to the German border via Pilsen. At the border, we presented our phony Index Cards and were allowed to get on the train to Germany. After a very short ride, we crossed the border and for the first time I felt that I finally really was out of the Soviet Empire. This was the beginning of a new adventure and it was exciting in spite of my blistered feet and apprehension about what might happen next.

We stopped at a station called Cham, where everyone got off the train.

An unarmed German border guard asked us for identification and we showed him our Index Cards, which he handed over to two American military policemen. They wanted to know whether we had any other identification and we replied that this was all that had been given to us upon being freed from a labor camp in Germany, and that we had gone to Poland to search for surviving family members. Not having found anyone, we decided to return to Germany in the hope of being able to emigrate to some peaceful country. The military policemen eyed us with suspicion and told us to open our suitcases. Not finding anything suspicious, they told us to raise our hands to be frisked. I felt blood draining from my face, but there was nothing to be done. The policeman frisked me from top to bottom, including my boots, but he did not reach far enough in the back to feel the packets of money.

"All right," they said. "Tomorrow you will be questioned by an official of UNRA [the United Nations Refugee Agency], who will decide what to do with you. In the meantime, you will be taken to jail."

They packed us into a van and drove us to the German jail, which was a low, gray, sprawling building not far from the station. We were registered and taken to a large cell, which contained about a dozen narrow iron beds along two walls and a long table with benches in the middle. Two small windows with iron bars were close to the ceiling. From the middle of the ceiling hung a single naked lightbulb. Several people lay on the beds in various positions. Some were reading while some just stared at the ceiling. They gave us a quick glance and continued with whatever they were doing. We found four empty beds in a row and sat on them, looking at one another and hoping that we would not be searched again. While we were apprehensive, we were not really frightened: according to my companions who had been back and forth several times, the German authorities did not have much say with regard to foreign refugees, while the UNRA officials were mostly sympathetic.

The walls of the cell were covered with graffiti in several languages, to which I added my name in Russian. Some time later we heard the clanking of a key in the lock and looked at the iron door. It swung open with a creak and a young man wearing a Soviet soldier's uniform and holding a small bundle entered the cell. He turned around and watched the door close behind him, then stood in the middle of the cell as if unsure what to do next.

I spoke to him in Russian and motioned to a bed next to mine. He looked at me with surprise and sat down.

"How did you get here?" I asked him.

"Just walked across the border," he answered in Ukrainian, "and gave myself up." He must have been about eighteen, and his speech told me that he was from a village.

"Why did they lock you up?" I asked this time in Ukrainian.

"I told them that I want to go to America; my uncle lives there." He looked around the room at the barred widows and the iron door. "They said they will send me back tomorrow . . ." His eyes filled with tears, as we both knew that this would mean, even in the best case, many years in a Siberian Gulag and, in the worst case, a firing squad. At one of the Summit meetings, Stalin had prevailed upon Roosevelt and Churchill to agree to return all former Soviet citizens to the Soviet Union.

The iron doors screeched open again and a metal cart with steaming food was wheeled in. We all received a metal dish of thick noodle soup, a slice of bread, and a metal cup of ersatz café, which means "coffee substitute," and is a brew made with roasted barley. I was very hungry and wolfed down the tasteless soup and drank all of the bitter coffeelike concoction.

The soldier did not touch his food. He just sat at the table staring into space. I wondered how to distract him and asked whether he would like to play cards, which I knew one of our men had with him. He nodded and I borrowed the cards. We began a game called "The Fool," which was known to every child in the Ukraine; however, it was obvious that his mind was not with it and, after a few minutes, he quit.

"A fool . . . a fool . . ." he mumbled a few times and lowered his head onto his arms, face down on the table.

We all went to bed without undressing. All through the night I heard the soldier twisting and sighing.

In the morning we received another cup of ersatz café and a slice of bread. At about ten o'clock our names were called. We were brought out to the entrance hall, where a man from UNRA, who wore an American uniform but without any military insignia, awaited us. He examined our "Index Cards" and asked us the same questions as did the policemen, to which we gave the same answers.

"Since you came from Czechoslovakia," he said, "you cannot be recognized as refugees. Only those who were liberated here and stayed here are considered to be refugees."

Oh, oh, I thought. They are going to send us back, too.

"But," he added, "we will recognize you as 'infiltrees.'"

We did not have the slightest idea what that meant but were not about to ask him.

"You wait here outside the door, and I will send a van to take you to a Displaced Persons Camp. They will be here within an hour."

We thanked him profusely and said that we would wait, but as soon as his jeep disappeared around the corner, we grabbed our belongings and rushed to the railroad station.

Chapter 8

1946–1949

Not wanting to disclose our destination, we bought tickets to Munich. There we would take the train for Landsberg, where Itche's wife and son lived in a camp for Displaced Persons (called DPs). The train was not due for a couple of hours, and because we did not want to attract the attention of the policemen who patrolled the station, we tried to be as inconspicuous as possible. This was not easy, because we did not want to walk the streets where we could run into the military police patrols, and the restaurant near the station was still closed. Even if it had been open, it would not have done us much good because we did not have any ration cards, without which we could have bought only a cup of ersatz coffee. So we mingled with other passengers and hoped for the best.

Finally the train came and we arrived without further problems at the bombed-out train station in Munich, where we boarded the train for Landsberg.

The DP camp was on the edge of town. It was reserved exclusively for Jewish DPs because the populations of other camps contained, in addition to people who were sent to Germany to work, those who came here with the retreating German army. Some of those refugees came because they did not want to live under communism; others because they had collaborated with the Germans or even served in elite SS units. The Germans had recruited SS personnel from some occupied countries when they began running out of their own people. Having such people cooped up with their former victims would have created a highly explosive mixture.

The camp occupied former army barracks and consisted of about a dozen two-story stucco buildings with large rooms and bunk beds, subdivided by curtains made of green army blankets. Luckier surviving families lived in small apartment houses with single rooms, formerly officers' quarters—a family to a room. Every room had a sink and each floor had a bathroom.

There must have been close to two thousand people in the camp. It was set up by the United Nations Refugee Agency, known by its acronym UNRA. With the exception of the American director, the camp was managed by the DPs themselves. It had a hospital staffed by DP doctors and nurses, and its own unarmed policemen who resolved local squabbles and maintained general order and peace.

Itche lived in one of the rooms in the officer's building. It contained two beds: one for him and his wife, and the other for his young son, who now had to share it with me. I did not care for this arrangement. After becoming friendly with some young people from the camp, I slept and ate in the barracks most of the time. On Solomon's instructions, I gave the smuggled money to Itche for safekeeping; of this he later retained a substantial amount for presumably having housed and fed me, even though neither housing nor food cost him anything.

Most of my new friends were older than me—some had already been students or had just graduated from high school before the war, and now hoped to continue their studies. Many were in terrible physical condition—they were covered by purple burn scars, or were missing toes that had been amputated because of frostbite suffered while hiding in forests or sewers during winter. Many had numbers from concentration camps tattooed on their forearms, and most had lost their entire families. They came from every country of Eastern Europe now under Communist control: Estonia, Latvia, Lithuania, Poland, Czechoslovakia, Hungary, Bulgaria, Romania, as well as from the Soviet Union and Yugoslavia.

There was not much to do in the camp. There were soccer and volleyball teams and an occasional movie supplied by the Joint, mostly tear-jerking melodramas in Yiddish. Most people just sat around all day, playing cards and waiting for some country to admit them. Some went to religious services; some got involved with one of several Zionist organizations, ranging from Socialists on the left to the right-wing Revisionists, who were followers of the late militant Zev Zhabotinsky. In general, the old adage that wherever two Jews get together they form three political parties proved very true here. Some people got involved in black-market activities because the stores were empty and there was demand for everything, from food and cigarettes to clothing and pencils, but the majority just sat around.

Landsberg itself was a medieval Bavarian town with a well in the middle of a cobblestone-paved square, remnants of a city wall, and a gate-tower with a clock. Its claim to fame was the prison, where Hitler had spent several years after his unsuccessful putsch in November 1923, and where he wrote *Mein Kampf,* "My Struggle," in which he outlined his philosophy and plans that, at the time, no one took seriously. Most of the people in Landsberg were Catholics, and the state of Bavaria was mainly agricultural outside its large cities. This was unlike highly industrialized and Protestant northern Germany.

There were several beer halls in Landsberg where one could see grayhaired men in lederhosen and with pheasant feathers or goat-hair brushes in their green felt hats, guzzling beer from huge steins. Many had beer bellies and fist-size goiters on their necks, which were caused by lack of iodine in the drinking water and in their beer. A large beer belly was presumably also a sign that they suffered from *Beerherz,* or fattening of the heart, which caused heart attacks. The beer was not very good—in fact, it tasted like burned molasses and left an unpleasant aftertaste.

Germany was divided into four occupation zones: American, British, French, and Soviet. The eastern part of Germany was added permanently to Poland, and East Prussia was divided between Poland and the Soviet Union. Each zone had a military government supervising the local German administration that ran the day-to-day activities. There were occupational military forces, but order was maintained by unarmed German police; in Landsberg, only American military policemen, who occasionally drove by in their jeeps, were armed.

Some of my friends had made inquiries in Munich about the possibility of studying there and the procedure for applying to the university. In addition to the ancient university, which did not teach technical subjects, there was a technical university that for some historical reason was called Technical High School and also a university operated by UNRA, where both the students and the faculty were DPs. To be admitted to the technical university I needed a certificate of graduation from high school, which I did not have. Since most of the DPs did not have any documents, we could take a test and obtain an equivalency certificate at the Jewish Students Union, which had been accredited by a department of the Bavarian *Kultusministerium,* or the Ministry of Public Worship and Instruction. This was an arrangement for helping the former *Rassisch und Politisch Vervolgte,* or victims of Nazi persecution on racial and political grounds, to make up for lost time.

The man in charge of this *Viedergutmachung,* which literally translates as "making good again," was Dr. Auerbach, a corpulent, middle-aged German Jew who was constantly reviled in the German press, ostensibly because he was fat while most people had very little to eat. In reality, it was because he demanded and obtained more assistance for the victims of Nazis than was given to German refugees. He was eventually arrested on charges of corruption, which were presumably trumped up, and died in prison only about three years after surviving a concentration camp.

I went to Munich to see what could be done about studying. One of my friends knew someone who lived there and who might let me stay overnight. The Munich railroad station and surrounding area was bombed out, but other parts of the city appeared to be more or less intact. After about an hour of wandering, I finally found the Students Union, which was in a walk-up apartment near the Maximilianeum Palace. The infamous Munich Agreement that gave part of Czechoslovakia to Germany had been signed there in 1939, after which the British Prime Minister Neville Chamberlain declared "peace in our time."

As I entered, a woman gave me a number, and I joined a mass of young people crowded into the small rooms and chattering in all the Eastern European languages. After a long wait for my turn, I finally faced the examiner—an intense man with a distracting twitch who appeared to be taking the job of screening out unworthy applicants very seriously. I later met several people who had been students before the war, but were unable to answer some of his questions, and whose lives had been very adversely affected because he did not pass them and they were unable to continue their studies.

The examiner was from Poland and had been a senior in college before the war, which means that he was about thirty years old. Since my German was very limited, he asked his questions in Polish. I did rather well until he asked me to name the capitals of all the Central American countries. Political geography was studied in the ninth grade, which I had skipped, and except for Panama City I could not think of the names of any other capitals. He said that I probably never went to high school and that he was going to flunk me, but then I answered all his questions about physical geography such as the names of rivers and lakes on various continents, which we had studied in the eighth grade, and he grudgingly passed me. I was elated: it looked as though my dream of becoming an engineer might actually come true!

By the time I received the certificate it was too late to do anything else that day, so I found the streetcar that took me to the Grillparzerstrasse where my friend's friend, named Yablonski, had a small apartment. Fortunately, he was at home. He was already enrolled in the dental school at the university, and was very helpful with advice on the bureaucratic procedures of finding a place to live and obtaining food-ration coupons. I had not eaten the whole day and he shared with me a can of tuna fish.

The next morning I went to the *Kultusministerium* and, on the strength of my having passed the test, was given another certificate stating that I was entitled to free tuition. Furthermore, I was entitled to housing and food rations. Armed with these two certificates, I found the college, which was in a partially destroyed block of gray stone buildings near the railroad station and, without many questions asked, was enrolled as a mechanical engineering student. I actually wanted to study aeronautical engineering, but its teaching was prohibited by the American Occupation government because it had military implications. The school year was going to start in a couple of weeks, and I would need to find a place to live before then.

I returned to Munich the following week and went to the city's housing authority, called the *Wohnungsamt,* where with my student identification I obtained a permit to live in Munich, called *Zuzugsgenehmigung.* I was also given a letter addressed to Herr Koob at 39 Schneckenburgerstrasse, requesting that he rent me a room in his apartment. The apartment was on the third floor of a four-story building, part of which had been destroyed. When I knocked on the door and identified myself, I was told through the door that they had no room for rent, and no matter what I said they refused to even open the door. I went back to the *Wohnungsamt* and they sent an employee to resolve this impasse. When he knocked and received the same answer that I had, he raised his voice and said, "You were a Nazi *Oberpolizeiinspector,* and your room is being requisitioned. If you do not let us in immediately, we will return with the police!" Hearing the man being called an *Oberpolizeiinspector,* I was not sure that I wanted to live there, but the door was opened and we walked into a semi-dark hallway, where stood a tall, gaunt, elderly man and a short, pudgy woman, whose gray hair was tied in a bun on top of her head. They were very nervous.

"But we already have one foreign student living here," stammered the woman. "He has the living room and all we have left is a small bedroom, the kitchen, and this small room with the window covered by cardboard." She opened the door to a small room and turned on the light. The only window was indeed covered with cardboard, but there was an old couch, a small table with a chair, and a tiled coal stove. "Can you find for me a room with a glass window?" I asked the agent. "No, this is all we have available at the moment," he replied. "We will arrange for you some transparent plastic, so that you will have some light." He turned to the landlords: "You have to give Herr Konstantinowsky a key and allow him to use the kitchen. I advise you not to give him any trouble!" At this, Herr Koob became visibly angry and left the room, murmuring something under his breath.

The official left and I remained sitting in the room illuminated only by a low-wattage lightbulb, not knowing what to do next. I did not have a book, any food, or any of my things. After a while, there was a timid knock on the door and Frau Koob came in. She must have been older than sixty and wore round glasses that gave her an owlish appearance.

"Let me show you the bathroom," she said, obviously resigned to my presence, and I followed her into the hallway. The bathroom contained a tub with a shower and a water heater that required coal. I had heard a lot about how immaculately clean and neat the Germans were supposed to be, but judging by this apartment, it was not universally true—there was dust all over the place.

"You have to get a coal ration for the stove and you can also use it here to heat the bath water," she said. "There is a coal storage bin in the basement." The toilet was in a separate room that was long and narrow; shipping cartons were stacked along one wall from floor to ceiling. "Also," she added, "I would prefer it if you would let me make your tea or whatever, rather than using the kitchen; this is what I do for the other student. My daughter sleeps in the pantry off the kitchen." She sighed deeply. "One of my two sons was killed in the war. The room you are in was his." I agreed with her requests and told her that I would try to get a hot plate for my room.

I opened the window and inspected the U-shaped courtyard, which had several entrances to the apartments. It was pretty much intact, except directly opposite my window, where a bomb had taken out a large section of two upper floors, permitting me a view of the buildings on the next block. The skies were gray and a cold, raw wind rattled the cardboard window-panes. The single lightbulb, suspended from the ceiling in a matted, tulip-shaped glass lamp shade, did not give much light, but it did not make any difference since I had nothing to read. I locked the door from the inside: being at the mercy of a Nazi *Oberpolizeiinspector,* even an old one, did not do anything to relieve my apprehension. I certainly did not feel at all like a top dog, the way I felt when dealing with Germans in Poland.

The tiny amount of light seeping through the cracks around the edges of the cardboard panes had disappeared and, not having anything else to do, I was getting ready to curl up on the couch, when again there was a knock on the door, this time much firmer. I had no choice but to open it. I found myself face to face with Herr Koob.

"May I come in, Herr Konstantinowsky?" he asked stiffly, pronouncing the "s" before "t" as "sh," the way it is pronounced in German.

"Please," I responded. He entered and, much to my astonishment, I saw that he was formally dressed in a suit and white shirt with a bow tie, while before he had been wearing an old sweater. He looked at me sternly through the thick lenses of his wire-rimmed glasses. Although his face was wrinkled, his posture was that of a military man. Shivers ran down my spine; the last thing I needed now was a confrontation with a Nazi.

"Here is the key to the apartment," he said, handing me the key. "Also, since you are going to be our tenant, I will shine your shoes, if you will put them outside your door at night."

To say that I was flabbergasted would be an understatement.

"Thank you," I mumbled, and as I looked at him, I suddenly saw before me not a Nazi *Oberpolizeiinspector* but an old man with watering red-rimmed eyes and trembling hands. Demeaning him was not part of my make-up. "Thank you very much, but I will shine my shoes myself," I said.

"As you wish," he said formally. "We will accommodate you according to the rules of tenancy. Good night." He turned around on his heels and left.

"Good night," I mumbled, still unable to collect my thoughts.

In the morning I met the other student in the hallway. He was a balding Byelorussian named Petra who studied law and was a nationalist, waiting for the Soviets to collapse and for Belarus to become independent. His room was twice the size of mine and contained nice furniture. He said something about having trouble with his throat and wrapped a woolen sock around his neck, pinning its ends together with a safety pin. He told me that he had no problems with the landlords and occasionally did put out his shoes to be polished.

About a month after our arrival in Germany, Berek went back to Poland and returned with Ruzka, who told me that Mother was coming over next with another group; then Vilya would come with Solomon. Several weeks passed but we had not heard from any of them. I assumed that their departure had been delayed for some reason and did not think much of it. Then, to my great surprise, Vilya and Solomon arrived, but Mother, who had left two weeks before them, turned out to have disappeared together with her companions. We were very worried. All of them carried money, and we were afraid that they had met with foul play or had been detained by the Soviets. We did not know what to do or where to go to look for her.

Even though the distance from Gliwice to Landsberg was only about four hundred miles, two border crossings were involved, one of which had to be negotiated at night through a forest, where they could have been killed by either Polish or Czechoslovak border guards.

Finally, after about two weeks of extreme anxiety and helplessness, two of Mother's companions showed up and told us that they had been imprisoned in Czechoslovakia for smuggling money, and that Mother was still in prison in Prague.

Solomon immediately went there, but several days later returned alone. However, he was able to find out where she was held and who had to be bribed for her release. He went back again and this time returned with Mother, who after having been in a prison for close to six weeks was thin and haggard but very happy. It was a great day!

As we had expected, the Soviets were trying to stem the outflow of people through Czechoslovakia and had tightened their control over the country. The train to Prague, on which Vilya and Solomon had traveled, was halted by Soviet soldiers in a field between stations and everyone was ordered off together with their belongings. Solomon had a big argument with the Soviet officer, telling him that he could not possibly jump off a train that was not at a platform; he showed him certificates from the Soviet military hospital stating that he was an invalid and had been a partisan. Finally, the officer gave in and had their luggage searched without their getting off the train. Their money was in a double wall of a suitcase and gold coins were hidden in the heels of their shoes, and the search did not uncover either. Through the window they saw people being searched and some being taken away. Others were allowed to get back on the train.

Because Solomon could not walk across the border through the forest as we had done, he and Vilya went to an official border crossing in the middle of the night. Being an invalid on crutches and accompanied by a child, Solomon hoped to cross the border by telling the guards that they were going to Germany to search for the child's mother. However, when they came to the border the gate was down and there was no one around. There was light in the building on the other side, and Vilya crawled under the gate and peeked through a window. Several guards sat around a table, playing cards. Vilya signaled Solomon to come over, but when he tried, his backpack caught in the gate and he was stuck until Vilya came back and freed him.

Mother, Vilya, and Anatole in Germany, 1947.

Anatole, student in Munich, 1947.

They walked away from the border but then had no idea how to find the railroad station. The village streets were deserted, so they knocked on the window of the nearest house, but no one responded. They tried the next house—someone opened the window but told them to go away. At the third or fourth house a woman opened the window; seeing a man on crutches and a boy, she invited them in. She made tea and sandwiches for them and pointed them in the right direction.

Unlike my group, Mother and her companions did not walk to the third station away from the border. They tried to board the train at the very first station, and were apprehended and searched by Czechoslovak border guards. The search was very thorough and money was found on all of them. Her two companions, who had only paper reichsmarks, were released after three weeks. But because the border guards had found gold coins on Mother, they kept her in prison, probably anticipating a ransom.

Once Mother was safe, I could concentrate on getting settled in Munich. Eventually the *Wohnunsamt* came through with the promised plastic windowpanes, but they were only translucent, not transparent, and all I could tell by looking through them was whether it was daylight outside. The room was still too dark to be able to read without turning on the light.

I went with trepidation to my first class at the university, not knowing whether I would be able to understand the language. It turned out that my fears were justified, since my German was limited to the everyday vocabulary of a high school textbook.

Most classes that were common to all branches of engineering, such as math and physics, were held in the main auditorium, where about twelve hundred students were tightly packed together on semicircular rows of benches and tables. Classes on specialized subjects, such as metallurgy, were held in a smaller auditorium where one wall was missing, and those who sat at the end were only a couple of feet from a drop of two floors. My problem, however, was fear not of falling but of failing—of not understanding the terminology. I had only a vague idea as to what was going on. Also, in math, the German students had already taken basic calculus in high school, which I had not. In addition to this, there were no textbooks available, and we were promised transcripts of the lectures only at some time in the future. There was no way that I could keep up with the lectures, and the situation would have been totally hopeless if it had not been for the fact that the first exams were not to take place until after the second year, by which time I was hoping to be able to catch up.

Most of the professors were distinguished elderly scientists, some of whom had been called back from retirement, because the younger ones had been members of the Nazi Party and were considered unfit to teach. Later, some of them who had undergone *Entnazifizierung*, or denazification, were allowed to teach if it was established by the special denazification court that they were only *Mitlaufer*, or fellow travelers, not ardent Nazis.

Our professor of thermodynamics, Dr. Nusselt, was world famous. A constant factor in heat transfer calculations is named the Nusselt Constant in his honor. He was quite old, with a white goatee and thick glasses. He would shuffle into the auditorium and, without saying very much or anything at all, begin to write formulas in the upper left-hand corner of the blackboard, which was at least thirty feet long. He continued writing in small, tightly packed letters and symbols until the end of the class, or until someone who had a transcript of his previous lectures would shout, "Herr Professor, you have made an error!" He would then step back from the blackboard, take off and wipe his glasses, look at the formulas, and, obviously hopelessly lost, would smile with embarrassment and dismiss the class. I tried to copy the formulas as they were being written, but could never keep up. In any event, without understanding his murmured explanations, I would not have been able to decipher them.

Professor Loebel, who taught descriptive geometry, was somewhat younger and had a military bearing. With some colored chalk, a string, and a ruler, he drew magnificently precise drawings on the board so rapidly that I could not copy them fast enough. Neither could I keep up with the formulas that he printed in his precise hand so that they marched down the blackboard like soldiers on parade.

Design of steam power plants and locomotives was taught by tall, white-haired, jovial Professor Loschge, who entertained us with stories of his engineering apprenticeship in Manhattan, at the construction of the Hell's Kitchen power plant. He was quite forgetful; at the end of the last lecture of the semester, when everyone was looking forward to vacations, he raised

his arm in the Nazi salute and shouted, "Heil, meine Herren!" We all burst
out laughing. After confusedly blinking a couple of times, he realized what
he had done and hastily retreated through a side door. No one took this seriously.

As I fell more and more behind and grew desperate, a savior appeared in
the form of Herr Radikevich, a Yugoslav tutor who had set up shop a block
away from the university. He ran tutoring classes in all major subjects several times a day, so that one could fit them into the school schedule. He had
been doing this for many years and knew the curriculum. But, unlike the
university method, which was to teach general theory from which solutions
of specific problems were to be deduced, his method was inductive, that is,
he gave us examples of problems that were likely to appear on an exam, in
such a way that the theory behind them frequently became self-evident.

Even so, by the time I caught up with calculus I was hopelessly behind
in physics, in which calculus was used from the very beginning. Fortunately, I found a physics textbook designed for a two-year engineering school
that covered the same ground as ours but used only algebra; with its aid I
managed to pass the exam with a better grade than some of my colleagues,
who became entangled in the higher math. I was very much interested in
physics, but since I was not planning to become a physicist, the simpler textbook gave me an understanding of its concepts that was adequate for my
purposes.

Most of the German students were in their mid-twenties because the university admitted only those who had lost time during the war. The DP students were exempt from this rule, but even among them, I was one of the
youngest. While we did not develop close relationships with the German
students, I did not feel any particular animosity toward them. Everyone was
preoccupied with studying, and there were no social or sports activities. At
one point I did study with a German student who lived in the neighborhood, and a few times I visited his home. While many of the German students undoubtedly had been Nazis—one was even a Swiss Nazi who had
volunteered for the German army—I was not aware of any political activities. The prewar dueling societies, whose members proudly displayed their
facial scars, were outlawed.

I was surprised at some of the weird, pseudo-scientific lectures held for
the general public at the university. In one of them, a learned Doctor of Sci-

ence disclosed that his *Gedankexperiment* (thought experiment) and calculations showed that an imaginary straight line laid on the surface of Lake
Geneva would touch the water at both shores rather than just in the middle. He concluded from this that the surface of the lake was concave rather
than convex. This meant that we live on the inside surface of a sphere, rather
than on the outside. I thought that the university was carrying the newly
reinstated academic freedom a bit too far.

The DP students were from all the countries of Eastern Europe, and
most had histories of persecution either by the Nazis or the Communists,
or by both. Ironically, some of the Jewish students had been saved from the
Germans by Soviet persecution, because if they had not been banned to
Siberia when the Soviets occupied eastern Poland, they would have perished
at the hands of the Nazis.

Most did not talk about past horrors except with close friends, but after
a while, one friend told another and their stories became known. One of
the more gruesome stories was that of a Jewish student named Leon, who
was in the *Sondercommando* of a concentration camp, which means that he
was in the brigade that burned the bodies of gassed inmates. The comman-
dos themselves were periodically killed off, and they knew it. Leon found
the identification papers of a dead man and somehow managed to escape
with this new identity. He then hid out in a sewer for more than a year until the Germans retreated.

In general, these tales covered almost every kind of tragedy and misfor-
tune known to man, from death to broken hearts, such as the story of the
wife of one older student who all through the war in Poland was hidden by
a young woman at the risk of her own life. After the war she and the student were married and escaped to Germany. But she was a simple soul and,
after a couple of years, their marriage began falling apart, and she was at a
loss whether to return to Poland or try to tough it out here alone.

In addition to the technical university, there was the UNRA university,
and I decided to enroll there too, just in case I could not hack it in the other one. All the professors at the UNRA university were refugees. They spoke
German with various degrees of proficiency, but always slowly and more un-
derstandably than the professors at the other school. Some were quite good;
I especially remember the professor who taught Elements of Machines. He
had a problem with his neck, and his head rested horizontally on his shoul-

der. His classes helped me to better follow those at the technical university, but unfortunately, my schedule only permitted me to attend a few classes a week. I tried to be at the UNRA university around lunch time, so that I could have a cooked meal in the students' cafeteria. I could eat there without spending ration coupons, which was very important, because in restaurants they required coupons for fat, meat, bread, and sugar and, if I were to eat there every day, the monthly coupons would have lasted less than two weeks.

Since all the students at this university were refugees from Communist countries, it attracted the attention of the Soviets. One of my friends, who came to register as soon as the university was opened, told me that as the long line for registration approached the office, he noticed some Soviet officers inside. Not wanting to attract attention by leaving abruptly, he asked the person behind him to hold his place in line while he went to the bathroom, and he did not stop walking until he was miles away. It turned out that the Soviets were trying to talk the students from the Soviet Union into returning home by promising that everything would be forgiven. In the meantime, they collected names and addresses, which was very dangerous, because right after the end of the war the American and the British authorities forcibly repatriated to the Soviet Union thousands of former prisoners of war and forced laborers. They were rounded up in DP camps, packed into freight cars, and shipped to the Soviet Union, where they were undoubtedly sent to Siberia or shot. Some of them tried to resist, and there were even cases of mass suicides. For some never-explained reason, President Roosevelt and the British Prime Minister Churchill had committed themselves to Stalin at the conference in Yalta, in February 1945, to forcibly return all former Soviet citizens to the Soviet Union.

The UNRA university was housed in the empty building of the *Deutches Museum,* the once-famous German Museum of Technology. The front part of the building contained a very large hall where Hitler had held the pep rallies of the Nazi Party—the NSDAP—*Nazional-Socialistische Deutche Arbeiter Partei,* or the National-Socialist German Workers' Party. Now, on the day of Passover, the Jewish members of the American Armed Forces held a Passover Seder there, to which we, the students, were invited. It was nothing short of phantasmagoric to see a rabbi standing on the same spot where only two years before stood Hitler. Sometime later, Yehudi Menuhin gave a concert for a general audience in the same hall. He was criticized by some in the world press, who did not think a Jewish musician should entertain the Germans. As I recall, his response was that music is international and that he was bringing back to Germany the music of the German-Jewish composer Felix Mendelssohn, which had been prohibited during the Nazi regime.

Unfortunately, unlike the technical university, the UNRA university held exams after the first year, and since I did not seriously study there, I had to drop out. I lost my lunch privileges, but by that time I had already discovered the tutor Radikevich and felt reasonably sure that I could manage at the technical university. Also at that time, the Students Union informed us that we could eat lunch at a kosher canteen, two of which were maintained in Munich by religious Jews as a good deed, to help the faithful observe tradition. The food was prepared and served by bearded men with hairy arms, who wore black skull caps. Except for Fridays, when a traditional potato dish called *chulent* was served, it was not very tasty, but it was cheap and did not require ration cards.

Ration cards did not provide very much, and even the rationed food was not always available. Then, on June 18, 1948, a miracle happened. There was a monetary reform and everyone was entitled to exchange a small amount of reichsmarks for the new deutschmarks, at the rate of ten old ones for one new. The next morning I could not believe my eyes: the store windows that were bare the previous evening now overflowed with goods of all kinds. There was food and clothing and even wine, which had not been available for years. It was like the biblical miracle in which Christ turned water into wine.

Even things like pencils and paper and so-called French curves—plastic templates needed for drafting—and, most of all, technical books, appeared as if by magic. I wondered, where had it all been until now? Foolishly, I spent most of my new money on two French curves, which I had always wanted, and on some technical books, for most of which I never had any use.

Once a month I went to Landsberg for a good home-cooked meal, and

Mother supplied me with a few cans of Spam and whole bricks of American cheese, which were included in their camp rations. The Students Union also gave us rations of canned food, soap, and half a pack of American cigarettes a month. The cigarettes were particularly valuable since the German ones were awful, and they also served as a sort of alternate currency. These goodies had been provided by the American Joint Distribution Committee on a monthly basis until someone decided that it was improper for us to study at German universities and that we should join the underground army in Palestine and fight the British. Great Britain had controlled Palestine since World War I under a mandate of the now-defunct League of Nations, since replaced by the United Nations. A large group of students did head for Palestine. Many wound up on the ship called *Exodus,* which was intercepted by the British; they spent more than a year behind barbed wire in an internment camp on the island of Cyprus.

When our arguments for reinstatement of rations fell on deaf ears, we held a meeting and decided to take the matter into our own hands. Several students had been officers in the Soviet or the Polish armies and our actions were planned with military precision. About two hundred of us assembled at precisely ten o'clock and surrounded the Joint building. Then several husky students entered and pulled out all the telephone plugs at the switchboard, to make sure that no one summoned the police. We did not let anyone in or out of the building, and told the head of the Joint that we were not going to leave until they reinstated our rations. We pointed out that most students had lost several years during the war and their whole future depended on obtaining an education. The officials gave all kinds of excuses, but at about three o'clock they gave in to our demands, maybe because they had not been able to go to lunch and must have gotten hungry.

There were several dozen students from our union at the technical university in various grade levels and specialties, but for some reason, five or six of my closest friends were medical students at the University of Munich. Perhaps it was because we all spoke Russian. I had noticed that many students formed cliques based on their common language. The big-shots at the Students Union were Polish-speaking students, who were in the majority and managed to retain their offices and control of the ration distribution at every election.

Having medical students for friends was a mixed blessing, because whenever we met at lunchtime at the canteen, one or another of them tried to test my intestinal fortitude by describing their autopsy experiences in the most excruciating detail. But as hard as they tried, their stories did not affect my appetite and they eventually gave up.

The oldest friend, Misha, was close to thirty; we all looked up to him as to an older brother and sought his advice. He and his younger brother, Sasha, had spent the war years in Kirgizia, near Kazakhstan. Another friend, Volodya, had been a lieutenant in the Soviet army, serving as an aide to a general. He loved to tell stories about his experiences, and we kidded him that his stories improved with every telling. Grisha had been a lieutenant in the Polish presidential guard. He had a problem with total amnesia after a few drinks, and whenever I met him on the day after a party, he asked me whether there was someone to whom he should apologize. At a guard party in Poland, he had pulled a gun on a Soviet officer because he thought that the officer was making a pass at his girlfriend, and later woke up in jail not remembering a thing. His fellow guardsmen let him escape before he was to be court-martialed.

Then there was Ira, a young woman with a baby, whose husband knew how to obtain food. She became sort of a den mother to us, and we knew that in case of emergency we would always be fed at her house.

Another friend, Pavel, an older engineering student, remained alive only because whoever had circumcised him had not done a good job; by using a rubber band, he was able to conceal his circumcision for the few moments of the *Schwanzappel* or "tail roll call." He had been a soldier in the Soviet army, was wounded and captured by the Germans, and told them that he was a *Volksdeutch,* or a German colonist in Russia. Because he was blond and had blue eyes, they accepted his story. But to make sure that there were no Jews among the prisoners, the Germans periodically made them drop their pants to see if they were circumcised, since only Jews and Muslims followed this custom.

Fortunately, Pavel did not speak any Yiddish that would have left a recognizable accent in his German, which he learned very quickly and so well that he was given a job as an interpreter. When I knew him, his most prized and valuable possession was a full-length gray leather coat. One day he hung the coat on the wall in a restaurant, and when he looked a few minutes later, the coat was gone. He had graduated two years ahead of me, married his

German girlfriend, and moved to Bad Reichenhal, a resort town in the foot-hills of the Alps, where he got a job as an ORT trade school director.

On a visit to Pavel, I discovered that he lived near an airfield where the Luftwaffe had tested new airplane designs. I went there and wandered among a hundred or so airplanes, trying to figure out what was innovative. Since I had always wanted to be an aircraft designer, it was like being in a fantastic amusement park, the likes of which can only be seen in a dream. I climbed in and out of the airplanes, sat in the pilot's seats, and did not no-tice the passage of time until a German guard came running and told me that I had to leave because some of the armament in the planes still had live ammunition. As we were leaving, I noticed a Messerschmidt fighter plane with American stars on the wings; the guard told me that some American pilots were flying it for fun.

Even though my room was not exactly deluxe even when, after about a year, I obtained real glass for the window, it was in a very good location. I could walk to the university in about forty-five minutes when I did not feel like taking the streetcar, and the Prinzregenten Theater, the temporary home of the Munich Opera, was only two blocks away. The tickets were cheap and I saw most of the standard repertory, with my favorite being Bizet's *Carmen*. Then a Russian girl I was dating at the time talked me into going to hear Bach's *Matthaeuser Passion* or "The Passion of St. Matthew." I had never heard music like this before, and it was a revelation—man com-muning with his God through music, which one could describe only as di-vine.

Another revelation for me was a visit to an exhibition of modern paint-ings. I knew of Picasso and the Impressionists, Cubists, and painters of oth-er modern schools, but had never seen their paintings, other than some poor reproductions. Just the fact that they were prohibited in the Soviet Union was enough to make them interesting. I did not see much in Picasso's work but was fascinated by Impressionist paintings, which showed how each painter conveyed images of familiar objects or scenes in his own way, and I could see the working of his imagination.

Before Hitler, a Munich district called Schwabing was the home of an artist colony, one of whose members was Vassily Kandinsky, a Russian émigré. Even though Kandinsky's paintings did not depict recognizable objects, they were unmistakably Russian, because of the colors and shapes reminiscent of Russian folk art. These paintings made me realize that impressions and moods can be conveyed by colors and shapes alone, just as they can be conveyed by music, and that abstract paintings may be, in effect, the visual equivalent of music.

While I liked baroque music for its regularity and orderliness, and jazz for its freedom and imagination, I disliked modern music for its gritting chaos. In my opinion, the baroque, classical, and romantic periods were followed by the musically neurotic period.

I continued to learn English, and eventually was able to read American pocket books issued to soldiers. I loved Hemingway and Steinbeck, managed Fitzgerald, and struggled with Faulkner. Humor was quite difficult to understand, but I loved James Thurber, perhaps because I could identify with his daydreaming Walter Mitty. I also subscribed to *Der Monat,* an excellent magazine issued by the Americans in German. It featured articles from American publications on politics, economy, philosophy, and many other subjects, by authors ranging from the journalist Dorothy Parker to City College of New York philosophy professor Sidney Hook, who, while a Socialist, understood the nature of communism and strongly opposed it.

There were several repertory theaters in Munich, and the operetta theater had been rebuilt and featured the wonderful romantic operettas of Lehar, Kalman, and Strauss. There were also numerous movie theaters showing prewar European and American films. But with all this almost normal student life, we never lost sight of who we were and where we came from. One day I saw the documentary movie of the liberation of the Buchenwald concentration camp, showing mountains of emaciated corpses and the technology used for mass slaughter. As the throng of spectators was leaving the theater, there was not a single sound to be heard from the mostly German crowd. It was as if we were coming from a funeral. I understood that this film had never been shown in the United States. Then there were the war crimes trials in Nuremberg, which I followed in the newspaper *Muenchener Mercur,* to which I subscribed.

After about six months of being almost totally immersed in the German language, I was listening to a public lecture when I suddenly realized that I understood almost every word. The everyday language I had acquired from my landlady, Frau Koob, who was rather chatty, particularly on her favorite subject of astrology and about the discrimination that her family, being Lutheran, experienced at the hands of the Catholic majority. Every evening she brought me my chamomile tea or ersatz coffee and we chatted until I picked up a book, which indicated to her that I wanted to study. One day I obtained some real coffee, and there was no end to her joy, because she had not seen any since before the war. Bohnen Kafe! Bohnen Kafe! she kept repeating—real "bean coffee!" I did not have any conversations with Herr Koob, but I chatted with their son who visited them from time to time and found him quite friendly.

Frau Koob recommended a woman who took in the wash—a friendly middle-aged woman with large, strong hands who was married to a bald-headed elderly man with the biggest ears that I had ever seen. Whenever I came to pick up my wash in the evening, she practically forced me to have tea with them and to discuss the latest news, which they heard reported on a huge old wooden radio set. While she and I sipped herbal tea and talked about the latest street crimes, he periodically took large gulps of beer from an enormous stein and nodded. Occasionally he would emit a deep sigh, interjecting *"Ach ja, was wird den geschehen?"* ("Oh my, what is going to happen?") in his Bavarian dialect.

When the sentences were pronounced at the Nuremberg trials, Frau Koob ran into my room all excited and waving a newspaper. "What do you think of that?" she asked. "Most of them will be hanged!" Somehow, in spite of the horrors revealed by the tribunal, she did not think that the sentences were justified. "All of them should be hanged," I responded. "But they were just following orders," she mumbled, and I heard her excitedly telling her husband in the kitchen that I thought they should all be hanged. I did not hear his response, but I assume that "just following orders" is how he justified whatever he had done as a high-ranking policeman.

Upon closer examination of the cardboard boxes stacked from the floor to the ceiling in the room with the toilet, I noticed that they were parcels from countries that had been occupied by the Germans, and that the sender was Lieutenant Koob, the son who had been killed in the war. When I asked

Frau Koob about them, she said that indeed he had been sending them parcels from all over. I wondered whether he had bought those things or looted them.

One day, I noticed that on the soap in the bathroom were stamped three letters: R.J.F. I remembered reading somewhere that in some concentration camps the Germans had made soap from human fat and stamped it with these letters signifying *Rein Judisch Fett,* or "Pure Jewish Fat." I saw red and stormed into the kitchen with the soap. "Where did you get this soap?" I shouted. "Do you know what these letters mean?"

"I got it on my ration coupons," Frau Koob mumbled, obviously at a loss on how to react to my rage. "They have it at the store around the corner; go see for yourself!" I told her what I thought the letters stood for and left, slamming the door. Otherwise we were getting along rather well, and it did not take me long to realize that, as individuals, most Germans were not much different from anyone else.

Occasionally, friends from the DP camp came to Munich and stayed with me overnight. There being no other place to sleep, we shared the narrow couch. After several such visits, Frau Koob was visibly upset and mumbled something mentioning the number 300 every time she brought my tea and cake, which she baked from my ingredients and which we shared. I had no idea what upset her, so I asked my friend Paul whether he knew what she could possibly mean by "300." He burst out laughing and explained to me that it was the statute of the Nazi Criminal Code that declared homosexuality a crime punishable by imprisonment. I immediately took steps to clarify the situation and brought home my girlfriend, which I had hesitated to do before, because I thought that the landlords would object. I made sure that Frau Koob saw her, and the next time they saw me, both Herr and Frau Koob had big, benign grins on their faces. However, I was not sure whether they were happy for me, or glad that they were not harboring a criminal.

I did not have much to do with the other student, Petra, who continued to wear a sock around his neck and who, because of his throat problem, had the revolting habit of coughing into a handkerchief and examining the sputum while continuing to talk. Occasionally, we discussed current events, until I expressed my opinion that I did not think the Soviet Union was about to collapse and that even if Belarus someday did become independent, I doubted whether it could survive on its own. This made him very angry and ended our discussions.

After the fourth semester, I began taking the halfway exams called *Vorpruefung,* which covered general subjects such as physics, chemistry, metallurgy, etc. I was allowed to postpone the dreaded math exam until the end of the next semester, which gave me more time to prepare for it. My grades were not great, but I passed everything.

At about that time came the great news that a delegation of the American Hillel Foundation was coming to Munich and would be selecting students for scholarships abroad. The Foundation appeared in the person of Miss Serkin, a small, quiet, middle-aged woman who interviewed all applicants and asked us to write an essay on our favorite book. We could write it in English, German, or Russian, since she could read all these languages. I wrote in Russian about Tolstoy's *Anna Karenina,* which I had recently read, but wondered what this had to do with the ability to be an engineer and whether good engineers had to be good essay writers.

The results were posted at the Students Union, which, according to Miss Serkin, was the American way. This publicized for all to see who was smart and who was stupid, or rather, who was good and who was not good at writing essays. My name was somewhere in the middle of the list, which coincided with my view of myself, so I did not feel any embarrassment, as did those at the bottom. While I was not considered worthy of a scholarship in America, I was deemed good enough for a scholarship in Switzerland at the *Ecole Politechnique de Lausanne.* I would have preferred going to the United States, not only because I was already studying English but also because going there had been my dream. But beggars cannot be choosers, and there was no certainty that it would be possible to go to the United States, because the Eastern European immigration quotas were filled for many years ahead.

Miss Serkin assembled us and told us that one of the conditions for emigration was that we must present certificates from the German authorities stating that we were in residence at a certain time. "Sure," we said. "Just tell us what kind of certificates you need." Miss Serkin raised her eyebrows.

"You seem to take the requirement for documents very lightly," she commented. We looked at one another but managed not to burst out laughing at her naïveté. We did not want to tell her that for one pack of American cigarettes one could obtain almost any kind of German certificate.

There was nothing left for me to do but to start learning French, which I would need to know in the part of Switzerland where I would be living. In a store next to the university I found a French textbook in two volumes by someone named Louis Marchand. The reason I remember it so well is that it had free-hand line drawings in the margins illustrating some of the rules. An example of the passive mode was the sentence "Un chat pendu" accompanied by a drawing of a cat hanging in a noose with its tongue flapping on the side of its mouth. However, before I even had a chance to get through the first volume, I was informed that the Swiss *Fremdenpolizei,* or the police in charge of foreigners, had refused to let me into the country because I was stateless—if upon graduating from the *Ecole Politechnique de Lausanne* I were to refuse to leave the country, they would not know where to deport me.

One of my fellow students mentioned that he had an uncle in Argentina, and I remembered that my father's sister also lived there. The problem was that not only did I not know the city where she might live, but I did not even know her married name. Nevertheless, I asked him to ask his uncle to inquire about her, and to give only her maiden name. Several months passed and I had forgotten all about this, when I received a letter from Argentina, written in Yiddish. I found a friend who could read it. It was from Aunt Aida, and she was asking whether I was a son of her brother or of her sister. It turned out that my aunt's daughter-in-law happened to be visiting her mother, on whose kitchen table lay a newspaper, open at the announcements page. She casually glanced at it and noticed the name Konstantinowsky, which she recognized as the maiden name of her mother-in-law.

A friend wrote out the Yiddish alphabet for me and, writing from right-to-left, I managed to put together a response that she could understand. She lived in Buenos Aires and had three grown children: two sons, Raul and

Issac, and a daughter, Perla, all of whom were married and had children of their own. In a subsequent letter she informed me that, unfortunately, they were not in a position to help me financially, which did not upset me. I was happy just to know that I had an aunt and cousins with whom I could communicate; I did not think it was safe even to try finding my relatives in the Soviet Union.

One weekend a month I visited Landsberg, arriving Friday night and leaving on Sunday afternoon. Mother was a very good cook and I greatly enjoyed her dinners. She, Solomon, and Vilya lived in a two-room apartment on the second floor of a small private house just outside the DP camp. They were able to communicate with their German landlords, who lived on the ground floor, in Yiddish. Vilya was an inquisitive boy and one day, looking into the toilet water tank that was near the ceiling, he found a packet containing a small loaded pistol that was wrapped in wax paper and was in good shape. The German landlord, who was not told about this find, said that the previous tenant had been a young man. It was illegal to possess firearms, but who was to know?

We were very concerned about Vilya's education. Mother engaged a German tutor for him, but he did not show much interest in learning German or in going to the Hebrew school in the DP camp. He hung out all day with kids in the camp, or at the warehouse with truck drivers, for whom he ran errands. I had taken him to the circus and to the zoo in Munich, but there was nothing I could do about his studies.

One day, he was passing a fenced-in garden down the street from his house and noticed a ripe pear close enough to the fence that he could reach it. As he picked this pear, the German owner ran out and slapped him very hard on the face. Crying, Vilya ran to the warehouse, and several truck drivers returned with him to confront the German. They ripped apart the fence and broke off branches from all the trees in the garden. The owner ran away and returned with the German police, who were unarmed and, not wanting to start a riot, tried to calm down the situation. The truck drivers told the owner that if he would hit a child from the camp again, they would do to his house what they had done to his garden.

A pal of Vilya's from the camp happened to notice that Vilya was not circumcised and told his religious parents about it. They spread the horrible
news to the religious community, and a whole campaign to save Vilya's soul
was put into motion, with people harassing him whenever he showed up in
the camp and pressuring Solomon to have Vilya circumcised. After a while
the pressure became unbearable and Vilya agreed to the operation. On the
appointed day, a ritual specialist called the *moyel* arrived at the camp infirmary and Vilya, who was ten, and another heathen boy discovered in the
camp were brought in by their parents. The other boy went first. Apparently
the *moyel* did not apply enough local anesthetic, and Vilya heard a horrible
scream. He jumped up and ran into the street pursued by men with side
curls, who had come to form the group of ten men necessary for the appropriate prayer to be heard by God. Solomon could not chase after Vilya
on his crutches. Vilya ran into the room of someone he knew, and it took
several hours of cajoling and the promises of adequate anesthesia to talk him
into submitting to the procedure.

When I found out that Mother was pregnant, I was concerned because
she was in her late thirties, and in those days it was considered to be dangerous to have a baby at that age. However, her pregnancy was normal, and
she looked well and appeared to be happy. Then, on November 5, 1948,
when I came home from school, I found Solomon's son-in-law Berek waiting for me in my room. He was grim and told me that Mother was in the
hospital and I should go there immediately. He would not give me any details. We rushed to the station and he did not sit next to me on the train.
He went with me to the hospital but remained outside. When I asked to see
Mother, the receptionist looked at me for a moment before saying quietly:
"She is in the morgue."

I became completely numb and followed her outside to a small building,
which was dark. She turned on the light and I saw Mother lying on a stone
slab. Her face was peaceful as if she were just asleep. I bent over and touched
her forehead with my lips—it was ice-cold. Only then did I become fully
aware of what had happened and tears began rolling down my cheeks. I

don't know how long I stood there; finally Berek came in and led me by the arm, as one would lead a blind man, to their apartment.

Vilya was there and I tried to hug him, but he pulled away. There were some friends of Solomon standing around, and he was sitting on a chair that was down on its side. I noticed that the front of his jacket was torn, and I yanked as hard as I could on the lapel of mine. It tore off partially. No one said anything. The mirror on the wall was covered by some kind of cloth. It was dusk and the room was dim.

Someone led me to a chair and I sat down. The tears never stopped rolling from my eyes; I wondered how many tears a human body can hold and where they are stored. Solomon told me that the baby was all right. He said it was a girl and that she was still in the hospital.

Some more men arrived and someone turned on the lights. One of the men wore a black hat and had side-locks coiled up in front of his ears. He also had a wispy beard. He took out a prayer book and everyone stood up. Someone put a black skull-cap on my head. The bearded man began to read in Hebrew; I did not have the slightest idea what he was saying. As he read, the upper part of his body swayed back and forth. I noticed that some of the men did not sway back and forth but twisted their bodies from side to side. Some twisted only to the left and others only to the right. I thought that Mother would have found this scene amusing.

This went on for some time. Then someone handed me a prayer book and pointed to a prayer written in Latin letters. The prayer was recited in unison and I desperately tried to keep pace in pronouncing the unfamiliar words. It was the prayer for the dead. Then two of Mother's friends brought some food, but I could not eat.

I must have fallen asleep in the chair. When I opened my eyes, gray light was seeping through the windows. Then Vilya and Solomon got up and we had some tea. Later someone came and told us that Mother's body had been brought into the camp. They did not think that it could be brought to the apartment because the stairs were narrow and curved. We all went to a warehouse where Mother was lying on the cement floor, wrapped in a shroud. Two candles were burning at her head and a man in a black hat was praying, swaying back and forth with rapid, jerky movements. I overheard one woman telling another that she had performed the ritual ablution and that

Mother had a girlish figure. Two young German policemen came in and said that they had to sign something. They had taken off their hats and stood there, ill at ease. They saw that all the men in the room had their hats on, and after a while also put on theirs. I felt embarrassed that Mother was lying on the cement floor—back home, the dead were laid out in the house and were surrounded by flowers.

Someone took Vilya to their house to feed him and he brought me something to eat. In the evening, more men came and read prayers, and again I was handed a book with the prayer for the dead in Latin letters. I noticed that different people pronounced the Hebrew words differently and wondered whether I was doing it right. I wanted to believe that it was important and that doing it right would somehow help Mother. I stayed with Mother all through the night. Solomon must have hired some religious people to keep vigil and to pray all night. They kept coming and going.

In the morning Mother's body was placed in a plain wooden box. It was loaded onto an enclosed pickup truck and Vilya and I sat next to it. Solomon rode with the driver. It was raining and someone said that this was a propitious sign because, presumably, it always rained at the funerals of Hebrew sages. I thought that it was just nature crying with us.

The cemetery was on the outskirts of Munich, and it took us some time to get there. It was surrounded by a high stone wall and, as we entered it, I was surprised to find it full of old monuments and saw that it was in good order. I thought that probably no one had given an order to destroy it and it was left alone right here in the *Hauptstadt der Bewegung,* the Capital of the Nazi Movement. Over the gate to the cemetery there was an inscription in large metal letters: *Wir sind nicht von Ihnen sondern nur vor Ihnen gegangen.* ("We did not go from you, only before you.") I could not concentrate on it, but somehow it sounded comforting.

The coffin was taken into a small chapel where some more prayers were recited. Then it was placed on a cart and we, with the twenty or so people who came from Landsberg, followed it to an open grave. After another prayer, the coffin was lowered into the grave, and I led in throwing a handful of soil, the impact of which reverberated in my ears for a long time.

We returned to Landsberg and did not leave the house for five days, which is a ritual called sitting *shivah.* Mother had many friends, and they all came to express their condolences; every morning and night men came to recite prayers. They brought prayer books, one of which had a German translation of the *kaddish,* the prayer for the dead. It turns out that actually it is not a prayer for the soul of the departed, but a recitation of the praises of God. I wondered whether my little sister would feel like praising God when she understood what had happened.

Upon returning to Munich, I made myself a black armband, which I was to wear for a year, according to the German custom. Then I went to the cemetery. It was snowing. Large snowflakes swirled around in the air, and it took me a while to find the grave, which was white and had blended in with the landscape. It was absolutely quiet, and I was alone in the kingdom of the dead. I wondered whether Mother felt the cold; I told her about her daughter, who would carry her name, and promised to take care of her and Vilya.

About two months after Mother's death, one of my medical friends, Volodya, and I went to see the doctor who had performed the cesarean section. We had been told only that Mother had bled to death and, the doctor being German, we had a lingering suspicion as to whether he did everything possible to save her, or perhaps might have been trying to complete what Hitler had begun. The doctor was rather young and aloof. I told him that my friend was about to graduate from the medical school and that he could use medical terminology.

"Ach, ja," said the doctor. *"Das war ein interessanter Fall."* ("It was an interesting case.")

I felt blood rush to my face. To him my mother's death was nothing but an interesting case! Did he run an experiment on her to make it more interesting? Perhaps my suspicions were not completely unfounded. Was he a Nazi? What was he doing during the war? I thought of the gun that Vilya had found.

The doctor began talking about muscles of the uterus that did not contract and about the transfusion of Solomon's blood, but I was thinking only about how I could find out whether he had performed experiments on concentration camp prisoners.

I was shaking with rage as we left the office, but Volodya thought that in spite of the doctor's poor choice of words, he did not contribute to Mother's death, even though a hysterectomy might have given her a chance to survive.

Solomon had found a German woman to take care of the baby, but this arrangement did not last very long. After a couple of months they did not get along and the baby was placed in a convent, whose nuns were caring for about forty babies. The convent was a short train ride from Munich, and I visited my little sister at least once a month. Care there consisted of feeding and cleaning the babies, but no one held or played with them. They were swaddled in diapers in such a way that they could not move their arms: the two edges were wrapped around their arms and tucked under their backs. This was done presumably to prevent them from scratching their faces. All the babies were in one large room, in rows upon rows of bassinets, hollering and screaming their heads off. Later, when Rachel was six or seven years old, a psychologist who did not know her history concluded that she had missed her first year of life.

I wondered whether I should try to notify my grandfather about Mother's death. It was not a good time for Soviet citizens to receive mail from abroad. The Soviets had blockaded the roads to Berlin and the Allies were supplying the city with food and even with coal by airlift. We saw American troops moving toward the border, and we were afraid that the blockade of Berlin might lead to war. Nevertheless, I decided to do it, hoping that notice of a death would not be construed by the Soviets as an enemy act. I wrote to the woman who had been my grandfather and uncles' landlady in Zaporozhie before the war, whose address I happened to remember.

A couple of months later, I received a letter from the old landlady. She wrote that my letter was not delivered to their house; instead they were notified that there was a letter from Germany that they had to pick up in person. They were very excited because her husband had not returned from the war, and they thought that the letter could be from him. They had to do a lot of explaining as to why they were getting this letter, which, since they had not read it, was quite a challenge. But they got it and brought it over to my Uncle Samuel, who had returned to Zaporozhie after the war and lived on the other side of the city.

About a month later, I received a letter, addressed from my grandfather, who being old was less likely than my uncles to suffer any consequences. He and my uncles had escaped to Siberia, where Uncle Samuel got married and now had a baby boy named Joseph. Grisha-the-Elder had been killed at the front, leaving his wife with a baby boy named Vilya. Grisha-the-Younger remained in Siberia, where he became the chairman of a *kolkhoz* and had two boys by a new wife. Grandfather was ailing, and the family was not going to tell him about Mother's death. There was no suggestion that I should write again, and I did not.

Not having had any vacations at the university, we managed to squeeze a four-year course into a little over three years, and I graduated in the summer of 1949. My landlords immediately began addressing me as "Herr Diplomingeneur." My grades were nothing to brag about, but I still thought that Mother would have been very happy and very proud of me.

At about the same time, the U.S. government had decided to admit three hundred thousand displaced persons from Europe, outside of the national quota limits. My friends and I applied to NYANA—the New York Association for New Americans—which helped the prospective immigrants with the formalities and provided job sponsors who guaranteed that they would not become a burden on the government. Because engineers were not in demand, I was registered as a sheet metal worker, and NYANA lined up a job for me in Wilmington, Delaware.

To be admitted to the United States, we had to pass several screenings by various counterintelligence agencies, at one of which I was told that someone had reported to them that I was a Communist. I was dumbfounded. In a long interview with a middle-aged agent who carried a pistol, it became clear to me that my accuser was my apartment mate Petra, who must have been trying to get even with me for my lack of faith in his cause. The agent was very friendly, complimented me on my English, and, after we chatted for some time about my plans for a career in engineering, said in a fatherly tone that he did not believe the accusation and wished me good luck in the United States.

Another screening was by a congressional committee, during which a very arrogant and hostile young congressional staff member repeatedly asked me about various dates, then commented to the German translator that he thought he might confuse me enough to say that I was born before my father. The translator laughed obsequiously. I did not let on that I understood English.

We were X-rayed for tuberculosis and then had to stand stark naked in line and pass before a German doctor, who made us bend down and turn around in front of him as he scribbled comments in our files. He was rather gruff and made me think of the Nazi doctors who did the same examinations in concentration camps, with the movement of a thumb either to the left or to the right sending people either to the barracks or to the gas chambers.

After this, there was nothing to do but to wait for authorization to travel to the port of Bremen. Vilya had already left with Solomon and the baby, and so had most of my friends. Some went to the United States, others to Australia or Canada. My friend Misha, who was the first to leave, wrote from New York that he was trying to get an internship position at a hospital. He found the skyscrapers very imposing, but what impressed him most was the sight of blue-haired old ladies ice-skating at Rockefeller Center— in Europe they would have been sitting in rocking chairs.

At long last, in November I received notice to be ready to leave in two weeks and began making preparations. I sold my food supplies and bought a large suitcase that I filled with books to such an extent that I could barely lift it. I had about sixty American dollars, forty of which I foolishly spent on a beautiful yellow leather briefcase; I was told it was absolutely essential for making a good impression when looking for a job in America. The remaining twenty dollars I sewed into the lining of my trousers because I was informed that it was against the law to bring currency into the United States. I do not know whether this was true and, even if it was, whether it applied to such small amounts. I had been told that to check whether the money was counterfeit, it should be folded so that the large capital letter in the round Federal Reserve stamp was on a sharp corner. When this point is rubbed on white paper, the ink should come off on a genuine bill. According to this test, my bills were genuine.

The special train with DPs left Munich and headed for Bremerhaven, where we were assigned to former army barracks to await the ship that would take us across the ocean. There was not much to do other than serve on cleaning brigades for a couple of hours a day and check daily the lists of those who were to leave on the next ship.

One day I took the train to the city of Bremen and visited the medieval cathedral, which stood unscathed amidst the rubble of bombed-out buildings. It was overwhelming; I felt like a small ant. Even so, no matter where I looked, the lines of its walls and arches pulled my eyes upward in the direction of heaven to the distant peak of the Gothic ceiling, and the overall effect was not oppressive but uplifting.

Finally, after about two weeks, my name appeared on the list. The following day I was to board the S.S. *General Muir,* which was heading for Boston. It was a troop transport, somewhat larger than the Liberty class; I believe it was Victory class. The men were directed to four large windowless holds with four tiers of hammocks, while women and children were placed in smaller cabins with beds, a family to a bed. Fortunately, we were not overcrowded, with only two men occupying each stack of four hammocks. I picked the second hammock from the top. My travel companion, who took the lowest hammock, was a very gentlemanly elderly Russian concert pianist who had escaped from Russia during the Revolution and had lived in Yugoslavia.

The transportation of DPs to the United States was managed by UNRA. A lean, chain-smoking elderly Frenchman in the UNRA uniform greeted us over the ship's intercom and informed us that, because it was the end of November and we might encounter rough seas, he had spent a large part of his budget on anti-seasickness Dramamine pills rather than on food. He assured us that in spite of this, there was enough food on board to last for the approximately seven days of the voyage, and wished us *bon voyage.*

The rest of the administration was selected from the passengers. As his chief assistant he appointed Boris Ivanovich, another Russian emigrant from Yugoslavia who, with his attractive blonde wife and an equally attractive sister-in-law, formed the top level of management—the autocratic aristocracy of the temporary social order. The ladies, who spoke French, swooned over the French UNRA manager, who melted in their presence, bowing and smiling and giving them free reign over the rest of us. We referred to them as the princesses. They combed the passenger list of about five hundred people for suitable names for various positions on the organization chart to assure smooth functioning of the ship. I, being a young engineer with a Russian name, was a natural candidate for a good position. Indeed, the princesses smiled at me benignly and presented me to the chief assistant, who gave me an armband that established my authority. I was assigned the choice job of maintaining law and order on the foredeck, from the bow to mid-ship. Another young man with a Russian name had the same function on the aft-deck, from mid-ship to stern. Others were made supervisors of areas below deck or put in charge of cleaning crews, which consisted of people with mostly non-Russian names.

The first day at sea was wonderful, in spite of the fact that the small portions of food consisted mostly of celery, raw or cooked, mixed in with various kinds of unrecognizable mush. This delicacy left such a lasting impression that I have not been able to eat celery ever since.

We halted at Dover and admired the white cliffs. The ship rocked gently, and I had never felt better in my life, heading for a new land, a new life, and new adventures. But I still did not quite believe that I was actually going to America, that this was not just a dream. Bits of a ditty that I remembered from childhood floated through my brain:

> America is a unique but banal country,
> Where money litters the streets . . .

Having read *Grapes of Wrath* and similar books, I did not believe that money was easy to come by in America, but was amazed at how many people did believe it. A friend of mine, a former officer in the czar's army who spent the years between the wars in Paris, in all seriousness assured me that in America when someone's car, no matter how new, stalled in the street, the owner would just abandon it and anyone was free to take it.

I learned that the ship was powered by a gas turbine, and the constant hum and throbbing made me feel as one with this giant living machine. I noticed every valve and every gadget and tried to figure out its purpose. This was my kind of environment.

After we passed the English Channel and entered the Atlantic Ocean, the sea became rough and the small ship rolled and pitched, meeting the foam-crested waves head on. While many people became sick and were throwing up into tin cans that were handed to them for this purpose, I felt wonderful and loved to stand at the bow to be raised up and dropped low as the ship climbed the waves and dived into their troughs. To prevent seasickness, I periodically took small sips from a flask of gin, which I carried in my back pocket, in spite of a prohibition against alcohol on board. I do not know whether gin was proper medication, but I did not get seasick.

I had to be on deck all day long but there was nothing to do, since everyone was on his best behavior, not wishing to jeopardize admission to the United States. I watched a short, religious Jew with dangling side curls approach a big, Scandinavian-looking officer and in distorted Yiddish, which he obviously tried to make sound like German, anxiously ask him whether the storm was dangerous. The tall, blond, blue-eyed officer looked down at the little man and, shaking his finger under the man's nose, sternly answered him in pure Yiddish: *"Eymytser hot nisht gedavnd!"* ("Someone has not said his prayers!") I could not stop laughing.

Breathing the fresh sea air all day long made me ravenously hungry and, knowing that food portions were small and the removal of the ubiquitous celery made them even smaller, I borrowed the dinner card from my neighbor, who did not feel well, and received a double portion. Still it was not very much, and on the next day I borrowed two cards from other yellow-green victims who could not even think about food.

On the morning of the fourth day, as I happily took up my post on the foredeck, my counterpart from the aft-deck told me that Boris Ivanovich was ordering me below deck to the cleaning crew that was cleaning women's cabins. I was flabbergasted. "Did he tell you why?" I asked. "No, he just said that you should do it right away."

I headed for the office, but the princesses, instead of smiling at me as usual, pursed their lips and told me that the chief assistant was not to be disturbed. I threw my armband on the table and walked out. As angry as I was, I did not want to disobey the order, fearing that it might cause a problem; the whole thing would be over in a few days anyway. I found the cleaning crew supervisor, who checked off my presence and handed me a mop and a pail. The women's cabin contained about ten beds arranged in two rows. On each bed sat a woman with her children, whatever number she happened to have. The floor of the cabin was completely covered with vomit from one end to the other, which the half dozen of us in the crew were supposed to clean up.

The ship was heaving and rolling, making the stuff flow back into the areas that we had just mopped up, the bucket was sliding away, and the kids and some of the women were adding to it faster than we could clean it up. The stench was unbearable and I began feeling queasy myself. I told the supervisor that I was not feeling well and went to the infirmary to get some Dramamine, which was given to me together with a note freeing me from this work. I went to my hammock and indignantly told my pianist neighbor what had happened. He laughed and said, "The princesses have checked out your sponsor and discovered that it is an agency that sponsors many Jews. They asked me whether I knew your religion but I told them that I had no idea."

I did not take the Dramamine but instead took a sip from my flask, and the fragrant gin cleared the unpleasant taste from my mouth. It was against the rules but no one ever noticed and besides, when I was still on good terms with the "royalty," I had noticed an empty wine bottle in their office, probably a tribute from the Frenchman.

I spent the rest of the voyage reading in my hammock and bobbing up and down on the bow. Then, on the early morning of December 2, 1949, I woke up because it was absolutely quiet: no hum, no vibration, and no rocking. I went on deck and saw what I thought was a small skyscraper, which I later learned was the Customs Tower in Boston harbor.

I was finally in the land of my dreams.